MY COUNTRY is HOCKEY

How Hockey Explains Canadian Culture,
History, Politics, Heroes, French-English Rivalry
and Who We Are as Canadians

Brian Kennedy

argenta
press

The Publisher: Argenta Press is an imprint of Dragon Hill Publishing Ltd.

Library and Archives Canada Cataloguing in Publication

Kennedy, Brian, 1962–

My country is hockey : How hockey explains Canadian culture, history,
politics, heroes, French-English rivalry and who we are as Canadians /
Brian Kennedy.

ISBN 978-1-896124-52-0

1. Hockey—Canada. I. Title.

GV848.4.C3K45 2010   796.9620971   C2010-905139-4

Project Director: Gary Whyte
Project Editor: Kathy van Denderen
Cover Image: Illustrations by Roger Garcia
Photo Credits: Courtesy of Hugh Kennedy, p 9.
Text permissions: Poems "Road Trip" & "Tie Game" (pp. 7, 8) reprinted with
permission of Richard Harrison. From *Going Top Shelf: An Anthology of Canadian Hockey Poetry* ("When I Was a Boy," p. 84, John B. Lee; "Road Hockey,"
pp. 84, 85, Bruce Meyer; "Rheaume," p. 325, Richard Harrison) reprinted with
permission of Michael P.J. Kennedy. Poetry of Randall Maggs (p. 130),
reprinted with permission of Brick Books, publisher.

Produced with the assistance of the Government of
Alberta, Alberta Multimedia Development Fund

**Government
of Alberta** ■

We acknowledge the support of the Canada Council for the Arts, which last
year invested $20.1 million in writing
and publishing throughout Canada.

Canada Council   Conseil des Arts
for the Arts   du Canada

Dedication

For Daniel and Sarah, with hope that your country will always be hockey

Contents

Acknowledgements

Each time I send in a manuscript, I believe it is polished. I have generally gone over it a dozen or more times looking at the voice, the message and the style. Invariably, I tell myself that this time, my editor will have less work to do. And each time, I get back a document with a million markups, every one of them calculated to make the book better. Editors make writers who they are, and I am fortunate to have one of the best. Kathy van Denderen could be plying her trade in Toronto, Vancouver or London (England) at any publishing house she wanted to. Fortunately for me, she works in Edmonton. Each time I work with her, I recognize more the accuracy of her insights. Thanks, KV, for another stellar effort.

Thanks also to my publisher for believing in me. Your faith, I hope, will have been paid off again in this book. And to the talented production people, graphic artists and others at Argenta Press, please know that I understand that producing a book is a collaborative endeavour, and I offer you a giant share of the credit.

To Gaby, my wife, for her patience; to my dad, Hugh, for his pride in me; to my sister, Sandra, and my brother-in-law, Phil Reimer, and their kids, to whom this book is dedicated, for the way they support my love of hockey—thank you. I owe this book to all of you.

A lot of good people in hockey have helped me—so many I could not name them all. But I want to acknowledge the Anaheim Ducks and LA Kings hockey clubs and my friends in the media (Josh Brewster, Doug Stolhand, Eddie Garcia, Gann Matsuda, Kat Kealy, the late Jon Moncrief, Charles Smith, Dennis Bernstein, Dave Joseph, Ted Sobel, Keijo Jolli, Jim Fox, Bob Miller, Kevin Greenstein, Samuel Savolainen and others) who have all supported my books in any way they could. Thanks to each one.

Road Trip

When the manager of the gallery in the Hotel
Ivoire sees the flag on my pack, he tells me he
loves my country, and he plays hockey on the rink
that lies chilled like a pie in the middle of this hotel
on the equator where leaves rot as they grow and
the air is sweet as apples with their dying. I say,
What position? He says, Left wing. I say, Like
Bobby Hull! And Bobby's name makes it. He draws
his hand up and it smiles at the end of his arm.
This is The Shake, the one that begins with the slap
of palm against palm, the one between men
who've found enough between them to confirm
the world for a day and go on. Tomorrow I will
skate on this rink like the pros back home, way
ahead of schedule and nature. I will tell you
I touched the ice, and I could be any boy in love.

–Richard Harrison

Tie Game

–for the Team

A good game repairs the boy inside me—I mean a good
game as spoken in the language of men. Everyone
knows—win or lose—you did what was asked, the guy
with the puck counted on you in position whether he
passed or not, and the one that rang off the post was still
hailed as a good shot in words heard round the rink,
when the better shooter says to you, Take it! This is
impersonal love, this movement of men on the ice,
thinking, talking all the time, playing the angles and each
other, the love the mind has for the body, the key for
the lock, the one men express for machines they've owned
that always started in the cold. Today, because of how
we felt, we let the game end in a tie. You don't see that
every day, but one of us was leaving town next week,
and we couldn't let him go with that good game dying
in victory or defeat.

–Richard Harrison

Richard Harrison is the author of *Hero of the Play*, the first book of poetry
launched at the Hockey Hall of Fame. He currently teaches English and
Creative Writing at Calgary's Mount Royal University.

Left to right: Hugh Kennedy, Marshall Rogers, Philip Kennedy

Introduction

"Hello, Canada, and hockey fans in the United States and Newfoundland."

For decades, Foster Hewitt intoned these familiar words as *Hockey Night In Canada* came on air. The words sound simple enough, and people listening would have taken them as the signal that it was time to stop whatever they were doing and hunker down in front of the radio—a night of hard-fought action was about to commence. But hidden beneath the words' simplicity is the truth about Canadian national identity. Hewitt doesn't say, "Hello hockey fans in Canada, the United States and Newfoundland." Rather, he assumes that to be Canadian ("Hello, Canada") is to be a fan. Then he goes on to address those from the other country, and Newfoundland, which became a province in 1949. If they have tuned in, they must be hockey fans. But by calling them out as he does, Hewitt makes the tacit acknowledgement that they are a select group among a larger whole.

The fact that Hewitt could lump all Canadians together as hockey fans simply wasn't questioned. But could he say the same thing today? If he could, what set of shared values would be reflected? And what would it mean if he could not? These are the questions this book will try to answer as it explores the place of hockey in the Canadian mind and soul and ponders both the changing contours of contemporary Canada and the place of the U.S. in the creation of present-day hockey culture.

It might at first appear that the thoughts in the pages to follow draw upon a background, geography and frame of reference that are distinctly Canadian, and that is true, to a degree. But in fact, the country of hockey is larger than the country of Canada, and so my hope is that wherever you live in hockey country, you'll find something to interest you here. And to make the point that I'm not going to take the whole "I'm Canadian" thing too seriously, here's a joke that puts a Canadian as the butt:

Q. How does someone from Toronto change a light bulb?
A. He holds it, and the world revolves around him.

Toronto? Light bulbs? Put into hockey terms, that might go something like "How does the Canadian hockey fan understand the game?" The answer might be "as if it were played just for him (or her)." We all know that point of view is much too ethnocentric to be tolerable today. But still, people who live north of the 49th parallel (or who, like me, have left but still retain ties) tend to think of hockey as their game and to believe that any changes that happen to pull it south are evil and destined to fail. Hence the tension inherent in the sentence, "My country is hockey."

On the one hand, the sport does define Canada in ways that I will describe and diagnose in the next few hundred pages. On the other hand, hockey at present reaches beyond its ties to Canada, since the sport has been relocated (some would say "dislocated") south over two generations, so that it is now played (at all levels, not only the NHL) in places as far-flung as California and Florida (and obviously, in Europe and other parts of the world, but that's not the focus here).

The traditional centres (Toronto and Montréal) no longer hold sway over what goes on in the game. For Canadians, that fact is both disconcerting and begrudgingly accepted as beyond easy remedy, but that's not to say it feels right. Hence, one goal of this book is to figure out where the game came from, what it means in Canada today and what its future significance for the Canadian culture might be.

A question that might be posed is whether Canada will be able to claim ownership over hockey in the years to come, or what the inability to do that might mean, both for Canadians and others. To put it bluntly, what if the Americans steal our game from us? To start off your thinking, consider that Wayne Gretzky, the ultimate Canadian hero to the majority of Canucks, is now American. Stephen Brunt points out in his excellent book *Gretzky's Tears* that Gretzky has "spent more time of his life outside of Canada than in it."

Further, The-Great-One-as-prototypical-Canadian-boy ideal is, as Brunt explains at various points, much more a myth than the truth. It might have been that, when his career ended, Gretzky's fans wanted to view him as the small-town kid from Brantford who would come home and make a life down the street from where he was raised, but Brunt says that "wasn't him anymore, by a longshot.... [I]t was what Canadians wanted him to be."

Hockey, too, is not what it was 20 or 30 years ago. The "romantic attachment to teams and uniforms and owners vanished with the Gretzky trade," Brunt claims, explaining that the NHL has inevitably become Americanized, at least insofar as its business model and the majority of its teams being in the U.S. reflect U.S. values. Should you read Brunt's book, you'll find yourself admitting that he's right. But as a Canadian, you won't want him to be, or you may not want to accept the truth of what he says. Canadians want hockey to be the pure epitome of Canadianness, the embodiment of who we are and what we believe in as a nation. Those who are honest, however, will admit that it is more difficult than ever to make these claims. And it is in that spirit that I offer you *My Country Is Hockey*.

This book is not just a discussion of the state of the game today, though I include many contemporary examples that illustrate my argument. Nor is it simply a trip to the past, though I will make frequent reference to history. Beyond both of those, this book is a call to recapture the old-time spirit of hockey as the reflection of the Canadian psyche and to understand that psyche as a product of devotion to the game. Is that hard to do? Probably, because it depends at least in part on the reader's willingness to shut an eye to the fact that the business of hockey is now conducted in New York rather than Montréal or Toronto and instead focus on the magic elements that lie beyond what the players' contracts say or the amount of TV revenues generated. The magic I want to remind you of and excite you to is found on the ice and in the line that connects the youngest hockey hopeful playing on a shinny pond to the moment when the Stanley Cup is handed over to a waiting captain. I'm also going to ask that you confront some of the negatives of the game today, including its violence.

Is this book for Canadians only? No, it's not. Rather, it might serve as an invitation to all hockey fans, whether in Canada, the U.S., Russia, Finland or elsewhere, to understand that the game they see at the local arena has a much larger context and longer history than is apparent at a glance. Those who understand the game only in the present may enjoy it and find it a satisfying part of their lives, but my hope is that by getting deeper into the history and inner world of the game, this book will allow hockey to take on new dimensions and thus become a more worthwhile pastime. However, having said that, I must confess that *My Country Is Hockey* was written from a Canadian point of view, with the idea that the people who might most clearly recognize themselves in it are Canadians.

By the way, I mention Gretzky's Americanness because you're going to figure out that I, too, am now a U.S. citizen, and you're going to wonder why I wrote this book—and why I so often say "we" when I talk about Canada. It's because I, like Gretzky, am Canadian first, and forever, and though we both work in the States, and for reasons that are our own, ended up getting a U.S. passport, that doesn't take our Canadianness away. In fact, in some ways, living in the U.S. enhances our connections to our roots. When I moved to California, I learned pretty quickly to introduce myself to new people by saying, "I'm Canadian." Invariably, this statement makes them perk up a little bit, and it's not long after that they ask my favourite question: "Do you play hockey?"

Because I no longer live in Canada, you might say that the Canada I write about—where hockey is the predominating motif and the defining aspect of our culture—is a fantasy version of the country. Maybe it is, but I would argue that a lot of Canadians hold on to a similar idea, and that while my time in Canada these days is limited to about a month a year visiting family, my contact with home through hockey, which I cover in Los Angeles, is the defining feature of my life. I am thus more Canadian now than ever.

This is a bit of a "chicken-and-egg" question, however, when expanded to Canada and Canadians as a whole. Is who we are reducible to the game of hockey, or is hockey ever expandable, always big enough to contain Canadians and give us a sense of identity? Think about how many expressions of the game exist, from table hockey to fantasy leagues to various electronic versions to the NHL, and how much time we devote to playing, watching, thinking about or talking about the game. Is it any wonder that most Canadians could say without contradiction, "My country is hockey"?

One of the struggles in writing a book like this is that it's easy to generalize the "truths" it discusses and apply them to all Canadians. In fact, only about half a million kids play in leagues at any one time, which is less than 10 percent of those eligible. Almost none of us make it to the NHL. And even the most hotly contested game is *not* watched by approximately 25 million of our fellow citizens. (About 10 million watched the U.S.-Canada gold medal game in Vancouver.)

But hockey is so much a part of who we are that even people who don't watch the game closely, or casually, might have to admit that it permeates the atmosphere in which they live and informs the worldview they share. Hockey is more solidly rooted at the centre of the Canadian psyche now than it ever was. To understand contemporary Canada at all, and to predict what the country will look like in the future, hockey must be considered as one of the prime sources of its history, identity, imagery and values. That is one key premise of *My Country Is Hockey*. The other, I suppose, is that those reading this book do so precisely because they are trying to find out more about themselves, the hockey-mad—they are looking for a way to describe who they are, not trying on an alien identity for size.

So at least some of what you encounter in this book will be familiar—the 1972 Summit Series, the Richard Riot of 1955, the Olympic victories of 2002 and 2010. Some stories, of course, may be less so, because they're drawn from prior eras. The idea is not necessarily to surprise you—there's perhaps little in hockey history that could surprise most of us. Rather, I offer new ways to think about these well-known events, putting them into a fresh context and also allowing you to revisit what might otherwise be forgotten in the rush of following the contemporary game at its many levels.

My country is hockey. It's not simply an idea but a product of history and myth interacting, all within a setting where natural elements make following the game the most sensible means of expressing the essence of the Canadian soul.

chapter one

A Country Called "Canada"

Complicated Origins

G aze down at any Canadian city from an airplane, and you'll see the architecture of hockey. Arenas sit in downtown neighbourhoods, at the edges of suburbs and along rural highways. In winter, outdoor ice, or the local river or pond, supplements the indoor league games. When summer arrives, streets are taken over by the shouts and scrabbling after tennis balls that make up the game of road hockey. And everywhere, there are ties that connect people to each other and to the game present and past—fantasy leagues, hockey card shops, booster club meetings.

Given the ubiquity of the game and its many expressions, it's easy to imagine that hockey is eternal. That the game as we know it comes from some prehistory now unrecoverable. Of course, that simply isn't so, but neither is it true that a clear and visible line exists from present to past. Yet by understanding the history of the game, we can begin to get a sense of how Canada developed into the country it is today.

Just as the nation is a collection of disparate regions and multiple identities, so hockey has origins that are anything but singular. Not much more than 150 years ago, Colonel Byron Weston was playing a version of the Irish sport of hurley with "friends and Mi'kmaq Natives on the frozen lakes of Dartmouth and inlets of Halifax," and it was this game, if you believe the Nova Scotia–centric view, that was the predecessor of modern ice hockey. Even still, several of Weston's rules would be unfamiliar to modern-day fans. For example, teams changed ends whenever a goal was scored, all players played the whole game and the goalkeeper was not allowed to leave his feet to make a save.

However, the game played in Nova Scotia wasn't the only version of "hockey" that existed at the time. The Halifax Rules, as they were later called, were the basis of the ones used in the first public game in Montréal, played on March 3, 1875. The man who organized that game, held in the Victoria Skating Rink in front of a crowd of about 40, was James Creighton. He was born in Halifax in 1850 and grew up "with hockey surrounding him."

The Montréal game had nine players per side, and it followed the Halifax Rules with one exception—no forward passing was allowed. The puck could move only laterally or backwards, unless a player was skating it. As in Halifax, there were no lines on the ice, so offside was determined the way a soccer offside is nowadays, with no offensive player being allowed to go behind the defense.

The game that Creighton organized has come to be viewed, by many people, as the beginning of hockey as we know it today. The contest is important because it was played indoors, as an "event," and also because it was recorded in a *Montréal Gazette* article the next morning, thus taking its place as not simply an idle pastime but a significant moment in history. In Halifax, by contrast, early play was less formally arranged, and the rules were not written down, though Weston explained the rules to a local newspaper reporter, who left a record for us. The members of the Metropolitan Club, a men's sporting club in Montréal, recorded the written rules of the Montréal version of the game in 1877. They were called, not surprisingly, the "Montréal Rules."

But even these two competing histories don't finalize the story of the birth of hockey. Kingston, Ontario, also has a claim to make, with the story being that players from Queen's University and the Royal Military College had the most important early rivalry, one that is still going on.

Then there's Windsor, Nova Scotia, which has a tradition that dates back to an 1833 painting of people playing hurley on ice. The CBC bolstered Windsor's boast as being the originator of hockey by broadcasting *Hockey Day in Canada* from that city in 2003. This claim is weakly supported, however, with no documentary evidence existing from the time to suggest that hockey was born in Windsor, although newspaper sports editor Joel Tichinoff recently claimed that many of the game's recognizable features come from the play of local King's College students. "Incorporating physical elements of the local Mi'kmaq first-nations' sport 'dehuntshigwa'es' and the Scottish ball-and-stick game of shinty, the Kingsmen devised not just the name but essential elements such as the position of goalie, shaped sticks and bench clearing brawls," he says.

What can be concluded from this mishmash of competing claims? The comforting truth that hockey is our game, invented by Canadians anywhere from 130 to 175 years ago.

Not so fast.

As noted hockey historian Michael McKinley so nicely puts it, "James Creighton didn't invent hockey on that winter's night under the roof of that Montréal rink, but rather, he had found its temple." In fact, McKinley points out that a Dutch painting from the middle of the 16th century shows people on skates playing a game with a ball and sticks, on ice. In addition, in 1740, a report in the *Dublin Evening Post* talked about teams playing "a match of 'hurling' on the frozen Shannon River." Later on, but still predating the Canadian history of the game, poet William Cowper said in 1785 that the boys in a small English town "have likewise a very entertaining sport…. They call it 'hockey.'"

Native people were also playing a similar game when Canada was first settled. And British explorer Sir John Franklin left evidence "describing his men skating and playing hockey on the ice, while wintering at a fort on Great Bear Lake [NWT] in October 1825." The strength of this claim is that it is the oldest original documentation of all of the Canadian versions of the birth of hockey, according to journalist Randy Boswell.

These examples predate the pickup games played in Nova Scotia, the apparently organized games in Kingston and the first formal "by the rules" game in Montréal. To make it even messier, two Swedish researchers recently "unearthed the first seemingly unassailable evidence that Canada's national winter sport…originated not in Nova Scotia or the Northwest Territories in the early 1800s, but in the British Isles decades earlier." And horror of horrors, there is also "compelling evidence that rudimentary forms of ice hockey were played in New York and Philadelphia before such games were documented in this country [Canada]." It must be noted, however, that while the U.S. seems to have some claim to the birth of hockey, fortunately for Canadians, at this point, nobody in the States seems nearly so keen as we are to take credit for the invention of the game. (Nor does any Canadian want to be the one to awaken the Americans to this fact.)

English, Scottish, Irish, Dutch, Native? Somewhere in Nova Scotia, in Kingston or in Montréal? The Northwest Territories? Someplace in the U.S.? Suddenly hockey's history becomes more cloudy and complicated than brief TV features can document, and the Canadian seeking the truth of the origins of the game is left wanting.

Two things must be said by way of correction. First, when the Scots are mentioned, it is in relation to shinty, which was apparently a game played with all comers on the ice scrambling after a ball or other object. There is no organization into teams, as in hurling. This claim is substantiated further by looking at various historical documents that seem to point to large groups of players, perhaps as many as 20 on a team, playing a game descended from shinty, called "ricket." The Irish game of hurling was less a free-for-all scramble than an organized team game where players sought to propel an object into the other team's goal. It thus bears a much closer resemblance to the modern game than does shinty.

Second, whatever the origins or precursors of the game, hockey as it is now known and played all over the world is distinctly Canadian, because it was here that the game was organized and systematized with a set of rules that have been refined over time.

McKinley makes two pertinent points on the matter. First, "[t]he prototypical game that the world knows as hockey…was born somewhere in Canada, and probably due to the migration of the Irish and their game of hurley." Second, while the tendency is to want to clarify and simplify the origins of the game, or to find its pure "father," the truth, according to McKinley, is: "Early hockey probably achieved its greatest degree of sophistication in Nova Scotia, then was housed, regulated, and established in Montréal, with Kingston being an important hockey centre through the years...." In other words, hockey does not have a singular originating moment (at least, not one that is traceable), but rather is the product of a number of histories enacted over time. It is thus not a game that speaks to the needs or interests of one region of the country but is something that all Canadians can share, and which reflects many aspects of Canada's history. Hockey, to put it another way, is a lot like many of the people in modern Canada—from elsewhere, but happy living here.

Researchers will continue to ponder the question of who should be credited with the origins of hockey. And someday, maybe they will come to a consensus on the matter, but for most Canadians, the question is an interesting diversion and not a vexing problem. What matters more are the ways in which hockey has come to provide contours and meaning to the Canadian way of life. If we are to understand ourselves, or give others a glimpse into who we are, we could do worse than to examine the sport and its codes, both formal and informal.

The Warrior Mentality

Hockey is played by rules, but it is also a struggle for survival. To do well, a player must wield a weapon successfully, waging a battle with the enemy and triumphing by sheer force of will. Coming to the defense of a teammate is often needed in the ebb and flow of the game. And in the end, victory is the prize, and with it comes glory. Canadians learn this warrior mentality through playing or watching the game, and the consequent mindset is so ingrained in our psyche that it seems natural, though it is not. But this attitude was crucial to Canada's participation in World Wars I and II, events that allowed the country to forge its place in world affairs.

At the time of World War I, Canada was still under the umbrella of the British, and hockey as we know it was less than 40 years old, with the six teams of the National Hockey Association all coming from either Ontario or Québec. Yet both the country and what would become its predominant sport were beginning to take on modern contours. The connections between the game and Canada's coming of age through war are crucial, because the ethos formed on the ice and tested on the battlefield has survived to define Canada in the present.

If you believe that Kingston gave birth to the game in the 19th century, hockey grew out of an ongoing rivalry between Queen's University and the Royal Military College (RMC) of Canada. The military college saw the sport as a good way to enhance the physical training of their men. The first official league is thought to have been formed in 1885–86, with teams from the RMC and Queen's University joined by the Kingston Athletics and the Kingston Hockey Club. Historian Bill Fitsell claims that "Kingston was pivotal to the development of the game from Montréal west into Ontario and south into the States as well," primarily through the Queen's team. With their game hardened by competing against the team from the nearby RMC, the players were, if somewhat indirectly, carrying on the military tradition, using hockey as a metaphor for war.

The Ontario Hockey Association followed in 1890–91, made up of the Queen's University team and clubs from other colleges, universities and athletic associations, as well as military clubs. What better place than the confines of a military system to develop rules and order in a game that was previously something of a free-for-all? A few centuries earlier, the Scots converted their war club into the golf iron. Now, as the 20th century dawned, their descendents in Canada expressed their aggressive instincts through hockey, but who's to say that it didn't work the other way as well; that is, Canadian military men converted their sporting instincts into a predilection for battle?

"The Great War for Civilization" as World War I was then known, saw approximately 600,000 Canadian men, and a significant number of women, answer the Empire's call to duty. The enlistment papers of the Canadian fighting man read in part: "I will as in duty bound honestly and faithfully defend His Majesty, His Heirs and Successors…against all enemies." My grandfather made this promise when he signed up in 1915, and he spent the four years of the war, and then another six months after that, tending to wounded men in a field hospital in France.

His sacrifice was not extraordinary, nor something uniquely Canadian. It is something that has been shared by generations in the years since, notably in the more than one million who left the country to participate in World War II, and those who served and died in Kosovo and Afghanistan. For these soldiers, in each of these wars, a common theme exists: that it is simply right to sacrifice yourself to defend something you believe in or to defend someone who is being unfairly targeted. For Canadians, that value sprang from hockey.

In 1915, kids did not join local amateur teams in the numbers they do today, though pond hockey and other outdoor forms of the game were common. I have only the sketchiest information on the hockey my grandfather played. His service in the Canadian Expeditionary Force owed a debt to the game nonetheless, and the toughness with which he played hockey in those days might have served him well as informal training before he even entered the more formalized situation of boot camp (that's him on the right in the photo on page 9). The same would be true for other Canadian soldiers. Being in the fields of France and Flanders while the cold set in and the ground froze probably didn't faze them all that much. Many of them had been donning hand-knitted toques and mittens since they were tots and heading out to the nearest frozen pond or patch of ice cleared on the river.

Americans might have had their football, though back then, it was not the savage game it is now. Tackles were done waist-level and below, more rugby-like than NFL-like. Canadians, however, had hockey to teach them how to take a beating. The game frequently got rough, with the violence not only confined to the players but also occurring between them and spectators. The hockey stick, a weapon to this day, was used as a club on occasion. Not to disparage the toughness of rugby players, but when you add in the speed generated by skating and the elements of a Canadian winter, you're going to get a hardy breed of man, one who might make for a pretty leathery brand of soldier.

On a more positive note, hockey developed teamwork. The game was different in the early days, with seven players—the extra one was called a "rover"—used until 1911, but it was still the group that worked together that won. Round up enough men who would find such a sporting endeavour entertaining to play, and you might have a decent army on your hands. Put those guys in military uniforms, and you've got the equivalent, in their minds, of the Victoria Cougars or the Montréal Wanderers headed out to do battle, only in true life-or-death situations.

The battle probably seemed somewhat less hockey-like once the shelling in Flanders began, but it's not a huge stretch to think that while the British were hunkering down against the noise and the French were drinking their daily combatant's allotment of wine, the Canadians were trading stories of their local hockey heroes and imagining for themselves a little bit of glory, albeit on a vastly different field of battle.

Hockey was the proving ground for manhood. Cultural critic Michael Robidoux argues that the game came to stand in for Canadian identity at the turn of the 20th century, saying, "play was aggressive and often violent, providing men the opportunity to display [the young country's] emergent notion of masculinity." This robust spirit was expressed as Canada proved itself as a nation, particularly at the battle of Vimy Ridge.

By the time of World War II, professional sports were all the rage. Upwards of three million people a season were attending games in what was shortly to become the six-team NHL. Granted, four of those teams played in American cities, but the majority of the players were Canucks. And once again, Canadians went to fight a European war.

This time, Canada's contributions wouldn't be so famously concentrated into one battle as was the case at Vimy. Rather, the nation's efforts stretched across Europe and beyond. But the principle was the same. The Canadian spirit of teamwork, determination and toughness was initially forged in these fighting men on the outdoor rinks and in the local arenas where they played hockey.

Perhaps the exemplars of this spirit were three boys who grew up near each other in the Kitchener-Waterloo area, which has a large number of people of German heritage. Bobby Bauer, Milt Schmidt and Woody Dumart played together on Boston's Stanley Cup–winning teams of 1939 and 1941. The team dominated again in the 1942 season, being 20–12–5 by February, when the three men decided that country was more important than hockey and enlisted in the Royal Canadian Air Force.

As those who study hockey history likely remember, the Bruins did not win the Cup again until 1970, and in fact, the rest of that 1941–42 campaign saw them get only four more wins. That season, the Maple Leafs won the Cup for the first time since 1932, though who's to say if they would have had Boston retained its high-scoring trio? At the time the "Kraut Line," as Bauer, Schmidt and Dumart had been nicknamed, left to join the military, they were averaging .934 points per game apiece. This was in an era when a point per game put a player at the top of the scoring race.

The night the linemates said their farewells, the Bruins beat the Montréal Canadiens 8–1, and the line got 11 points between them. But more surprising was the response of the fans, and the Montréal team, after the game. The three players were presented with commemorative watches and paycheques for the rest of the season, then, to the applause of the crowd in Boston, they were carried off the rink on the shoulders of both their teammates and the hated Montréal rivals.

After serving time in the military, each man returned home. Schmidt played another 10 years for Boston, while Bauer got another two years in, plus a game in the 1951–52 season. Dumart played nine more seasons in black and gold before a half-season campaign with the Providence Reds of the American Hockey League.

When interviewed at age 88, in 2006, Schmidt recalled his happy memories at the sendoff the line received, although he was reluctant to talk about the specifics of his wartime experiences. Nevertheless, he and his linemates represent the sort of robust Canadian whose vigour both reflects the game and allows him to play it to the fullest. Perhaps that's the kind of hero every hockey player ought to be, the kind who forged a country that has embraced hockey at the core of its soul.

The Centre Shifts South

Looking back to the time immediately after World War II, many see a golden age in the game that reflected the prosperity of the country. Sure, two-thirds of the teams in the NHL were American, but most of the players were not. The hockey world, like the seats of Canadian politics and finance, was centred in a space between Toronto and Montréal, a little more to the one side or the other depending upon where your loyalties stood.

For most fans today, the far reaches of the hockey past are represented by the "Original Six" era, which is what we now call the time after the NHL consolidated to half a dozen teams after the Brooklyn Americans exited the league in 1942–43. When this happened, clubs such as the Montréal Maroons and the Ottawa Silver Seven, not to mention Stanley Cup winners the Winnipeg Victorias and the Victoria Cougars, were consigned to history, because most fans' memories don't go back far enough to see past the "Six."

Perhaps the enduring hold these teams—Montréal, Toronto, Boston, New York, Chicago and Detroit—have on hockey fans has to do with the coming of television, when the game went from being an airy figment of the imagination played out on the living room floor every Saturday night while listening to a radio broadcast, to a game where the players became alive, their faces glowing on the black-and-white TV screen for kids and adults alike to memorize. This shared experience, in turn, reinforced fans' identity as Canadians. When Foster Hewitt began his broadcast, "Hello, Canada," it was simply assumed he was talking to everyone. And perhaps those fans of Montréal, Detroit and Toronto who saw their teams trading the Cup back and forth through the '40s and '50s thought that hockey would stay this way forever.

But when colour TVs became the norm, the old black-and-white of the NHL quickly grew dated, and the idea came about for a cadre of new squads. In 1967, the modern (12-team) NHL was born, and with it came the first great challenge to the Canadian habit of defining hockey as coincident with the country. Canadians had to figure out how to absorb the increasing Americanness of the game, because the conversations surrounding the 1967 expansion focused on putting teams in the U.S. rather than in Canada.

Anyone with foresight would have known that going from six to 12 teams, with all six of the new clubs based in the U.S., would irrevocably change the game, and it did. The fear at the time was that Canada would lose hockey, swallowed up like so many other things by the voracious and irresistible appetite of the giant to the south. Pretty soon, the pundits thought, it wouldn't be our game anymore. One positive result of the change was that Canadians were forced to acknowledge the strength of the western provinces, one of which would gain an NHL team in a second expansion. But that wouldn't happen until 1970.

With expansion from six teams to twelve, in one stroke, the professional game was nearly 85 percent located in the U.S., including the most unlikely place of all—California. Perhaps most shocking was that the NHL did not put just one team in the state, but two, with one playing in the San Francisco Bay area (Oakland to be precise) and another in Los Angeles. Hockey was now on the Hollywood stage, against the backdrop of mountains and sea that had been the playground of the stars since the 1920s. It was the land of Clark Gable and Marlene Dietrich, and later, Bob Hope and

the Rat Pack. And nobody cared about what was happening
on the ice.

The joke people tell about the early days of hockey in
LA goes something like this: A guy calls the Forum and asks
what time the game will start that night. The person on the
other end of the phone responds, "What time can you be here?"

Paul Medved, an immigrant from Winnipeg in the
early 1970s, told me in January 2010 that his dad used to take
him to Kings games, and during the period breaks, they
would wander the concourse. It wasn't just to get a hot dog,
though they did that; it was to meet people from back home.
"We'd be out there scouting for people my dad knew. It was
all Canadians back then at a Kings game, and he'd always be
amazed at the people he ran into."

Meantime, in Canada, fans wondered why they
had been overlooked while teams went to California and
to St. Louis, Minneapolis, as well as to two cities in
Pennsylvania—Philadelphia *and* Pittsburgh. The change
in the NHL was more than an expansion—it was a sign that
the game at the professional level was not going to stay comfortably located in its past (that is, the Canadian) way of
doing things.

To see the NHL take an American turn was an insult
to the nation that was at that exact moment affirming its identity through celebration of a century of Confederation. So why
was Canada ignored in this first expansion? Maybe part of

the reason was that in 1967, the country was not yet big enough, metaphorically speaking, to embrace another team. The nation hadn't even adopted its own flag until two years earlier, when the maple leaf won out over two other competing designs and finally superseded the Canadian Red Ensign with its prominent Union Jack logo in the upper left corner. Expo '67, the World's Fair that corresponded with the 100th anniversary of Confederation, was held in Montréal. At the time, the city already had a team, with another one in the other important Canadian metropolis, Toronto.

In the Canada of the mid-'60s, the West was an outlaw zone, or a space too far, despite the song so often played on the radio in the summer of '67 that said that this land is your land and mine, "from the snow capped mountains to Prince Edward Island," itself a version of Woody Guthrie's popular American folk number.

If anything, the West was a place for boys' dreams to take place, with the old mantra "go west, young man, go west," originally an American coinage, being appropriated by a generation of young people who were starting to see the opportunities available to them in the wide-open expanse that started somewhere past Sudbury. In 1967, maybe Canada wasn't ready to see its western region as mature enough for an NHL team, although those who resented the NHL's neglect of the Canadian West could have pointed out that hockey had a rich history there. The challenge version of the Stanley Cup had been won by Western teams, including the Vancouver Millionaires and the Kenora Thistles. The Patrick brothers had started the Pacific Coast Hockey Association in 1911, and its teams contested for the Cup every year between 1914 and 1922.

In any case, it didn't take long for things to change, or, to speak from a Canadian point of view, for the NHL to wake up. By 1970, when the Vancouver Canucks (along with the Buffalo Sabres) came into being, a shift was taking place. No longer was it possible, or so Canadians must have hoped, to expand the league and ignore the homeland. No longer could the NHL try to shoehorn the game into places where it made a poor fit (that wouldn't stop further mistakes, of course). This was exemplified nowhere better than in Oakland, which by 1970 had changed the name of its hockey team from the California Seals to the Seals to the California Golden Seals. Shortly after, the team traded in the yellow skates their owner made them wear for white ones. The franchise finally abandoned the Golden State for Cleveland in 1976, and the wary Canadian looking on had no trouble casting an "I told you so" glance in the NHL's direction.

The West Is in the Game

If the NHL was going to expand again post-1967, it was inevitable that part of the bounty be placed in Canada, and where better than Vancouver? By the start of the "Me" decade, the city was home to about 400,000 people. Many, perhaps to the surprise of those in the East, were rabid for the great

Canadian game. Getting a "real" hockey team was a mark of the city's having made it, but more important, it was the sign that the country's identity encompassed more than just Toronto and Montréal. The Canucks made their debut in the fall of 1970, and suddenly, BC was a part of big-time hockey in Canada. Perhaps more accurately, the distribution of power to the West in the face of the region's increasing population and growing economy was mirrored in the emergence of a western NHL team.

Did this move garner respect from fans of the league as a whole or from those devoted to the Original Six? Let's just say that if a kid who lived in Toronto or Montréal opened a pack of Esso Power Player trading cards after his dad threw them across the vinyl bench seat of a station wagon in the fall of 1970, and the kid saw images of the Canucks' Andre Boudrias or Gary Doak, the look of disappointment would be clear. The effect was the same with regular hockey cards. Flashing a Rosaire Paiement or Jocelyn Guevremont (who broke in with the Canucks in 1971) as fodder for a trade meant certain death for a kid whose classmates followed the Habs, Leafs or Bruins. Of course, this may not have been the case in the West, or Vancouver particularly, but kids in the East could not be blamed for not knowing that on the far left edge of their country, the local NHL franchise was creating heroes for those living nearby. That kind of worldview shift doesn't happen quickly.

The Canucks, furthermore, didn't make it easy to be a fan, with a record of 24–46–8 in their inaugural year of 1970–71. The next season was worse, with the team posting 20–50–8. Nor did the franchise feature any superstars in its early years. In contrast, on the U.S. west coast, the Kings snagged Marcel Dionne from Detroit in 1975 and put him on a line with Charlie Simmer and Dave Taylor. Known as the Triple Crown line, these players became one of the highest-scoring trios in NHL history, though playoff success was never in the cards.

But whatever the Canucks' record, the average Canadian, whose worldview is always inevitably shaped by hockey, could no longer believe that Canada was contained in the 480-kilometre corridor along the 401 that took someone from Rue Ste-Catherine to Yonge Street. Instead, in order to understand the entirety of the Canadian hockey universe, you had to get on the great Trans-Canada Highway, point yourself toward the Pacific, drink a gallon of coffee and push the pedal down. More importantly, the tipping point that put Ottawa as the fulcrum between the two great eastern cities was now upset, and the West could view itself proudly as a place where history happened, at least insofar as history was coincident with what went on in the NHL.

The power of that transition is seen in my own experience as a Montréal Canadiens fan. As a kid, I, along with every other kid I knew, waited and watched for Frank

Mahovlich to score his 500th goal. We were too young to have seen it happen for Jean Béliveau, the man who did it before Mahovlich (and only the fourth in history), and so witnessing the "Big M's" accomplishment was, along with experiencing the 1972 Summit Series, the highlight of our lives. The goal would matter more than any history lesson we would sit through in school, we were sure.

Finally, on a March night in 1973, it happened, and the goal was a bit anticlimactic, rolling off the heel of Mahovlich's stick and past the goalie. But what's more telling, in terms of the place of the West in the eastern hockey fan's imagination, is that for 30 years, my memories of that goal had it being scored against the New York Rangers. But it wasn't. The opponent on this night was the Vancouver Canucks, a team that to my friends and me was on the outer margins of the hockey universe.

The Shift West Continues

Throughout the 1970s, the economies of the former seats of power declined, but at the same time, a new West was born. These changes were not reflected simply in political or economic realities, but in hockey, too.

Québec lost much of its corporate might during the middle part of the decade in the shadow of the FLQ crisis and the fear of a successful referendum powered by the Parti Québecois and their chain-smoking leader, René Lévesque.

Companies, including a number of the major life insurance firms, moved their corporate headquarters out of the province, many to Toronto.

In the late 1970s, Ontario took a huge hit to its industrial economy as the U.S. Rust Belt, just south of the province, declined. With places like Pittsburgh, Youngstown and Detroit in slowdown mode, the automobile industry began what was to become a 30-year slide to bailout, and steel was an industry from the past.

Meanwhile, young people who felt the need to explore new territory were once again hearing the call of the West, and this, too, indicated a change in the Canadian worldview. Alberta was a place to earn big money in the oil and gas industry. Hockey was there, too, in the form of hardcore interest in the junior leagues, with BC's New Westminster Bruins winning the Memorial Cup in 1977 and 1978. Perhaps more significantly, teams in Edmonton and Winnipeg joined the Canucks in the NHL. Both newcomers were holdovers from the World Hockey Association (WHA), which had been the NHL's rival for most of the decade (1972–79).

The WHA, of course, had gained early fame by convincing the most revered player in his prime at that time, Bobby Hull, to sign with the Winnipeg Jets for their inaugural season—for one million bucks. That was in 1972, and Hull's run in the NHL had been 604 goals, 1153 points and one famous slapshot that was helped along by a stick that he, along with teammate Stan Mikita, had figured out how to curve. Hull would add another 638 WHA points to his record and then go back to the NHL to boost his numbers by a further six goals and 11 assists.

Initially, the Winnipeg franchise was all pizzazz. During the WHA era, the team had the West to themselves. Other teams were out there, including Edmonton, Vancouver (the Blazers, who played from 1973 to 1975) and Calgary (the Cowboys, who played from 1975 to 1977), but the Jets were the powerhouse.

Winnipeg's success was achieved not only because of Hull but also because they nabbed a couple of European players—Anders Hedberg and Ulf Nilsson. The notion was a strange one, especially in a world where hockey players were gritty, tough men who had no shame when it came to displaying a four-tooth gap in the middle of their celebratory smiles. Hull, who himself didn't possess a full set of pearly whites, was also known as a bull of a man, with forearms the size of most athletes' biceps and biceps more akin to Popeye's than to a human's. A famous photo of him pitching hay on his farm proves the case.

Employing Europeans was an idea ahead of its time, one that would work 10 years later in Québec with the import of three brothers, the Stastnys, who were defectors from Czechoslovakia. Strengthened by the unique combination of Hull, Hedberg and Nilsson, the Jets won the Avco Cup in 1976,

'78 and '79. And with winning came stability, which few WHA teams possessed. Even the Toronto entry, the Toros, moved house at one point, becoming the Birmingham Bulls. They had started out as the Ottawa Nationals, playing in that city for the WHA's first season.

It might seem, then, that Winnipeg's success in this new league, and their move into the NHL when the WHA folded in 1979, portended a new life for Canada's West. It did in some ways, but not quite with the flash that the WHA suggested, because the Jets neither mirrored a larger reality of prosperity in their region nor created one. Maybe Winnipeg wasn't quite far enough west to partake in myth, but its image was more farmer than cowboy, and in the 1980s, the city was a place that people left, rather than a place that drew newcomers with its promise.

However, that's not to say that NHL hockey's centre wasn't shifting westward, especially when Atlanta's team moved to Calgary in 1980. By this time, the NHL consisted of 21 teams, with seven of them Canadian, a percentage of the total NHL not matched since the Original Six era. More teams existed in the west (Vancouver, Calgary, Edmonton and Winnipeg) than in the east (Montréal, Toronto and Québec), again a unique situation and maybe a sign that Canada was assuming its grown-up identity as a nation spread from sea to sea.

The West's place in the Canadian imagination changed forever when Wayne Gretzky started his tear through the record books, and with that came the visible rise of hockey (first the WHA, then the NHL) in the region. Gretzky's emergence as a superstar in Edmonton was no accident, but rather coincided with the emergence of the West as a dreamscape where anything was possible. Oil money beckoned in Alberta, and in BC, a new movement, Green Party politics, was about to be born.

The irony was that Gretzky might have played anywhere, were it not for a series of events that bound him, not via a player contract but by a personal services agreement, to Peter Pocklington. Gretzky first signed a deal in Indianapolis that spelled out that he was offering his services to owner Nelson Skalbania for a period of seven years. Skalbania sold Gretzky to the Oilers after Gretzky had played a handful of games with the Indiana team (which, in any case, folded in December 1978).

As the Gretzky legend grew throughout the 1980s, so, too, did the province of Alberta, though perhaps fewer fans thought of him as an Albertan than as an Oiler. His myth, as is well known, was always much more closely tied to a humble suburban upbringing and the fact that his dad was a regular guy, a telephone company installer, who somehow saw his son's potential at a young age and devised precisely the right drills to maximize his hockey sense. This was in an era when coaching was, for the most part, anything but scientific.

Gretzky quickly became the iconic Canadian figure. In Edmonton during the glory years, everyone who watched him felt as though magic possessed the city. Whenever he had the puck, fans felt their expectation rise. This quiet, gentle folk hero could defeat the big thugs, fooling them with his deft moves and leaving them wondering what had happened. Just a few years earlier, it had been the roughnecks who dominated hockey. Now, it was a new game, and Gretzky's often-flowing hair and darty quickness seemed to perfectly fit the spirit of the moment.

Being out west gave the whole phenomenon a further dimension. In a sense, Gretzky is the perfect image of the lone rider who strikes out, long leather coat blowing behind him, in search of something new. The result at a team level was that the Oilers couldn't be contained because when one player wasn't scoring, the others were. The offense was like an oil gusher—impossible to turn off once it got started. Similarly, Alberta was on an upswing, with money flowing in as the crude flowed out. Forget the old days on the farm—this was a new era, and the rest of Canada was starting to notice.

From the staid, moribund and recession-crippled former centres of the country—Toronto and Montréal—this new West looked like a wild place open to any possibility. Gretzky and the Oilers only reinforced that notion. Gone were the brutal ways of '70s hockey, when teams pummelled each other as a way to overcome their lack of skill. Gone, too, was the Montréal system of the latter part of the Me decade, which involved the carefully scripted speed of Guy Lafleur or Yvan Cournoyer streaking up and down the wings. This hockey, this Western hockey, was a whole new game. Why, this Gretzky guy even played from behind the net!

Gretzky's style of play, placed in a larger sociopolitical context, proved that the "Canadian Establishment," which Peter C. Newman identified in his 1975 book as controlling the money in the country, was about to lose its hold. No longer would the Mount Stephen Club in Montréal or the Bayview Golf and Country Club in Toronto be the place, as in *the place*, to see and be seen as part of Canada's elite. There was a new breed of Canadians, maybe a little more brash than easterners, who were confident in their way of living. And the money had found them. It was against this backdrop of infinite possibility and seemingly endless riches that the hockey of the 1980s played out and that a new Canada, one that truly stretched from Atlantic to Pacific, was born.

And then the whole thing crashed. First Gretzky moved to LA, then, in 1996, the Jets were relocated to the desert in the southwest. In the face of overwhelming change, Canada once again had to ask itself where its strength lay. The Jets, like their counterparts in Edmonton, had survived the disintegration of the WHA and thrived for another decade. But as the

1980s gave way to the Grunge decade, the Jets lost their ability to draw sufficient revenue to stay in Winnipeg, and when they were packed off to Phoenix, their history was overshadowed and the Avco Cup bearing their name was stored safely away in the Hall of Fame in Toronto.

Most Canadians resented the move, although with the Canuck buck somewhere around $0.73USD in those days, it seemed inevitable. Still, many wondered whether it could have been avoided. What if the NHL had been run by Canadians who appreciated Winnipeg for the arts and culture centre it was in the process of becoming? What if, somehow, the wacky films of Guy Maddin had gotten famous a decade earlier? What if the message that the West is not a monolith but a series of nuanced and varied landscapes, each fostering a different set of ambitions and ways of understanding the world, had been acknowledged?

Maybe NHL hockey would have stayed in Manitoba, rather than being sold by an increasingly desperate league in a place where, basically, nobody cares about it. (The Coyotes' good seasons and playoff appearances of 2010 and 2011 notwithstanding, if Gretzky's hallowed presence couldn't interest people in the game out in Arizona, what might?)

Ultimately, hockey expansion from Vancouver to Alberta and Manitoba, followed by hockey contraction in Manitoba, a loss which took until 2011 to remedy, says a lot about how

Canadians have viewed their own western half over the past 40 years.

Maybe when the Canucks were born, most folks saw the West as a single entity, with perhaps the far reaches, Vancouver itself, being different from the vast stretch that separated it from the trailing edge of Ontario. When the Jets arrived, they were viewed as the space-age entity that their logo and super-sized hero suggested—somehow not of this place, and therefore not really representative of what Winnipeg, or the province, was in most people's lived experience. Maybe they were a bit ahead of their time in that respect.

When Calgary and Edmonton got big-league hockey, suddenly there were two "Wests"—BC, with its edgy, left-leaning hippy-holdover environmentalist culture, and Alberta, the home of the guys who roamed the range. Today, with hockey teams and heroes having come and gone from the region (and come again), it's clear that the West has many contours and many places where the power of the East, so long assumed to be coincident with the force of Canada as a whole, might be found to have a counterpoint. Canada is not solely the Leafs and the Canadiens anymore. This richness and diversity brings history full circle from the invention of the game over 100 years ago.

Hockey Is Canada

From roughly organized leagues to the professionalism of the NHL, through a golden age and into an ever-changing profile of expansion, contraction and relocation, the history of hockey in Canada as well as the current configuration of the NHL are inseparable from the makeup of the country. The game itself and its importance in the communities that embrace it—at all levels—are what define us.

Given this glorious if complicated history, why is it that Canadians sometimes forget or seem to be unconcerned with the origins of their game? Maybe because it's convenient to overlook bygone days in the rush of the present. It's also comforting to believe that this pastime in which many Canadians invest so much of their lives was handed down from the gods, sacred and immutable, rather than being a product of human invention and change.

To many, the game, like the Stanley Cup itself, is at its best when its past recedes into the mists of time, back to some kind of Platonic world of pure "hockeyness," played eternally in its perfect form. It hurts a little to recognize that our version of the game is but a shadow of that ideal—imperfect and changing. But at the same time, looking back with a critical eye deepens our appreciation for the game in its various manifestations over time and provides a lens through which we can understand who we are and how we exist as a product of our past and our regions.

The Politics of Hockey

Playing by the Rules

"**P**olitics makes strange bedfellows," it is often said. For the moment, assume with me that hockey has a politics. Should we ask whether "hockey makes strange politics" or whether "hockey makes politics strange"? Neither sounds quite right. How about, simply, "hockey makes politics"? If you look at the history of Canada, it's easy to see the connection between the game and the "sport" of governing the land. More than any other aspect of popular culture, hockey is integral to the history and politics of the country. The game both reflects what the body politic thinks and does, and sets a pace for it to follow.

Rule-making, obviously, has played a role in Canadian life since the country's beginnings. Whether it was reconciling the Montréal Rules–Halifax Rules split or refining the NHL's rules as time went on, it seems that at some level, Canadians have always wrestled over how to make play fair for everyone.

Take the present-day debates over the ultimate rule of the land, the Charter of Rights and Freedoms, for example. It's more than a little ironic that a country as organized as Canada took over 100 years to draft such a document (if Confederation is viewed as the starting point). By contrast, the Americans had their constitution ratified within about 10 years of declaring their independence. No matter. The Charter is a descendent of something much more important than neighbour envy if we read it as a set of rules akin to those of hockey.

Before 1982, it wasn't clear what a player (if you will) could do, but now it is, though it's also worth noting, as many have, that the Charter of late has become a bit of a boondoggle as various groups try to appropriate it to justify things such as polygamy or to support demands for higher welfare payments.

For those not so crazy about what the Charter is doing in contemporary Canadian courts, maybe seeing it like the Halifax–Montréal hockey rules would make more sense. The rulebook is not a fixed document. It's adaptable and changeable, given to shift when the game changes. So if at certain times it's necessary to give the refs more power to eliminate the clutching and grabbing, then let's try that. If that doesn't work, we'll go in another direction. No big deal. The question is, who will wear the stripes, metaphorically speaking?

Knowing how important the game is in Canada, you might think that hockey would yield benefits to this country that are both tangible (such as people who would make good governors) and intangible (like a spirit of action that replicates the forceful decisiveness displayed on the ice). Yet if hockey gives Canadians a template for their shared existence, the game's spirit informing the spirit of public debate in the country, that doesn't mean that we always proceed in the most rational way, or that the people most fit to lead—those imbued with the qualities that the game imparts—end up in prominent positions.

Strange Bedfellows Indeed

The great Shane Doan caper of 2007 illustrates how the politics of Canada can become the politics of hockey, or vice versa. While most North American hockey fans were focusing on the start of the Stanley Cup playoffs' second round in late April of that year, the Bloc in the House of Commons had noticed something fishy in Russia. Shane Doan, the supposedly culturally insensitive Phoenix Coyote, had been appointed captain of the Canadian team that was about to play for the World Championship.

Doan had been accused of making inappropriate remarks to an on-ice official in a game that took place a year and a half earlier, in December 2005. Now, in 2007, Bloc MP Luc Malo, according to a CBC report, proclaimed,

"[Doan] has said disrespectful things…. Québecers don't feel the team represents them at all."

To most observers, the response to Doan's alleged behaviour smacked, at least a bit, of absurdity. For one thing, Doan denied the charge. In fact, he had ended up suing the MP, Liberal Denis Coderre, who had demanded that Doan be excluded from the 2006 Olympic team over the matter.

Further, you might ask why this particular tournament was on anyone's mind to start with. The World Championship is, let's face it, almost always entirely ignored in Canada, mainly because there's no way we can send our best team. Most of our premier players are still competing in the NHL postseason. And finally, since when does Québec speak for all of Canada? Oh, right. Forget that statement.

Not content to leave well enough alone, the government suggested that the captaincy issue be resolved by a parliamentary committee, where it seems everything that matters goes. (Is the Gretzky trade legal? Did Mulroney take the money? In the case of Gretzky, that was suggested but not carried out.) Hockey Canada officials were asked to explain why Mr. Doan wasn't sent to Siberia and abandoned in a labour camp populated with leftover Solzhenitsyn-types of the Communist era. Well, not quite, but the government did ask that the incident be investigated.

By the way, the comment that Mr. Doan allegedly made was not the scorcher you might be imagining. It was, "You are a 'blank' Frenchman."

As insults go, that's pretty mild, but Québec MP Marcel Proulx has a point when he says Francophones deserve to be respected. Proulx opined that if such a statement had been said about an Anglophone, or anyone else for that matter, an explanation would be demanded, and if Proulx was talking about a comment made on the street, he'd have a point. But what Proulx failed to see was that Doan's comment, if it was made at all, wasn't directed toward a random Francophone; it was said to a referee in the context of a game.

No, that doesn't make it right to insult someone's culture, but maybe there ought to be a little bit of an exception clause built into a ref's job description. The barrel-bellied Mick McGeough likely heard a lot worse in his nearly 20 years in the league. Or how about Kerry Fraser? You think he was never insulted over that hair? Sometimes, things just need to roll off.

That didn't happen with the Doan caper. The New Democrats got involved by saying that "the controversy is making it difficult to feel much excitement about the World Championships." They might have started by explaining why this lack of enthusiasm was different from any other year. Jack Layton said that the team should be playing at its best, "not having to think about something else…. [I]t's unfortunate that

that [what Doan allegedly said] wasn't on the minds of the decision makers at the time." What Layton missed is that the NHL had investigated the incident and decided that there was nothing to it. In other words, Doan had been declared not guilty, but Layton was equating the charge with the crime. And he was being doubly shortsighted because he assumed that the team was thinking about "something else." No, they weren't. They're hockey players. What concerns them is what happens on the ice.

The government defended its meddling by saying that Hockey Canada is funded by the public purse, and thus accountable. The Bloc leader claimed in the *Toronto Star*, "Sports Canada has certain objectives—and that includes reflecting what they call the Canadian reality," and that might be the truest statement of the lot, because what can be said in the end is that several contemporary Canadian realities were surfaced through "Doangate."

For one thing, the level of sensitivity in relation to what is said (or not said, if you listen to Doan, his teammates and the NHL) has reached unprecedented heights in Canada. That might be the unfortunate part. But the flip side is that if something happens in hockey, even in a far-away tournament that nobody is really paying attention to, it will register on the Canadian radar, thus proving that no matter what else is going on, hockey means more to us. And as for the government officials who got involved, at least you can't accuse them of being so interested in the affairs of state that they don't have time to watch the games on TV. Or maybe that's not such a good thing.

Anyway, if they *were* watching the tournament, they would have seen that Doan took his team to the gold, scoring 10 points (5–5–10) in nine games on the way. The next year, he helped them win silver, and again in 2009. In 2010, Doan was too busy trying to get his Phoenix Coyotes through the second round of the playoffs to go to the tournament, and Canada ended up seventh. The loss may have had nothing whatsoever to do with Doan's absence, of course, but not having his leadership might well have cost the team.

His coach in 2007, Andy Murray, said, "Shane Doan has answered the call whenever Canada's asked.... [H]e never has said no to Canada. That's all I'll say about it—it's just the fact that I think he's a real Canadian." Enough said.

In Place of An Empire

Perhaps the connection of hockey to Canadian political life matters so much because the sport, to most Canadians, is one area where they have a say in what goes on in the world. Canada never had a colonial empire, although one might argue that Jacques Cartier and his lot exercised colonizing power over the Native people who were here before the British, Scots and French started calling the place home in the 16th century. From early days, too, it has been clear that the neighbour to the south was going to do its own thing and didn't need Canada's opinion or approval for its actions. That mindset has left a curious void in the national psyche. Not that exercising dominance over another group of people is a good idea—although it has been a large part of the European way of doing things over the centuries.

Canada, in contrast with Britain, the United States and other countries of the so-called developed world, has nothing to control. Nothing except hockey. As one historian describes the formation of the NHL in 1917, "[t]he goal was to establish dominance over the professional game." This was a uniquely Canadian project at the start, and it gave the country something to concentrate on that satisfied its latent colonial ambitions.

When the NHL was first organized, teams came only from Canada, and nowhere farther apart than Toronto and Québec City. The Québec City team was a non-starter, leaving just Montréal (with two teams), Toronto and Ottawa as the league. The first American team, the Boston Bruins, was added seven years later. By the time the NHL consolidated to six teams in 1942, a smattering of U.S. cities had had teams, some for as short as one season. These included Philadelphia, Pittsburgh, St. Louis and others. Further, of the Original Six, two-thirds were from south of the border, making it appear from an outsider's point of view that our little empire of hockey was slipping out of Canada's grasp. Not so.

It wasn't as if these new NHL franchises were in Tampa, Phoenix or Texas. Goodness knows, those would be strange places for hockey to thrive! Rather, these teams were in the northern cities, places where natural ice might form, making the whole idea seem at least somewhat sensible... somewhat Canadian.

And it wasn't a concern anyway, because nearly all the players were from Canada. Everybody knew that, and it was a source of pride that we could lend the Americans our best people for their entertainment pleasure. Doing so was our small attempt at creating a feeling of superiority, dominance even, over the Americans.

Despite more expansion into the U.S. in 1967 and 1970, Canadians' belief in their power over hockey remained throughout the '60s and '70s at least in one measure, because even then, the league's franchises were mostly populated by Canadians. So what if the Stanley Cup went to Boston in 1972? Phil Esposito, Johnny Bucyk and Gerry Cheevers were from here, as were Fred Stanfield, Bobby Orr, John McKenzie and all the other top 10 players in Bruins' scoring, except Ken Hodge. He was born in England.

Montréal brought the Cup back to Canada for the latter half of the 1970s, making it possible to forget that an expansion team, the Flyers, had owned it for a couple of years and to continue the illusion that hockey was still uniquely and specially ours, despite the fact that 15 of the 18 teams in 1975 were American.

However, decades later, a shift has occurred, as Canadians are starting to fear that their hold on the game is diminishing. It's common knowledge that the league is made up of players from all over the world. Nobody today would maintain that there is a natural, genetic predisposition to hockey somehow bred into the Canadian stock. At first, we rationalized that the best "foreign" players were from countries that endure cold winters, like most areas of our country do. Russia, Sweden, Finland, or even a state like Minnesota. But some of the best prospects in recent drafts have come from places where, by rights, there shouldn't be hockey—California, Texas and other warm-weather states. And that fact has been a bit difficult to accept. What happened to the whole myth—the old "we're beating back winter with this game, taming a wild land"? How unfair is it that the game that gives us comfort can also be played by a kid who goes to hockey practice in February wearing a T-shirt and leaves the rink to go back into balmy weather, even after dark?

It's not fair at all, but we can still take pleasure in that, statistically speaking, the majority of players in the NHL are Canadian. Thus, no matter where hockey is played, one might enjoy the comfort of hearing the Canadian accent come out of the mouth of a player being interviewed after an NHL game. When he talks, it's as if Canada still has aspirations to world greatness, because, after all, if this guy, who plays in North Carolina, can be a hero, can't we win on other fronts as well?

Because he plays in Anaheim, California, you might think that a guy like Corey Perry, being interviewed after a game, would talk like this: "Like, ya know, we, like played real well out there? Um, I mean, like, we played as a team tonight?" Snap of gum. The perfect Valley accent.

Instead, what Perry says is, "Sure, we played well. We played as a team. Uh, when they got ahead, we stuck with it." Read that with the classically clipped Ontario accent cutting the vowels short, and you'll have the sound just right. And hearing someone like Perry on *Hockey Night in Canada*'s late-night *After Hours* segment is comforting for those who believe that Canada is the home of hockey. Though this game is played by people in every corner of the U.S., and all over Europe, the best of the best still come from this country, and for that reason, Canadians can continue to imagine that hockey is their game, their way of contributing to the world, and maybe even their way of pulling the strings of political power on a global stage.

Big Stick, Soft Voice

U.S. president Teddy Roosevelt advised that you ought to speak softly and carry a big stick in your engagement with the world. When Roosevelt made that comment, the likely image that would have sprung to mind for Americans was that of a baseball bat. But perhaps Teddy had his northern neighbours in mind when he made his admonition. A hockey player uses his stick differently than a baseball player uses his. The ballplayer uses his "stick" for one purpose and for a limited time, then he drops it and proceeds to another part of the field to take up a different endeavour altogether—running. By contrast, a hockey player always carries his stick, even when he sits on the bench and waits for his next turn to play. Some players rest them blade down in front of them, with the butt end, the one with the big tape knob, sitting just above eye level as they survey the ice. Others put that end on the floor and let the business end hang out over the boards. Looking at the typical bench while play is on yields a view of intense faces, the sticks standing ready for more action.

Throughout the history of hockey, the greatest players have let their actions speak, in the form of their sticks, rather than their words, by combining strength of purpose with a soft voice into what might be a template for Canadian politicians. Sadly, most of those at the centre of Canadian political life do not follow this example.

Maurice Richard exemplifies the soft voice, big stick mode of engagement. He was taken from the parks of Montréal to the ice of the Forum with a brief stop with the Senior Canadiens team in between. The transformation occurred so quickly that even he must have been surprised by it. Once a member of the Habs, he found himself in a position where he had a say in things, in one sense. At least the media (on behalf of the fans) expected him to speak up on behalf of French Canadians. But his words were few.

As biographer Roch Carrier says, "He arrives as silent as if his soul were inhabited by a rage that's about to break loose and with a will that resembles an obsessive stubbornness." The Rocket spoke little English in the early days of his hockey career, and even later was reluctant to address the public through the media. Perhaps that's why he accepted Clarence Campbell's suspension after his stick-swinging incident in 1955 with quiet words, reading a prepared speech on television.

Instead, Richard let his play do his talking. Again, Carrier: "In this Canada that their [Toe Blake's and Richard's] ancestors discovered, the French Canadians are the servants, the hewers of wood and drawers of water. The language of their ancestors, their language, is looked down on. Winning the Stanley Cup is a proud revenge." This in reference to Montréal's victory in 1944.

Richard did carry a big stick, however. That was never truer than when he exacted revenge upon Toronto's Bob Bailey in 1954 by "smacking him with the stick so hard that Bailey [lost] a tooth." As Carrier tells the story, when Richard lands on Bailey and feels the latter's fingers in his eyes, "Maurice explodes. He wants to wreck everything. With his stick he mows down whatever is standing on the ice.

Five times [referee] Red Storey disarms him. Five times he comes back with a stick." The incident that got him suspended in 1955 also started with stick-fighting, though at that time, what got the Rocket kicked out for the balance of the season was that he punched linesman Cliff Thompson.

Similarly, Gordie Howe was a man of quiet confidence. He let his elbows do his talking for him, and several players missing their front teeth can confirm this, but Howe's savagery never extended beyond the rink. Off the ice, he was soft-spoken, with a slight lisp and no hint of the ferocity that made his counterparts in the league fear going into a corner with him.

The one time I met him, he was coming up the ramp to the bench of an NHL arena to coach in a charity old-timers game being played after the conclusion of an NHL contest. Seeing me there, he paused, maybe because he caught my expression of surprise. I told him I appreciated all he'd done in hockey, and that I also knew he was active in helping out in fundraising in the hospital where my mom had been a rehab patient after having suffered a stroke. I mentioned that he had been at an event there and that the foundation had later auctioned off some stuff he'd autographed. He just smiled, and said, "Boy, I hope I can get these guys to play hard," and then shook my hand.

He and I both knew this game didn't have a great deal of importance, and that he probably wouldn't actually do much "coaching." And sad to say, since the game was in LA, not many people had stuck around after the Kings game to see it, nor would some of them have known who Gordie Howe was, anyway. But none of that interested him. Rather, he was living this moment for all it was worth, and he was totally committed to the value of the hockey to be played in Staples Center that evening.

Gordie spoke softly to me that day, and I'll never forget that. But had I played against him, I might have remembered him for his big stick (metaphorically speaking). When I discussed the incident in 2010 with his son, Mark, himself a darn fine hockey player for a couple of decades in the WHA and NHL, he said, "Yup, that's my dad. Always got a minute for everybody, but never takes credit for anything he does."

President Roosevelt might not have been referring to his neighbours to the north when he talked about the big stick, but he was accurately describing men like Richard and Howe—players who let their actions, both on and off the ice, be their voices. Given the importance of hockey in Canadian culture, it might seem natural that Canadian political life would benefit from leaders who are like hockey players, combining strength of the stick with subtlety of voice. However, it must be remarked, sadly, that most Canadian politicians, especially of late, don't live by the hockey ethos.

Michael Ignatieff came back to Canada in 2005 after a long sojourn in England and the U.S. as an academic and writer. He took over a failing Liberal Party on an interim basis in 2008, full time in 2009, with the hopes that he would keep its place as the so-called natural governing party of Canada intact. Instead, he took it to historic lows, then lost even his own seat. Maybe one reason for his failure was that he was all "talk" and no "stick." His rhetoric was the kind of polished stuff that a university president might use with his or her provosts. But most people just saw Ignatieff as distant and unconcerned. Maybe they held his long absence from the country against him.

Stephen Harper pulled off the amazing feat of merging the Canadian Alliance with the Progressive Conservatives to form the Conservative Party of Canada, and he became PM in 2006. Early in his career, people saw him as someone who could bring the West into the fold, maybe even keep a handle on Québec at the same time. As PM, he was offered a chance to carry a big stick when the U.S. made overtures about involvement in Iraq, but he stuck to the policies of his predecessor, wisely and thankfully saying, "No way, eh."

Harper is a hockey fan and a member of the Society for International Hockey Research who also is writing a book about the game. But without a stick and without the ability to softly and profoundly utter words that would compel Canadians to embrace his vision for the country, he faltered. He picked up his game a notch and won a majority in his second election as PM in 2011, but still many agree that he does not possess the undertone of gravitas that the best hockey leaders display.

Hockey players blend the two characteristics that Roosevelt named into a package larger than either element could be on its own. Perhaps so many leaders of the nation have failed because they seem always to choose one or the other as their modus operandi. The ideal, rather, would be to combine the big stick with the soft words. This is the source of the greatest hockey players' power and ability to lead.

If there's one federal politician who does this, it might be Jack Layton. Coming off hip surgery and having battled prostate cancer, he led his party into the 2011 election with a cane in one hand. His "injuries" didn't deter him, nor did his condition stop Canadians in record numbers from voting for his party's candidates, creating a 66-seat swing for the NDP. Sure, the issues were complicated, and Québec's dissatisfaction with the Bloc Québecois had a lot to do with the change, but seeing Layton as a hockey guy, a battler with a stick in his hand, might be one way to account for his success.

Leaders and Potential Leaders

How often has a rag-tag bunch of players been taken from mid-level regular-season performance to playoff glory, if not all the way to the Stanley Cup? Such a miracle doesn't happen every year, but when it does, it's often people similar

to the ones that Roosevelt might have been imagining who
help pull it off.

Dave Andreychuk was a strong but quiet leader when
he finished his second stint with the Buffalo Sabres in 2001
and went to Tampa Bay to join the Lightning. At the time, that
team was led by a great goalie, Nikolai Khabibulin, and had
a roster of emerging stars. But nobody (perhaps outside of the
team) believed they could win a Cup. Andreychuk contrib-
uted to their 2004 playoff triumph with just one goal, but he
added 13 assists. His real strength, however, was in captaining
a young team and showing them how to sacrifice. And in typical fashion, he credited the team after the Cup-winning
game: "I'm so proud of our guys because we got a game 7 at
home because we worked hard all year long." Despite this def-
erence to the team, observers knew that he had been the key.
Would he make a good MP someday? Could be.

Perhaps neither Teeder Kennedy, nor Larry Robinson,
nor Trevor Linden would make much of a prime minister
because, having devoted their lives to hockey, they never
developed the savvy that a politician needs to survive the
jungle of voter opinion and the heat of the Parliamentary
Question Period. But that doesn't mean that there's no future
for a hockey player in politics.

Jacques Demers and Frank Mahovlich are senators.
Neither man has any education past high school. And to add
to that, Demers has been open in recent years about having

struggled with illiteracy. When he coached, he had an assistant fill in the lineup card and sign it, often pleading that he had forgotten his reading glasses or that his language skills in English were deserting him at a given time.

Imagine for a moment that Jay Leno was Canadian. What would he say on his show about this state of affairs? For sure, he would have a comment about the other members of the Senate having skills no better than Demers', or perhaps he would make a crack that maybe now, everyone could just stop pretending to read legislation that they never gave a glance at anyway.

At the time Demers was appointed to the Senate, *Sports Illustrated* quoted him as saying, "I've worked so hard these last four years to improve my reading and writing. All of a sudden, they name me senator. It's just incredible." Those are not exactly the kind of words one might expect out of the mouth of someone about to take an important role in government, but after all, "Demers is the last man to coach a Canadian team to the Stanley Cup," as the article so precisely puts it. What more important achievement could someone accomplish, especially to distinguish himself to a prime minister who is an avowed hockey nut, as is Harper?

The key question since Demers and Mahovlich found their way to Ottawa is what business they have running the country. The answer is simple—look at what they've done in hockey. To Canadians, leadership on the ice (or in the case of

Coach Demers, off the ice) qualifies a person for leadership in the government. Again, think Andreychuk. On the opposite end—Roberto Luongo. Too much talk, and, to this point in his career, not enough action, especially in the playoffs of 2011.

The U.S. also venerates its sports stars and gives them places in government. People like football player Steve Largent are elected to Congress. The one difference to note is that American student athletes generally get some university training behind them before they embark on their pro careers, and often, they earn degrees. In theory, then, they might be more prepared for a place in the government after their sports careers than the Canadian who played junior hockey and went to class after getting off the bus fresh from "the Sault," having ridden all night. (This not to discount the recent advent of scholarship programs in the major junior leagues.)

But looking at how both countries are run, it makes you wonder if it's really fair of Canadians to be down on their Senate for appointing hockey players. Where else but on the rink do you learn sacrifice and teamwork? Where else do you learn to make crucial decisions in the blink of an eye? To exercise leadership, which is a key component of governing?

Think about the decisions coaches make. Demers, for example, was in charge when the infamous McSorley stick incident occurred, and he demanded that McSorley's curve be measured, with less than two minutes to go in the second game of the 1993 Stanley Cup final series against the Kings.

The ensuing minor gave the Habs a goal, and had they not won the game, it's all but certain the series wouldn't have been as easy as it was for the eventual winner (Montréal, four games to one), because they would have dropped the first two games at home. Reading skills are not needed to quickly sum up a situation, take charge and make something happen using whatever power is available to you.

And if you want a worst-case scenario comparison in the U.S. Senate, look at the late U.S. senator Robert Byrd, who by some accounts served well past the time when his abilities had started to fail. He was subject to re-election every six years, so it's true that he could have been turfed out many times during his 51-year tenure. But early on, he established himself as someone who looked after the people who sent him to Washington. When he passed 80, then 90, his ability to govern was probably reduced, but did that matter? Heck no—by that time, the electorate had him permanently cemented into their voting mindset, and he died in 2010 holding his seat at 92, still directing huge mountains of funds toward West Virginia to support all kinds of government projects.

What's even more scary is that Byrd, serving as something fancily called "President pro tempore of the United States Senate" whenever the Democratic party was in control, was third in the line of presidential succession, which means that had anything happened to the president, VP and speaker of the House of Representatives, he would have become the acting president. More telling, in terms of how U.S. spending policies developed over the past couple of decades, is that he was the chair of the Senate's Committee on Appropriations three different times in the early and mid-1990s, the early 2000s, and from 2007 to 2009. Those periods, students of history might recall, coincided with enormous spending free-for-alls by the U.S. government.

Compared to Byrd, senators Demers (born in 1944) and Mahovlich (born in 1938) are spring chickens. And while Byrd might have had an advantage over them in that he had a university education and a law degree, as many U.S. politicians do, would this necessarily make him a better thinker than our two hockey senators?

Frank Mahovlich played for the Maple Leafs and Red Wings before he joined the Montréal Canadians in 1971. He won the Stanley Cup six times with Toronto and Montréal. He also played in the Summit Series against the Russians, finding his way into six games. He entered the Hockey Hall of Fame in 1981 and the Senate in 1998.

Demers started his hockey career where Mahovlich finished his in the WHA, as a coach rather than a player. He won the Jack Adams Award twice, for being the NHL's outstanding coach, back-to-back with Detroit in 1986–87 and 1987–88. He led Montréal to its 24th Stanley Cup in 1993. Sure, that victory might have been unlikely, as the team depended on OT wins to survive that whole postseason, but any man who can deal with the pressures of the Montréal hockey scene and come out on top must have a reserve of strength that he can draw on for a future in politics.

Mahovlich didn't have any particular leadership experience when the Senate tapped him via a Chrétien appointment, and he was known to have had a nervous disposition over the years that he played the game, but as a senator, he has acted with poise, which in many ways is part of his job. Currently, he serves on the committees on Agriculture and Forestry as well as Foreign Affairs and International Trade. The first appointment seems harmless, and the second, well, you could do worse than sit next to a guy at a summit meeting and have him lean over and say, "You know, those Russians really taught us a thing or two about the black market back in 1972. You talk about trade? There wasn't anything those guys couldn't get!" Okay, not really, but the government does describe him as "a great ambassador for the game of hockey and an outstanding role model."

It might be uber-Canadian to tap a hockey man to take a job in the Senate, but when you analyze the character these two men have displayed, it makes a lot of sense. Kind of makes you wonder who's next, though. These days, a player with any degree of visibility doesn't need to depend on a government salary or pension after retirement, so there may be less incentive to take such a position, but what kind of strong dignity would Jerome Iginla bring to this post? How about Mario Lemieux?

Of course, one advantage to having a hockey player in a political role might be that he knows when it's time to call it quits. Byrd stayed until the day he died, which was probably too long. Mahovlich quit playing hockey after trying to come back from a knee injury at age 40. Demers lost his coaching job in Tampa Bay in 1999 at age 55. Mahovlich and Demers had the sense to call it a day when it was time to move on to other things. Hopefully, they will use the same logic when deciding to take that fat pension they're entitled to for their service to the country as senators.

Here is one other comparison to ponder: who makes a better governing official—a former professional sports player or a movie star? You can name a long list of the latter in U.S. governing positions. Arnold Schwarzenegger, Ronald Reagan, Sonny Bono, Fred Grange, Clint Eastwood, Fred Thompson and Al Franken are only some. Jerry Springer went the other way, from mayor of Cincinnati to talk show host. In Canada, we have few examples of the same thing.

Richard Malcolm Thomas (not John-boy Walton) was a voiceover actor and TV presenter, and he ended up failing at a number of bids at public office until finally being elected reeve of Armour Township near Parry Sound, which might just rival Eastwood's mayoralty in Carmel, California, for power. Daniel Clark was an actor who played the lead on *OWL/TV*, a kids' show, in the 1980s. He then disappeared for a number of years while earning his degree and resurfaced as PC candidate in Timmins-James Bay in 2000, a race he lost. His failure may have had something to do with the good people of that riding not appreciating the fact that, until a week before the polls opened, young Clark had never even been in Timmins. Suffice it to say, there is no history of electing our showbiz stars to run the show in Ottawa, or any provincial capital, that mirrors that of the Americans.

What does this say? It tells us that we as a people believe that a person who has spent his or her life in front of cameras pretending to be someone else is probably not the best choice to trust with public policy decisions. We would prefer a person whose value system has been formed in the crucible of the game, someone like Bob Attersley. His name is not familiar to most, but he was at one time the captain of the Whitby Dunlops hockey team. With them, he won the World Championship in 1958 and a silver medal at the Olympics in Norway in 1960.

Attersley's experience suited him well to later become a politician. Witness the description of that 1958 game between the Soviet Union and a bunch of amateurs from Ontario:

> *The Soviet athletes competed for the glory of their motherland, as well as the superiority of their leadership's Communist ideology, while the Whitby Dunlops carried the weight*

of a nation's fear [that] it might no longer
dominate the sport it bequeathed the world.
All the skaters faced extraordinary pressure.

About Attersley particularly, the editor of the *Toronto Telegram*'s sports pages said, "[H]ere was a player who would be there when all the blue chips were piled on the table." He scored two goals, including the winner, and assisted on the insurance goal in Canada's 4–2 win. He had worked in a tire factory earlier in his adult life, and after finishing up with hockey in 1963, he opened a tire shop. After being a Whitby city councillor for a number of years, Attersley became mayor in 1980, serving until 1991.

It might not be as common for Canadians to elect sports people as for Americans to elect actors, but it does make a certain kind of sense when it happens. Think of it this way—what's the worst that can happen if Mr. Schwarzenegger and his type screw up a shot while filming a movie? They redo the take another day. But a hockey player who has played for his country's honour in a game that will surely and irrevocably be decided right here, right now, must understand how to succeed under pressure—and with no possibility of a do-over.

Ken Dryden is a great example of combining brains and hockey grit. He got his baptism by fire early, in the 1971 playoffs. He didn't even qualify for rookie of the year honours that season—that happened the next year. In '71, Dryden was a call-up who saved the day, leading the Habs to the Stanley

Cup in a seven-game nail-biting final that still gives at least one opponent on the Chicago Blackhawks, Jim Pappin, nightmares, as I learned by talking to him in the press box at an NHL game. The next year, Dryden was the Calder Memorial Trophy winner as the NHL's best rookie, and as the latter part of the decade unfolded, he took the Canadiens back to the finals, and won, four more times. Then he quit.

He was, of course, a different sort of hockey player. Whenever there was a break from games, and during one year that he suspended his career (1973–74), he studied law. So it isn't much of a surprise that in his post-hockey days, after a stint in team management with Toronto from 1997 to 2004, he ended up in politics as a federal MP. What better preparation than a law degree and having played in some of the most important and pressure-filled games in hockey history?

Question Period in the House of Commons might be a seriously anxiety-producing experience for some. Getting shouted down wouldn't be fun, and Dryden had his share of insults to bear while in his post. In his first term, as Cabinet Minister of Social Development, he was insulted as an "old white guy" by Conservative MP Rona Ambrose after his comments on childcare struck Ambrose as demeaning to women. A CTV report described the atmosphere in the House that day: "The Speaker had to call members to order several times after [Ambrose's] remark as government and opposition MPs hurled invective across the floor."

Did this faze Dryden? Probably not more than when the Chicago Blackhawks tried to avenge that 1971 Stanley Cup loss in 1973, when Dryden again beat them, only this time in six games rather than seven. And probably not more than having New York's Phil Esposito standing in the slot firing pucks off his curved wooden stick while the goalie stood there, his famous "target" mask the only protection for his lawyer-face and a sixth Stanley Cup on the line, in 1979. Hockey players know pressure, and when you combine that with the education Dryden has (Cornell and McGill), you have what in the U.S. would surely qualify someone as state governor material, at least.

However, this kind of success has eluded the former number 29. Dryden attempted to become the Liberal Party's leader in 2006, but he received only scant support. The CBC blamed his loss of the leadership bid on "Dryden's wooden speech delivery and lacklustre fundraising."

But who's to say that Canadians won't realize one day that we're a lot better off with a hockey hero as the head person than career politicians or academics, as were Stephane Dion (who of course won the leadership role against Dryden) or Ignatieff (who succeeded him)?

What looks better on a resumé, the first word of Dion's description, "Cabinet Minister," Ignatieff's "Professor," or Dryden's "Goaltender"?

Nationalism Taken Too Far

At times, our political will as a hockey nation is consumed by our will to win. In these moments, hockey becomes equivalent to national identity, and our focus is not on a player, from Ontario or Manitoba, say, who spends his life in Tennessee or Columbus, Ohio, but a team, an entire squad, with the maple leaf in bold red or white on the front of their sweaters. In those cases the country can rally, and suddenly, there's nothing un-politically correct about being xenophobic. It's now okay to take that little maple leaf off the backpack, wave some magic dust over it, and turn it into a giant Canadian flag, then go to the arena and wave it in the faces of whoever else turns up to watch the game.

World hockey tournaments will never mean as much to Canadians as winning the Stanley Cup, but over the decades, they have given rise to some galvanizing episodes both on and off the ice. To many, the Summit Series of 1972 was the high-water mark for Canadian national pride in an international tournament. But students of hockey history know that there were teams that represented Canada long before 1972. The Olympics of 1920, 1924, 1928 and 1932, for example, all gave gold to Canada. And in 1958, a ready-made squad, the Whitby Dunlops, went to Oslo, Norway, to contest for a World Championship gold medal in the name of the country, and won it.

Through the 1960s, too, there were teams that played in maple leaf sweaters, some quite well, others poorly. In fact, one reason for the initiation of the friendly eight-game series between Canada and the Russians in 1972 was to erase some of the bad reputation Canada had acquired because of its bloody and violent actions on the world's hockey rinks during the hippy era. Speaking about international tournaments that took place throughout the 1960s, scholars Donald MacIntosh and Donna Greenhorn say, "the diminution of good will for Canada that stemmed from the 'brutish' and 'reprehensible' conduct of many Canadian hockey players...[was] distressing to the Department of External Affairs."

In the Summit Series, and in every series since then, creating something called "Team Canada" may be one of our strongest metaphoric attempts to define Canadian nationalism and express our collective political will. In the 1970s, the equation was less well worked out than it is today. Then, the defining characteristic of Canadianness was to say that we were not American. In hockey terms, there was no question that we were better, with nothing to prove.

Hockey back then meant something simple—assembling the best bunch of Canadians and going out to win. The principle held as time passed, proving itself in 1972 and 1987 during the Canada Cup. But by the new millennium, a shift was taking place. It was no longer automatic that the 20 or 25 guys on a roster, because they came from Canada, would dominate players from elsewhere in the world. The Europeans were having their say, as when their various teams won Olympic medals between 1984 and 1998. Canada gained silver in 1992 and '94, but had a disastrous non-medal effort in 1998.

Those results meant that the situation had to be taken in hand, and Wayne Gretzky was the person to do that as the leader of the Canadian Olympic hockey program at the 2002 Salt Lake City Games. The U.S., meanwhile, was expected to make an effort almost as credible as our own, and it was the Americans who, on their soil, played the Canucks for the gold in 2002. Cheering the Canadian team on were tens of thousands of fans from all parts of Canada who had made the trip to Salt Lake. And in the ice at the arena, for good luck—though only a few people knew it at the time—was a loonie.

That loonie in the ice perhaps more than anything else tells the story of Canadian nationalism in the new era, a time when winning at hockey is not a given. We believe we should win. Our team must be at least as good as the others, and it probably has somewhat of an edge most times. We know also that we might not win, but for a little extra intervention by the hockey gods. But like the experienced fans we are, we realize that those same hockey gods don't like it when you sit back and let them do all the work. A little underhanded participation in the process goes a long way with them. Hence that loonie.

Sneaking the loonie into the ice also says a lot about how we relate to our southern neighbours. Going into the Olympic

year of 2002, we were the people with the expertise in ice making, and the Americans knew it. They, in turn, were not too
proud to ask for help when they needed it. Or rather, their pride
in all the other things they excel at is so great that it didn't hurt
them to admit that they might have to outsource something so
trivial as creating a surface for hockey. So they gave Edmonton
a call and got the best guys in the world to do the job.

Those men, namely Dan Craig and a couple of Zamboni
drivers he brought along for help, decided to seed the deck
with that coin, and they buried it deep enough that it remained
undetected during the tournament. Then, after the win, the
Canadian players, who by this time had heard word of their
good luck charm, were seen bending down to view it. Once
the men's match concluded the tournament and the gold
medals were safely around Team Canada's necks, they dug the
coin out, and it now sits in the Hockey Hall of Fame. This is
similar to the little kid on the block who secretly learns karate
so that he can beat up the bully. The only irony, of course, is that
Canada wasn't really the underdog.

The attempt to circumvent the normal course of
affairs with an underhanded good luck charm reveals that
even when we're probably going to succeed, the familiar
Canadian inferiority complex takes over. How insulting to
put a distinctly and unmistakably Canadian symbol under
the Americans' ice. How put out would we have felt had
they pulled a similar stunt?

To put it into equivocal terms, let's say that at a Summer Olympics in Toronto where baseball is a part of the Games, the Yanks win gold over the Dominican Republic, and afterward, they pick up home plate to reveal a U.S. silver dollar. Would Canadians feel violated? What if the win were against our team? Unless the game was hockey, it wouldn't matter, at least not that much. But when it comes to what happens on the ice, perspective can get lost because hockey is so intimately intertwined with the Canadian self-image.

That a sport can have a politics might not be surprising. Look at the reaction to the Tiger Woods scandal or the hubbub raised over Michael Vick and the problems he had with dog fighting and it's clear that games matter, and that they frequently overlap into public affairs. But in Canada, when it comes to hockey, a different standard is brought to bear. Everything that happens in the game has immense significance, from the smallest slight to the biggest win or loss. The politics of hockey reflect—no, they define—the politics of our country as a whole.

Rhythms that Make Sense

Patterns and Pastimes

Hockey exists in four basic forms: the game you play on the ice, the game you play on the street, the game you play in other forms, such as on tables and in fantasy leagues and the game you watch. In every instance, its easy rhythms and back-and-forth pattern offer a comforting sense of flow in the complicated whirl of life. Because hockey is so much a part of who we are, for Canadians, each manifestation of the game might be read as the answer to the fundamental question that humans ask themselves: what does life all mean, anyway?

How depressing!

Sitting around and wondering about the dark soul of the universe doesn't sound like much fun. True enough, and yet nearly all of us do it at some point in our lives. Some go through a teenage "Goth" phase. Others go through a mid-life crisis. In either case, a lack, or loss, of identity causes us to search for something that will offer life meaning, but maybe when we feel down we should look to a more obvious place than music, the club scene or a red sports car and younger girlfriend as antidotes to the blues that invade our lives. Maybe the answer lies with hockey.

From the time a Canuck is a kid, he or she has something to do. Whether it's heading down to the rink for a practice or game, taking shots in the driveway or maybe plopping down on the couch to watch a Saturday night game, hockey is there for them. The game is a willing companion and an answer to the dark night of the soul. Or even the dark night of a Canadian winter. Whichever you choose, the game creates the contours of the Canadian worldview.

The moment-to-moment reality of the action on the rink suggests the easy flow that life at its best can have. The rhythm that hockey gives to the yearly calendar provides life with anchors, making it easier to cope with the hectic times. For instance, Christmas vacation means family, holiday traditions and presents. But it also means hockey tournament time, with kids as young as six heading off in search of a trophy to take to school when the calendar turns to January.

These rhythms associated with the game are not all that old. The rise of tournaments for non-all-star kids probably happened fewer than 20 years ago. But they quickly became what Canadians do, and now we don't question it. Instead, we revel in being busy, and we are seduced by the idea that these games, even those played by the littlest kids, matter. And in that, we take comfort. Winter comes and goes. Our modern devices allow us to survive the coldest of seasons, physically, but hockey is what gives us emotional victory over winter, and in the many ways that the game becomes institutionalized into Canadian life and history, it creates the country.

Poet John B. Lee nicely describes the feeling in his piece, "When I Was a Boy and the Farm Pond Froze":

When I was a boy
once every winter the farm pond froze
wide as a field from fence to fence
we'd go down with skates, puck and stick
and play in the burning wind for days.

Bruce Meyer also gets to the core of it, talking about "Road Hockey" in his poem of that name, but a winter version of the sport:

Snow had settled
on the brown furrows
of the fall ploughings
the way a dusting of ice
clung to our corduroys
as we shouted and raved
in a dead-end street,
pushing and hacking
each other's spindly legs
until the night descended
blackening the game
and calling us home

to those tiny rooms
taped with clippings
of Howe and Hull
and silver grails.

The Geography of the Canadian Mind

The game creates the patterns that characterize the Canadian mind—a series of linear opposites. Canada versus the U.S., English versus French, Toronto versus Montréal—all are familiar dichotomies. Think about it—even the geography of the country mimics the east-west flow of a hockey game. The U.S., by contrast, mixes east-west with north-south in a complex set of movements that swirl and change with the times. At one point in history, the migratory flow in that country was west, to follow a dream, such as the Gold Rush. After that, it was north, to the factories promising good wages for manufacturing products such as automobiles. That movement has changed now, and the south is attracting people, but the path taken is not linear in any specific direction. Americans are always shifting their focus from side to side and from top to middle to bottom. Maybe the baseball field is a reflection of that constant swirl, with its diamond shape and its circular flow.

Funny that when the Americans couldn't find any more space to occupy between the borders that they finally decided would define their country, they got Alaska and Hawaii, then they went into space. In so doing, they continued the metaphorical whirl of geography, moving off-axis, creating a country with three dimensions, rather than the flat plane that we occupy.

Hockey play goes from net to net, with one side gaining the momentum, then the other. It's a simple game, in that sense, played back and forth, from goal line to goal line. That momentum is perhaps also one of Canada's problems. It has always been easy to see the divisions in the country in terms of two poles. First, it was Lower and Upper Canada. After that, the West and the East. All the while, the population huddled along the border with its southern neighbour. Somewhere along the way, we appropriated a game that mimicked that long, thin line.

But about a decade ago, our geographical imagination changed to include a new dimension. To understand that, zoom back, say 30 years, to when kids learned geography in school by memorizing the provinces. The teacher also explained that in addition to the 10 provinces, there were two territories. One territory didn't even have a name, really. It simply took on its geographical descriptor: Northwest, and it was plural, Territories. Students didn't imagine anyone actually living there except, perhaps, "Explorers" or "Eskimos."

Those unknown people lived in a region where it was so cold that they didn't talk—they merely touched noses in greeting. Their bodies were covered at all times against the cold, even indoors, because they lived in snow houses. What they did with their time was anyone's guess, because there was no TV where they lived. These were the certainties of the ignorant mind even as late as the 1970s. Maybe later.

Then came Nunavut. Suddenly, Canadians in other parts of the country had to reconcile themselves to the fact that the borders that defined Canada were not solely east–west. Now, the North was not just a far-off land of snow that simply ended in nothingness (or at Santa's workshop, postal code H0H 0H0), but was a place with a political structure and a set of recognizable values that extended *somewhere*. To us, that *somewhere* now had a name, a language, a culture and a government that made Canadians aware that these "others" had an identity and were a part of us.

Today, with Inuk player Jordin Tootoo a part of the hockey scene and with the promise of others to follow, the attitude has changed, because what was purely on the margin is edging its way more into the centre of our collective consciousness. However, it must also be acknowledged that no matter what changes occur, no matter how the geography of the country shifts, the fundamental Canadian way of reading ourselves is rooted in an east-west flow, with first one region surging, scoring and having the upper hand, then the other, just as in the game of hockey.

The Simple Beauty of Flow

The flow of the calendar through the year is also helped along by the country's favourite sport. If you live someplace like Flin Flon, Manitoba, say, where Bobby Clarke and a lot of other NHL players have come from, then the coming of winter, naturally, demands an antidote. But in modern, suburban Toronto or Halifax, most people have no need to beat back the depressing effects of the snow and cold. They just carry on with their activities, driving golf balls and practicing tennis serves indoors or studying karate or ballet. Watching TV or even jumping on a discount airline and heading to Florida are also options.

But while we've tamed winter in some measure through a focus on other pursuits, hockey has retained its place in the rhythms of our lives. Fall doesn't mean the World Series for most Canadians. It means the start of the NHL regular season, and of kids' hockey practices and games. It means the local major junior team will be on the ice in the long pursuit that might take them to their league championship and then the Memorial Cup tourney. It means that the eternal-seeming cycle of training camp/Christmas tournament/playoffs/end-of-season pizza party has begun again.

This rhythm has become so familiar to so many of us that, honestly, the year wouldn't make much sense without hockey as our compass. Of course, what stands above all the amateur and lesser-league versions of the game is the NHL and the pursuit of the Stanley Cup, and for Canadians, no matter where they live, watching those games from October to June in that quest is an abiding passion.

Hockey is a game that never stops. The casual or new fan often makes two observations about it: first, it's odd that players come on and off during the course of play, and second, it's neat that there's no out-of-bounds. Of course, it's possible to put the puck out of play over the glass, which in certain circumstances nets the player a penalty, or the puck can go up into the netting to stop the action, but overall, hockey is a game of flow, not pauses, and certainly not one that finds its expression in statistics, despite the tendency to reduce it to such in American television broadcasts.

What does the flow of our game say to us, thinking through the idea that my country is hockey? The argument could be made that the history of Canada, like the history of hockey, is one of flow. Taking exacting measurements—inches, or centimetres these days—has never been our way of doing things. Maybe it's because the land we tamed is so big; perhaps because it was always more important to guard against the ravages of nature than nitpick about the details of where boundary lines were to be drawn.

Whatever the case, Canadian history is more like a skate down the Rideau Canal than a burst to the 100-metre line in a track meet. Time past, for Canadians, goes back a long way, at least to the 15th century (Cartier was born in 1491). For Americans, the hallmarks of history are routinely cited as 1776 or 1787 (when the Constitution was ratified).

With flow comes simplicity. It's not that hockey is an easy game to play. Skating is a skill that even some NHLers haven't mastered as well as others. But the game itself is not built on complicated strategies. In other sports, baseball, for example, what appears to be a simple and self-evident play becomes overwritten with complexities. What does the runner on second do on a ground ball to right field with two outs? Baseball fans will respond with "run on contact." But there are always so many variations thrown in depending upon what the pitcher does and how the second baseman is playing the ball.

Football outdoes both baseball and hockey as being immensely complex. The average NFL team runs dozens of different plays, each of which is diagrammed in a playbook up to 800 pages long. The game is so complicated that the quarterbacks wear what amount to maps on their arms to help them remember what's what, and they have earpieces to get calls from their coaches.

Hockey looks refreshingly simple by comparison, at least in the traditional way it was played. There wasn't a right or a wrong move to be made in any given situation, just a set of reactions mixed with determination that governed a player's actions.

Hockey's simplicity might be an outgrowth of the Canadian mind, which focuses less on coming up with a cunning answer when faced with a difficult circumstance and more on doing the right thing. There's a sort of honesty, or maybe better, a naïveté, in acting this way. It's like the old joke that goes, "How do you get 50 Canadians out of the pool in an emergency?" The answer, of course, is to say, "We have an emergency. Would you kindly get out of the pool?"

Canadians do the proper thing, with no resistance. Flow, again, is the metaphor, and it's how hockey is experienced at its most beautiful.

The difference between Canadians and Americans can be boiled down to the difference between their great game, baseball, and ours. In baseball, inches matter. The typical play at first base is decided on whether the player's foot is an inch above the bag or is touching it when the ball gets there. It's amazing that 100-plus years into the history of baseball, that play is still as close as it ever was, and they haven't moved the base farther away from or closer to home plate. The game just goes on, static in its presentation. That is not meant as a criticism.

But because that play is the most-often seen one in baseball, it has been said that it's a game of inches. Think about the strike zone. If the pitch is a little bit outside, or low, the umpire calls it a ball. If it's a little high, he still might call it a strike. Fans over the years have debated whether to use replays or electronic pitch calling to correct for the occasional mistakes umpires make or to ensure that each call is precise to the millimetre, but so far, nothing has changed. The sport, in that way, relies on the human element, and that's okay. Because of its reliance on the human element, however, baseball takes on its greatest meaning through its manifestation in statistics. A game of inches becomes a game of numbers.

Football, on the other hand, is a game of pauses. In the average 60-minute game, something like four or five minutes are devoted to play where the ball is moved. That's one-twelfth, max. But hockey is a game of almost tidal flow. It has been so from the start and on up through the game's greatest eras.

In the 1950s, the Montréal Canadiens' style of play, called "Firewagon Hockey," was all about speed, with Maurice Richard and Jean Béliveau complemented by other greats, including Bernie "Boom Boom" Geoffrion. The Habs' "system," to use a word that is frequently invoked by players nowadays, was based on the rush. Their sole focus was to get the puck from here to there, with "there" being the other team's net. Defense be damned. Well, not quite damned, because when the other team did pick up the puck and carry it into the Montréal end, Doug Harvey and goalie Gerry McNeil, or Jacques Plante, were there to turn it aside.

A few decades later, the Edmonton Oilers took up the charge, literally. The game in the 1980s never stopped, and the points piled up for Gretzky, Jari Kurri and Mark Messier. It's interesting to note that despite the Cups, the Oilers didn't set very many team records during this era. They don't appear on the list of most points, most wins, most home wins or all-time winning streaks. The Oilers do, however, hold all of the top five spots for most goals in a season, as well as the top three in most scoring points (goals and assists) in a season. They are also the only team ever to have three 50-goal scorers in one season, doing that twice, in 1983–84 and in 1985–86, with the trio of Gretzky, Glenn Anderson and Kurri.

The Washington Capitals continue the tradition of banzai play, despite being led by a headlining Russian player and playing in the U.S. They are one of the more Canadian teams in the league today if you add up the nationalities on their roster, and they play the Canadian game in the most spectacular, damn-the-torpedoes, Canadian way. Their game plan is much like Montréal's of bygone days, or the Oilers' of the 1980s. It's based on offense first. In the 2009–10 season, the Caps won more games than any other team (54) and scored 313 goals, besting the second-place team, Vancouver, by more than 40. In terms of goals-against, Washington was in the bottom half of the league (with the lowest team giving up the most goals), with 227 allowed.

The Caps' style of play also replicated that of the great Firewagon teams because even their defensive stalwarts were really just offensive players in disguise. The Oilers had Coffey, who ranged from 29 to 48 goals in the five seasons between 1981 and 1986. The Caps have Mike Green, who scores 20 to 30 times, give or take a goal, most years.

Where did this get Washington? Into the playoffs in 2010, and right out again when super-hot Jaroslav Halak, then with the Canadiens, bounced them in round one on a spectacular goaltending display, including a game six performance that might rank as one of the best for any goalie, ever. Washington poured 54 shots at the Slovakian netminder, with 22 in period three alone (Montréal's total for the whole game). Halak gave in only once in a 4–1 win. Washington lost the next game, returning home much earlier than most fans would have predicted.

The point of that story is not to boast that Montréal won, but that Washington was picking up where the Canadiens of the 1950s and the Oilers of the 1980s had left off, although without quite achieving the same success yet. It is interesting that a 30-year gap exists between each of these dynasties, as if it takes that long to grow a new crop of offensive-minded superstars, or perhaps, it takes that long for teams to forget how to defend Firewagon Hockey so that a new team of offense-first guys can rise to the top of the league.

So far, Washington hasn't been able to capitalize (sorry for the bad pun) on their scoring strength, but history says that they will do so eventually because it has always been hard to hold a great offensive team down for long. (Note that when, in 2011, they played a more balanced game featuring more defense, they breezed into round two of the playoffs and were swept. Experiment failed.) And when the Caps do win a Cup, they will demonstrate that the best hockey to watch has the quickest flow, and that's what turns fans on, not tight defense, which stifles the action game after game—remember pre-lockout hockey? It's probably better not to.

It's disappointing to note, though, that even the post-lockout NHL, which was supposed to be based on a more lively style, has its blight of flow-killing in the form of "systems" play because professional hockey, perhaps in a reflection of the complexity of modern life, is becoming ever more complicated in its execution. (Washington aside—and who's to say they don't have a system too? It's just based much more on offense than anything else.) Having a plan is all fine and good, and any player in the NHL who is interviewed is prone to falling back on the old "we need to stick to our system" cliché when asked about why his team is not winning. But compare today's micro-scrutiny of the game to 30 years ago, when the technology to break down the game into microscopic units to be analyzed did not exist. It was played, as mentioned, in waves, with the best teams being the fastest and most flowing.

Video-based coaching, more or less invented by Roger Neilson, changed things. Now, players were not just told to make changes to their game, they were shown how to do so in next-day meetings. The camera offered a view that they did not have on the ice. Players could see the way the opposition was setting up its defense, for instance, and how much time and space they had, which is not immediately apparent in the thick of battle.

Suddenly, what had been a spontaneous act, playing the game, could be critiqued in millisecond intervals, frame by frame, to use the old term. And since it was all caught on tape, there was no way to escape, no way to take a shift off. The evidence of lapses or lazy play stared a guy in the face as he stared at the screen.

Perhaps seeing themselves on video replay made players more "responsible," to use another frequently spouted cliché. They couldn't get away with anything. And with other changes, such as the expansion of the roster to 20, which allowed for more rest on the bench and the consequent shortening of shifts to 45 seconds or less, every stroke of the skate blade suddenly became of grave importance. What happened to playing with uncaring grace? The blind recourse to the idea of systems might signal a change in worldview that is not necessarily for the good. That the Caps play with abandon, while not helping them with playoff success as yet, endorses the notion that the game is free, flowing and spontaneous, which used to be values that guided Canadians in the quests to tame their wild land and thrive on it.

The best players still flow from end to end with lightning speed, but now, the grinders, those third- and fourth-line guys who see eight, 10 or 12 minutes of duty a game, are the ones defining the tempo for everyone else. While they may play an energetic style—look at the way Jordin Tootoo flies around like a human pinball, bouncing off guys and forcing pucks in deep—something like Béliveau's sense of grace isn't evident like it was in the old days. The situation has its reflection in modern Canada, where federal politics have for a handful of years featured a fragmented House and a PM who can't quite seem to get everyone working toward the same goals. Instead, what he does is micro-manage, going from mini-crisis to mini-crisis and making the citizenry long for a day when the person in charge will once again project vision—a flow of a different sort.

The Surging Energy of Spectating

The tradition of being a spectator goes back to ancient times, when Roman gladiators were the athletes of their day and Greek theatre actors the object of fascinated gaze in theirs. The actors in Greek drama, unlike today's thespians, weren't recognized as personalities. They wore masks on stage, and often took on more than one role during a production. But the powerful feelings the actors evoked in their audiences caused the philosopher Aristotle to surmise that those watching the production were enabled to purge their negative emotions through a process he called "catharsis." Pity and fear, he thought, could be expurgated from the system as an audience stood or sat rapt by the events unfolding before them.

Hockey, for Canadians, has always served a similar function by allowing us to vent our energies in support of our favourite club. Having a team to root for gives us something to believe in. It has often been said that following the

Montréal Canadiens has all the elements of a religion. More recently, fans who venerate the Maple Leafs have dubbed themselves "Leafs Nation," perhaps to indicate that the rising and falling fortunes of their team replicate those of their country, or a mythical nation where the test of citizenship is shown in how much time and energy is devoted to the club.

Spectators help their team however they can. For hockey fans, this may come in the form of carrying lucky charms, performing repeated rituals, and, of course, turning up at the arena to be a part of the action. Think about the small towns that dot the vastness that is Canada and how they support their local hockey teams on a weekly basis. Think about the almost-mythical drive from town to town that fans of a team like the Brandon Wheat Kings make, headlights piercing darkened highways in winter, where a broken-down car might be an invitation to death. The energy between the fans and the game is higher when the opposition is viewed as the enemy. The threat is felt most intensely when the enemy comes to town, right into your own backyard, in order to engage in battle. It's all by invitation, and you know they're coming, but that doesn't make the engagement any less fierce.

True fans like to think that in whatever game they watch, something of great significance will happen. They buy tickets expecting the bad guys to ride into town and try to whoop up on their boys. Seeing a game like that is what gives fans a chance to practice the catharsis that Aristotle talked about. But sometimes, the game lets fans down. It's a weeknight contest maybe, and the visiting team is one from the other conference, or from a place that doesn't seem like it should have hockey to start with (in the NHL, Texas and Florida, for example). These visitors play in your building only once every couple of years, and it has been so long since the home squad and its fans have seen them that nobody even remembers much more than who the first line is, maybe the big D-man and the goalie. But who remembers the other squad's third line guys or their agitator? Most of the time, these players are shadowy figures with little face recognition, kind of like those masked Greek actors.

So the home crowd enters the arena without a great sense of expectation. The players, in their turn, feed off the energy in the building. If there isn't much, it doesn't take them long to figure that out, and they start to relax. The shifts lengthen on both sides. Nobody does a lot of forechecking. If the visiting team scores and the home side doesn't respond, the local boys might find themselves leaving the ice accompanied by some boos.

On nights like this, hockey is not doing for Canadians what it does at its best, which is to offer up the chance for spectators to shed polite, workday propriety and go a little crazy. But here's where the Americans can help, because they, perhaps only to an extent superseded by English soccer fans, have a way of conjuring up emotion at sporting events.

Baseball player Kevin Millar gave the phenomenon a name when he started using the phrase "Cowboy Up" (actually, the title of a song written by Ryan Reynolds) in 2003 while playing for the Boston Red Sox. Millar is a Texan, and he said at the time that the expression means to quit whining and get to the business at hand. For the Sox, that meant applying themselves in their quest to defeat the Yankees in the American League Championship Series (they lost, 4–3).

For a hockey player, to cowboy up might mean coming out in the second period and making a game of it. And while in the old Wild West movies the sheriff dispatched the bad guy, in hockey, it's not always the team captain who does this. Sometimes, it's the guy playing eight minutes a night who is called on to get the game back on track, and when he steps up, the crowd watches with a renewed intensity.

Dustin Byfuglien, then of the Blackhawks, knew how to cowboy up in the 2010 playoffs. A few years earlier, nobody had known how to pronounce his oddly spelled name. A couple of months before the playoffs, he played defense. But during the postseason, his coach, Joel Quenneville, changed his assignment to winger alongside Patrick Kane and Jonathan Toews.

"Cowboy up" might have been the challenge levelled at Byfuglien. You've got your chance now, so let's see what you can do. "Big Buff," as fans started calling Byfuglien, took the reins, and when the playoffs ended, he had 11 goals, five assists and the Stanley Cup.

When a guy like that gets going, fans, in turn, find themselves in a situation where that $32 top-row ticket they bought suddenly seems like it's worth a whole lot more. The energy reaches the few hundred feet up to them, and they feel it in their guts. This game matters.

But forget the playoffs. A game can rise from ho-hum to significant during the regular season as well. For example, something odd and interesting might happen, statistically. Despite Gretzky having nearly every scoring record in the book, some individual game records can still be overturned. And even in those contests where nothing of historical importance happens, satisfaction comes from beating a familiar rival—who cares if neither Edmonton nor Calgary is going to the playoffs or that it's January and 20 degrees below zero. It's The Oil, baby, and you'd better get off that butt of yours and show the other fans around you, not to mention the players far below, that you get it. As you get caught up in the moment, you reinforce your identity as a hockey fan, the concrete expression of being Canadian.

The hockey-bred audience knows that the Karma of the rink is one of absolutes, where the good guys are able to outshoot the bad guys, no matter the odds. The game is not one of statistics, but one of action spurred on by the genuine emotion of the crowd. Although the players seem to be in their own little world inside the glass, their play, in the best-case scenario, is really a product of their interaction with the bodies in the seats so that together, they can overcome the terrible force of the visiting team.

Connections

Connections don't happen only in the official confines of an arena where those present have paid for the privilege. In neighbourhoods throughout Canada, bonds are created by kids, hockey nets and yelling "Car!" when play on the street must be temporarily suspended. Or they are reinforced on outdoor rinks that parents or tireless city workers create and tend, using a mix of science and art to get the ice smooth enough to play on. The rhythm of the rink touches Canadians in a deep place, providing solace at some times, companionship at others, but always with a sense that life has more meaning here, with the skates on, than anywhere else.

The greatest proponent of the backyard rink, ironically enough, was an American: the late Jack Falla. He's the writer of *Home Ice: Reflections on Backyard Rinks and Frozen Ponds* and later, *Open Ice: Confessions of a Hockey Lifer*. Jack also wrote a really lovely hockey novel, *Saved*. "I'd write some in the morning, then go out skating," he said when I interviewed him in 2008. "While I was out there, I'd just ask myself, 'What would be likely to happen next?' Then I'd write it down the next day."

Makes pretty good sense—the cool stillness of the ice sheet, the scrape of the blades, the whack of the stick on the puck and the *thwack* of the puck off the boards. That quiet moment when you are the only one on the rink is magic. It's almost surprising that more of us hockey lovers haven't written novels. But who knows? Maybe for us, the Zen-like tranquillity of the backyard rink has produced better parents, more patient teachers or inventors who have changed the world.

When I spoke with Kevin Lowe in 2008, he told me that he spent glorious mornings alone as a preschooler on the indoor ice rink his father had built on the grounds of the family's milk processing plant. Bobby Hull has a similar memory of when he was six, but his version has him getting up at the crack of dawn, stoking the stove, putting on the porridge pot for the family and then heading out the door to the rink across from his house.

But the rink is more than a place to play alone. It's a place to get together with friends, and sometimes enemies, to bond via the ritual that is pick-up hockey. Perhaps the first ceremony a Canadian kid learns is choosing players for the teams, where two captains call together whoever is playing on a given afternoon and tell them to throw their sticks into a pile at centre ice. The first time I heard this, I was one of the smaller kids on my corner rink. "Throw my stick in there? There's no way. I'll never get it back," I thought to myself. Some bigger kid insisted that I do it, though, and when I realized that there was no denying him, I complied.

The captains then started tossing the sticks this way and that, picking teams. My stick flew out to the left, that of my friend—and the only other boy my size—to the right. I went to retrieve mine, still not sure what was going on. "It means you play for me," my captain said. In that moment, I had become a part of something, a team. And until the game ended, I would enjoy the fellowship of this group of boys.

You hear professional players refer to their team all the time. Often, spouting a cliché about "team" is a way of saying, "I don't want to say anything real or anything about myself," so they throw off something like, "We worked together out there, five-man unit, everybody doing his part." But every once in a while, you'll find that a player really has a sense of what it means to be part of a team. He knows that this group of guys is better as a unit than they should be, and certainly than they would be alone. Martin St. Louis of the Lightning is a guy like that. When I asked him in a locker-room interview about a pass that Vincent Lecavalier used to set him up for a goal against the Kings one night, he said, "These are plays we're used to making. He knows I'm going there, and I know he's looking there." The thing is, that bond wasn't obvious to anyone else in the building. It was teammates connecting in a magical way.

Bonding on the corner rink has that same quality. The players become a community. Hockey has given them a sense of togetherness. Contrast the "great American pastime," baseball, again. It's a team game as well, in a sense, but there's rarely more than two or three players in on a given play. Offense is a solo affair, one pitcher against one batter.

It's a contest of wills, where strength and trickery (the fastball followed by a changeup comes to mind) are deployed by one person in the effort to defeat the other—the other person, that is, not the other team. Sure, the result is that the team wins or loses, but in the moment, it's head to head.

Not so in hockey. "Let's get back and help out the goalie," someone might say on the bench. It doesn't matter if you're a right winger. Your job is not finished in the other team's end. It's done in yours as well, as you sprawl to pick a puck off the goal line, a shot that has eluded all of the others wearing your colour of sweater. It's the approach that a guy like Ian Laperrière lived every day, including when he had to block shots with his skull at great personal risk.

Playing hockey is never for an instant a matter of going it alone. Sure, every team wants a superstar. In the Oshawa kids' league my nephew plays in, the star one year was a boy named Aden. Every game, that little fellow would grab a puck in his own end, get his legs churning and work his way through the other team's entire on-ice roster. Once he got close to the goal, he would put the puck on his forehand and kind of shovel it up over the opposing goalie, who would, of course, be lying on the ice in a desperate gesture that either meant he was giving up or that he didn't believe it was physically possible to raise the puck.

Aden would skate back, semi-exhausted, toward his jubilant teammates, arms raised in celebration, and they would join him. It might have been his individual effort that got them most of their wins, but to them, it was a matter of team—they were good because of what he gave them. The idea embedded in their little heads goes to the core of Canadian culture—together, we can do it. It's not individual effort that we prize but what each person contributes to the larger whole that defines us. An inordinate percentage of Canadians play hockey growing up. This is what makes them good team players later in life. They are proud of their contributions to the team, at work or in other cooperative endeavours.

The focus on team versus the emphasis on the individual might be looked at as the great Canadian-American divide. Think of the Canadarm. Canada's contribution to the U.S. space program was the ultimate act of team play. Never mind that it's a lot cheaper to produce one part for a spaceship than the whole thing. The Americans couldn't have explored space the way they did without that piece of equipment, and in almost any picture of the space shuttle, the giant arm with the "Canada" logo and flag can be seen.

You can read our contribution to their conquest of "the final frontier" in two ways—as a sign that it's the best we could do, or as one that says they couldn't have done it without us. The Canadian Space Agency itself describes the Canadarm by saying that it "remains a sterling example of successful international space cooperation," which sounds a lot like the way a closely knit hockey team describes its strengths. The agency goes on to say that the "Canadarm firmly established Canada's international reputation for robotics innovation and know-how." Not as glamorous as going to Mars, perhaps, but important nonetheless.

Give and Take

Street hockey, for a Canadian kid, forms an important part of almost every day, other than when outdoor ice is available. Like outdoor shinny on the ice, road games allow kids to form relationships with others in their neighbourhoods. In my era, the kid who owned the net had the privilege of having the game take place in front of his house, usually. And he had the power, too, because if he decided to "go in," the rest of us had to play without the net that made our games feel like the ones we saw on TV.

The tradition of picking player names, such as Hull or Mahovlich back in my day, or Crosby or Kaberle in this one, was glorified by the fact that when we scored, we did so on an "official" goal. We weren't putting the tennis ball between a pair of shoes and chasing it over the curb and onto the lawn of a nearby house or smacking it against the garage door. We were scoring NHL goals because we had a net.

In these impromptu games of my past, when we wanted to up the ante, we wore our official replica sweaters, many of which had the name of our hockey hero emblazoned on the back. It bonded us to the far-off star who didn't have a clue that we existed, or that on this day, on this street, we were reprising his great goal of the night or weekend before. That he didn't know us wasn't important. What mattered was that we could channel him, creating a web of connections between ourselves, our buddies on the street and the heroes of the NHL.

Sometimes, a new kid would show up to play. Maybe he lived on the block but went to private school or Catholic school. Maybe he had just moved in or was a cousin visiting from somewhere else. That was fine, unless his preference in players was the same hero as one chosen by another established player on the street. Simultaneous utterances of "Orr" would be heard, the two voices overlapping one another as each kid looked around to see who had chosen his hero.

In that moment, a kid learned the measure of himself, and his social skills would start their slow progress toward maturity. The strong kids would get the first taste of their confidence as they stared down the other person so that they could "be" the player they had called. This trait, years later, would make them the alpha people at work, the ones who ended up in the corner office with the nice view. The weaker kids, and that was most of us, would recognize that life isn't always fair, and we figured out that, sometimes, it was okay. To again invoke the divide between Canadians and Americans, the willingness to give in is a reflection of our feeling that we don't have to surge to the front to feel like we've done something worthwhile. Sometimes, letting the other kid have his choice was more important.

My dad taught me how we differ from Americans. We'd be on vacation in the U.S. when I was a kid and see a car that was the same model of Ford or Chevrolet that my dad happened to be driving, except that it was a bit fancier. "The equivalent model in the U.S. is always more glicked up than the one we get," he would explain. This was in the day when power windows and air conditioning were not givens but luxuries. "That's because Americans don't mind spending more for their cars."

I probably heard this comparison a couple of dozen times growing up, and I was just as interested every time he said it, kind of like it was a Zen Koan I had to figure out. Or maybe it was the closest my dad got to the wisdom that TV dads seemed always to be dispensing right at the opportune moment, so I listened.

Now I realize what he meant. Canadians are like the kid who hears his player's name choice called and has to decide whether his preference is worth potentially fighting for. Most of the time, we realize that it's not, so we let the other kid have his choice. It's not that we can't defend ourselves; it's that we've learned, somehow, that to negotiate is always the better strategy. We act in a way that assures togetherness.

To accept the version that focuses on compromise, like having a car that does everything it needs to but has less shine, is to be Canadian, and that's not a knock. It's what makes it possible for us to have the kind of generous social system we have. It's what makes it acceptable for Canadians, despite the grumbling, to tax the middle class more heavily than would be politically possible in the U.S., and to use the money to help the less fortunate. It's what makes it possible to have universal healthcare, which, though not perfect, is a compromise we can live with—we let things roll off our backs, realizing that it's okay not to always be the dominant one.

Hockey may not be the perfect game, though many of us would have a hard time acknowledging that. But for Canadians, the game is our comfortable place, somewhere familiar and safe. It shows us that the give-and-take that is part of compromise is often the best way to get along in the world. Americans may have their "boys of summer," as baseball players are called. We're okay being people of winter, as long as hockey is there to guide us, create a pattern for our days and afford us comfort.

chapter four

Heroes to Believe In

Who We Worship

"**O**h the good ole hockey game, it's the best game you can name, and the best game you can name is the good ole hockey game" (Stompin' Tom Connors). The words are so simple that they're almost trite.

The rhythm of the lines is cheesy, allowing kids to draw out the words—"the goooood old hawwww-keeeey gaaaaame"—as they belt out the song one final time before Dad pulls the car over and gives them a "what-for." On the other hand, Dad himself might have hummed along the last time he went to an NHL game, which probably featured the song as part of the intermission entertainment.

What Dad realizes, and what the kids don't, is that within the verses of Stompin' Tom's classic is the truth: Connors has cleverly hidden history in the middle of hockey cliché. Anyone can remember the chorus, having heard it only a few times. But sing that, and soon you want to sing the verses. The "third period," as the song has it, goes like this:

Oh take me where the hockey players faceoff down the
rink
And the Stanley Cup is all filled up for the chaps who win
the drink.

Learn those words, and you're remembering something that needs to be preserved.

Then there's the core of the song, which goes, "Someone roars 'Bobby scores!' at the good ole hockey game." Hopefully, some who hear those words will be prompted to ask, "Who's Bobby?"

Maybe the first modern hockey player, and the one whose mantle Gretzky would later inherit, was Bobby Orr. His hockey wasn't the gritty grind that everyone except the Montréal Canadians played in the post-war era. It was a flashy, smooth whirl of motion, deceptive and confident. It was modern, the same way that the long hair and bell-bottoms of the time were a new take on what it was to look good.

He was the NHL's prime star in 1972 when Connors first recorded the song. Orr quit playing the game in 1979 (really 1975, since that was his last full season, though he limped on—literally—for a few more campaigns, the last couple with Chicago rather than his original Boston team), and while true fans never forget an icon, statistics show that only about 70 percent of Canadians now living were alive back then. Subtract from that kids under five in 1979, assuming they were too young to watch and remember what they saw, and you have a number that should frighten anyone who thinks of Orr as the greatest player ever. (And a lot do—ask LA Kings former player and now TV broadcaster Jim Fox who the greatest was, and you'll get an immediate and decisive answer. "Robert Gordon Orr. Name one better," he will say.)

Did I say "frighten"? Well, yes. Because those numbers show that a relatively small portion of the population now has any recollection of Orr as a player—maybe 60 percent at best. More recognize Gretzky, still more Steve Yzerman. Fewer perhaps know the names Bobby Baun, Gordie Howe, Maurice Richard, Howie Morenz, Fred Taylor and on back to the beginnings of the game. But each of these names has been, in its time and for years after, synonymous with hockey greatness, and for that reason, their histories should be preserved.

On-ice heroes have always galvanized the attention of fans, and hockey has been full of colourful ones from the outset. Think of "Cyclone" Taylor. Phil Pritchard, known to NHL fans as the "Keeper of the Cup," says that his favourite old-time player was Taylor, who played in the Pacific Coast Hockey League from 1917 to 1923. This, despite the fact that Pritchard's all-time favourite team is the Montréal Canadiens of the 1970s, with standout figures such as Ken Dryden, Henri "Pocket Rocket" Richard, Yvan Cournoyer and Guy Lafleur. Why was Taylor his favourite? "Just think of the name," Pritchard said to me during an interview I had with him in 2008. "His real name was Fred. There's nothing poetic in that. But 'Cyclone' suggests so many possibilities."

Taylor's era of the late 1910s and early 1920s was a high-flying time when leagues from the East and West competed for players, dollars and prestige. His strength was his speed, and he was revered by fans of the day. While there's probably nobody left alive who actually saw him play, his legend remains, in large part because of his nickname.

Since Taylor, many have come and gone. Howie Morenz was one notable. His story starts with reports that he was faster than Taylor and ends with, many say, a death caused by a broken heart suffered when he realized that he could no longer play the game after suffering a broken leg. After he died, his funeral was broadcast live on radio from the Montréal Forum. The minister described him by saying, "Howie Morenz was not only the idol of thousands upon thousands of fans who went to see him weekly play hockey, but he was above all the hero of his teammates" because he did not know what it was to give up.

Eyewitnesses to Morenz's exploits and those of the other greats of hockey's earlier days have of necessity passed away with time, yet each great player makes the transition from history to myth, and together they stand as a Canadian pantheon comparable to that of the Greek gods in ancient days. That is, if later generations of hockey fans have a way to remember them. Connors' song does that for Orr, or other famous Bobbys, such as Hull, Clarke or Ryan. But the history of NHL heroes goes far beyond these few.

How Are Heroes Made?

At first blush, the rise from humble beginnings to make it big in the world sounds like the American Horatio Alger story. That myth is named for the author of more than 100 rags-to-riches tales. But the key to these stories is monetary gain, and for Canadians, at least until recent days of mega-salaries in the NHL, hockey dreams centred around the Stanley Cup and the chance to touch it, drink from it and later see your name engraved on the side. Money wasn't the goal. Glory was, because nobody made much money in the NHL (except the owners).

For decades, the great shoot-to-the-top-of-the-ladder dream in Canada went like this: a kid from a small town finds that he has extraordinary talent at something that matters to everyone he knows—hockey. His parents see it, too, and encourage him to work to make it to the next level. Soon, he is discovered by a scout, who, having driven 450 kilometres through a blinding snowstorm on a tip, finds him playing on a frozen outdoor rink. (The distance, of course, would vary, but for the purposes of myth-making, farther was always better.) As the boy walks off the ice after the game, the man stops him. "Son, you're going to be a star in the National Hockey League," he enthuses. "Where are your parents? I need to talk to them." This was the first moment in the creation of the hero.

The NHL draft began in 1963, but until 1969, a team could grab a player's rights as soon as a scout could sit at a boy's kitchen table and get him and his parents to sign the "C-Form," which committed him to a professional club. What happened to the boy on his way up varied, but generally, the path went through major junior hockey. At the appropriate time, he received an invitation to the club's NHL training camp, and the next stop was Maple Leaf Gardens or Madison Square Garden, or whichever of the six rinks his NHL dreams might come alive in.

Sometimes, parents needed a bit of persuading to sign on the dotted line, and in that case, scouts offered an incentive package. Bobby Orr, as documented by Stephen Brunt in *Searching for Bobby Orr*, watched as his mom and dad bargained for new stucco on their house with the Bruins' scout who came to talk to the boy, who was 14 years old at the time. Bobby went away the following fall (1962) to play for the Oshawa Generals, a team basically created with him in mind. Four years later, he was in the NHL.

The dream up to Orr's time was simply to see yourself in an NHL sweater. Boys would fantasize about being the subjects in those old black-and-white player portraits, skidding to a stop with a spray of ice chips coming off their chromed skate blades. The few who made it became local heroes, though their lives during the off-season were not filled with luxury vacations, golf or intense fitness programs, as is the experience of

NHL players today. Instead, the kid would return home, like Bobby Hull did in the summer of 1958 after his first season with the Blackhawks, and work. In the Golden Jet's case, that meant a stint at a Coca-Cola bottling plant, which he drove to in the used 1957 Chevy he bought with part of his first-year salary of $6500, as he told me in a phone conversation in 2009. Today's rookies make that kind of money *per game*.

These days, the whole process has become much more professionalized, and, inevitably, complicated, perhaps because everyone knows how much money is at stake. Kids can't be approached by NHL clubs, but rather may be drafted by teams in the year they turn 18. Agents pursue boys as young as 13 or 14, trying to get them to sign on with them for the purposes of later negotiating NHL contracts. It sounds official and sterile, yet for some players, even generations apart, the dream remains rooted in faraway places. Bobby Clarke and Jordin Tootoo lived versions of this dream. Ditto for Dustin Penner and Ryan Getzlaf, though their stories didn't have quite the hardscrabble beginnings of the other two.

Clarke grew up in Flin Flon, Manitoba, and he believed that he had achieved all he needed to in life when he found himself playing for the local Bombers Junior squad and working in the mines. When I interviewed him in 2009, he also told me that he sensed that he could do more, and that was to make it to the NHL. He played in the league from 1969 until 1984.

Tootoo left home at 14 to go far south of his familiar territory of Rankin Inlet, Nunavut, and deal with life in a big city, Edmonton. He was drafted into juniors and eventually made the NHL in 2003. For him, playing hockey was something he simply had to do—a destiny.

His contemporaries, Getzlaf and Penner, are prairie boys, but they might serve well to illustrate the shift in the hockey dream. Getzlaf was picked by Anaheim in the first round of the 2003 draft. Penner made his way to the NHL via a more circuitous free agent route. How they got there didn't matter. When their lives collided in Anaheim, a few miles from the glamorous and money-soaked California seaside towns of Newport and Laguna Beach, they must have looked around and wondered how it happened that they, too, could participate in the Ferrari-driving luxury lifestyle of the California coast. What was Canadian-dreamy about this?

The Modern-day Dreamer

Indeed, the dream has lost some of its innocence as money has become a greater component of the NHL. To understand this, contrast the story of Rogie Vachon with that of Sidney Crosby. The former signed his C-Form at 15, in 1960, and went from his rural Québec town to Montréal to play for the Junior Canadiens three years later. Two seasons after that, he found himself in net for the Montréal Canadiens, amazed at the speed of his rise. When he tended goal in Palmarolle, Québec, where he was discovered, he often did so on boots—it was warmer than wearing skates. The Crosby-style dream is more common these days: a kid with talent is identified early and nurtured, his whole life focused on exacting development through precise, scientifically inspired coaching, leading to the NHL. The difference between "discovered" and "developed" is the key. Talent is still there, obviously, but it is now carefully nurtured to make the player who he becomes.

Crosby's experience, and that of other players, shows how the dream has shifted over the years as the geographic footprint of the league has expanded. The monetary rewards of an NHL career are much greater than in the past, but the irony is that big-time hockey, which in the old days was played in Chicago, Detroit or the other cities of the Original Six, is now spread to the four directions of the compass across North America. Tootoo ended up in Nashville, Penner and Getzlaf in Anaheim before the former went off (to a really big payday) to Edmonton. He later found himself back in the Golden State with the Kings.

For Steven Stamkos, playing hockey took him to Tampa Bay, and perhaps part of the reason for his uneven performance early in his career was the total alienation he must have felt there. How could someone who grew up in Markham and played junior hockey in Sarnia adjust when, at 18, he found himself thousands of kilometres away in Florida? Think about that first autumn. No hint of cold in the air. No sense of the hockey season starting except in the little bubble that was his team. The balmy Gulf breezes and the comfort of the beach a few miles in any direction would probably make the whole "I'm in the NHL" idea seem a bit unreal.

Crosby, of course, wound up in Pittsburgh, which could at least boast of two Stanley Cups when he got there. But playing in far-flung places, whatever its disadvantages, comes with the perk of getting paid more in a week than the average Canadian gets paid in a year, and thus the shift in the substance of the dream.

In the old days, it might have been the pure glory of playing one game in the NHL that motivated a young man. Then, no matter what happened, it would be okay to settle back into the life pre-ordained for you. Maybe that meant going into the family business or taking over the family farm. It didn't matter because you'd always have your stories to tell.

A few lucky ones extended their good fortune into a career like that of Pat "Whitey" Stapleton, a veteran of about 1000 WHA and NHL games. Interestingly, Stapleton remained unaffected by the dream he lived. He played professional hockey for nearly two decades, competed with Team Canada in the Summit Series, grabbed the last puck as the eighth game ended and, eventually, returned to Strathroy, Ontario, to farm.

That puck, which you can see him chase out of the film's frame if you watch the DVD of the last game of the series, sat in a box in a shed on the farm for years, although he denied having it until recently. It's most likely the puck that Henderson used to score the most famous goal in history with (at least until Crosby's overtime winner in the 2010 Olympics), but Stapleton is unimpressed by any of that. "Why all the fuss over a rubber puck?" he said to one interviewer some years ago. (More recently, Stapleton brought it out for display at a Junior B game, in 2008, according to *The Peterborough Examiner.*)

To cite one more example, in 1974, Vaclav Nedomansky, one of the greatest players in the game anywhere, left Czechoslovakia with his wife and young son for freedom in the West. Once in West Germany, he phoned a man he knew and told him he had escaped. Nedomansky's goal was to live in Canada, which he had visited a few years earlier, and to play in the NHL. After a detour through the WHA with the Toronto Toros (which became the Birmingham Bulls), he made it, joining the Detroit Red Wings in 1977. Nedomansky's story is relevant because it shows that the Canadian dream is so big that it can transcend the nation's boundaries.

Sadly, the purity of spirit that motivated Vachon, Stapleton, Nedomansky and others might largely be gone. Those who rise from humble roots to hockey stardom now do so for more than notoriety because material success is never far behind. Even the most humble four- or five-year NHL career should leave the player with enough money, if he has managed his earnings conservatively, to do almost anything he wants afterward. Of course, these guys don't retire to sit on their couches and do nothing for the last 40 or so years of their lives. (And they don't sit around and watch old game film of themselves either, which is what I always kind of thought they did, because that's what I think I'd do in their shoes.) They go into business, take a job in hockey or complete their education. But regardless of their direction, it must be said that the dream has, in an ironic way, turned into a kind of Horatio Alger story. Maybe even to a point that Canadians should be uncomfortable. Heroics are the ice still happen every season, but heroes are different today. They don't exist like they did in the days when the game was played purely for its own sake.

Quiet, Confident Leaders

Even though the dream has changed, those who make the NHL still exhibit superhuman qualities as they battle for the puck and score glorious goals (or defend against them). But what, exactly, is the prototype of the contemporary Canadian (that is to say "hockey") hero? American rock-and-roller Tom Petty offers an answer in the twist he puts on the cowboy motif in his song "Two Gunslingers." It tells the story of two guys who get to the centre of town to duel but then decide not to. "What are we fighting for?" one asks, and the other has no answer. Having failed to deliver the excitement that the gathered crowd demands, the men turn and head to their horses. A fellow in the crowd tells his wife,

"That's the last of these gunfights you're ever going to drag me to," and the two guys ride out of town. But if the crowd isn't happy, that might be because they don't grasp what's just happened. These guys have made a decision. They have determined their own destiny. Sometimes, as in Petty's song, that means not fighting.

The payoff line, which gets repeated a number of times in the song, is "I'm taking control of my life now." The crowd wants action, but they have to settle for the quiet confidence that proves that the captain is the boss. That's a lot like what those who follow hockey's heroes experience.

Along with being the best, the ideal on-ice leader must master a way of acting that softens the roughness of the message that he's in charge. Serge Savard, Mark Messier, Larry Robinson and Jean Ratelle, among others, were in fact better than everyone else. They just didn't let on that they were better. Instead, they went out and did their jobs, putting themselves on the line when necessary, going over it when they felt that was a good idea, but always with the grudging acceptance that this was their job, and they were doing it because they must.

That was the attitude of the captain of the 1989 Calgary Flames, the leader of a squad that wasn't thought to have the potential to achieve, but that won a Stanley Cup. A dynamic, older (36 years) captain with the world's most fantastic moustache, Lanny McDonald led those players. But it wasn't that one guy who made the team win. It was how he inspired the bunch of them to do more than they could as individuals. This was the team that had watched its neighbour to the north capture the Stanley Cup four times in five years, through what many must have thought was the pure good fortune of having snagged Wayne Gretzky.

Watching playoffs like the series the year Calgary won or hearing about them in the news as they happen and then as touchstones in the years afterward, is it any wonder that Canadians internalize the lesson that if we all pull together behind the strong one who leads us, we can do more than we could alone? It's the opposite of the Lone Ranger mentality that our U.S. counterparts hold up.

That ideal is about one man fighting heroically against the forces of evil. In the popular American imagination, this hero gets mapped onto U.S. presidents all the time. Sometimes, as in the case of Ronald Reagan, the man himself appropriates the image. Think of Reagan on his vacation. What did he do? He went to his Santa Barbara ranch and did cowboy stuff like riding horses. And his press people made sure the news stations saw him do it. George W. Bush did the same, except it was a pickup truck in Texas that substituted for Reagan's California Arabian steed and tiny Jeep Scrambler.

Mr. Obama is a guy from Hawaii and Chicago, and he doesn't camp it up like a cowboy—his off time is spent playing sports or going to the gym, the kind of stuff most suburbanites do when they're not working. Maybe that's partly why his public image doesn't have the kind of strength that Americans expect of their leading politician. Perhaps he would have made a good prime minister, because for Canadians, the cowboy image doesn't always resonate. Recall the publicity photo of Stephen Harper in the ill-fitting leather vest—it just didn't work.

We want leaders with the quiet dignity of Jerome Iginla or the staid confidence of Bob Gainey. Occasionally, when things are going really badly, we want the undertone of ferocity displayed by Dion Phaneuf. What we don't want is the arrogance of Roberto Luongo. Perhaps that's why Luongo hasn't become popular past the BC border, and a guy like Michael Ignatieff didn't cut it as a leader. There's a sense that each behaves like he's better than everyone else, and that's not the Canadian ethos.

A generation before Gretzky, the ideal player as presented to the NHL fan was Jean Béliveau. A perfect mix of fluid grace and strong determination, he could carry the puck through to the other team's net without messing up a single hair on his perfectly coiffed, helmetless head. Off the ice, he was the gentleman in all situations, someone who could diffuse the tension in the room when the conversation turned to French versus English. He set the modern pattern for leadership.

For Canadians, the best sort of leader is one who can form the right consensus—a captain, both in the literal sense and in the sense of a man brave enough to stick with the ship when it founders. Sometimes, too, the gunslingers don't walk away, and a duel does take place. In these instances, leadership means going toe-to-toe with the enemy, but even that is done as an example to the rest of the team rather than for self-aggrandizement. Think about Iginla and Vinny Lecavalier duking it out in the 2004 playoffs. They met during the third game of the Stanley Cup final, with the series tied 1–1. The Flames, as hockey fans know, eventually lost the series in seven games, but Iginla sparked them to take a 2–1 series lead by punching out the other side's captain and figurehead.

What about San Jose's Joe Thornton and Anaheim's Ryan Getzlaf? The Sharks won in overtime of game five to make their 2009 playoff series 3–2 (Anaheim's favour). As the two centremen met at the red dot at the start of game six, according to Getzlaf, Thornton asked him, "Do you want to go tonight?" Getzlaf, having thought about it beforehand, had decided that something had to happen, he told me during a postgame interview. Before the puck hit the ice, they were scuffling. It wasn't quite the clean-punching affair that Iginla–Lecavalier had been, but it was worth five-minute majors, as the crowd watched with a combination of shock and delight. Getzlaf's fight got the Ducks out of their funk and allowed them to win the series, 4–2. They went on to lose the next round to eventual champs, Detroit. A season later, with Scott Niedermayer having retired in 2010, Getzlaf was made team captain.

Other heroes who captured the imagination of onlookers include Mr. Hockey, Gordie Howe, who threw a lot of big elbows but also touched a lot of people over the years through participating in off-ice charitable events. (Recently, for those who keep up with such matters, he was crowned Dr. Hockey via an honorary degree from the University of Saskatchewan.) Tiger Williams—his nickname is much more sonorous than his real ones, David James—provides one final example. When such shorthand stands in for what a boy's parents named him, can fan adulation be far behind? Tiger earned his, playing nearly 1000 games and getting almost 4000 minutes in penalties. His brand of leadership was simple—go out and kick butt.

Other sports have their nicknames, too. Baseball has the "Big Unit" (Randy Johnson) and the "Big Hurt" (Frank Thomas), and boxing sports its share of "Sugars," but for Canadians, what swells the imagination will forever be connected to the great game and its larger-than-life personalities, who don't have to be cowboys to make us believe in their magic abilities. They just have to give the best of themselves and inspire their teammates to do the same.

Heroes or Madmen?

Goalies are perhaps not typical of the Canadian mind-set, which honours safety and lack of risk, but anyone brave enough to strap on the pads and play in an NHL net enjoys a good deal of admiration from fans. Go into most kids' rooms in any era of hockey history up to today, and you'll likely see pictures of netminders adorning the walls. Why is that? Because everyone likes to slow down to watch the aftermath of a car wreck, and goaltenders fascinate us because their job demands they have a touch of madness.

The joke I like to tell goes like this: in the 1960s, a Martian lands in Toronto. Wanting to find out more about Canadians, he picks up a copy of the *Star* and reads that there is a hockey game that night. Once there, he tells a fan who he is, and the man, being an avid reader of sci-fi books, takes the alien into the Leafs' dressing room to meet the players. As they go through the door, the guy turns to the Martian and says, "Ask anyone anything you want to, but see those guys over there?" He makes a gesture with his head toward the far corner, where Terry Sawchuk and Johnny Bower are getting suited up. "Stay away from them. They're insane!"

At least until the 1980s, when mask and equipment technology got better, playing in net was a precarious affair. Not that any position in hockey at the highest levels has ever been safe, but playing in goal was a sure way to end your career with fewer teeth and more scars than you started with.

Emile Francis, a goalie who played in the pre-mask 1940s and '50s, told me the story of the day when he got a puck in the mouth, went to the dressing room for half an hour and came back to finish the game—completely buzzed on the brandy he'd been given as a sedative.

In the U.S., baseball produces a few wacky pitchers from time to time, such as Mark "The Bird" Fidrych and Bill "Spaceman" Lee. But that position, although the most pressure-packed, isn't the most dangerous; it's the catcher's. And he is decked out in gear as elaborate as that of an NHL goalie, including the mask. However, you don't hear stories of catchers being eccentrics who enact strange superstitions to help them do their jobs, at least, not more than any other ballplayer.

Almost any goaltender, though, has a routine he (or she, to be fair to the many women who play the game) follows. It might be as simple as using the same stick game after game if there's a hot streak going. The good luck charm might be the comfort of having a family member's initials or name painted on the mask, as Cam Ward does in Carolina.

The "out" players are also highly into ritual, as anyone who follows the game should know. Putting on the left skate first, always taping four new sticks, using the same shoulder pads all through a career—all of these, to various NHL players, are the markers of good luck. But the goalie position has been the home of some true eccentrics.

Maybe, in the old days, it worked the opposite way around. Maybe the person wasn't crazy to start with, but the position made him so. Listen to these words from Randall Maggs' great book of poems on Sawchuk for a hint of the madness of the goaltender. Better yet, read them aloud, as poems should be experienced:

Goalies, *they mouth to one another cheerfully.*
Everybody knows they have their dark and bloody ways of
dealing with the world.

So why are we so fascinated with these guys? Because they give us the ability to project ourselves onto them, to be the warriors we really wish we could be, but can't. Canadians are conservative in many ways. They play for safety first. They don't take the big risk. Who wants to end up like Sawchuk did, nervous, miserable and alone? Again, Maggs on how the goalie—and particularly Sawchuk—feels after a game:

You couldn't just go home, your head still rattling over
the one you made at the end or didn't. Or something some
bastard
said from their bench. Bloody Pilote, the way he gets
under
your skin....
Some nights it hurt just to breathe.

From the early days, when they couldn't leave their feet and Clint Benedict was playing for the Senators and Maroons, through the era of Sawchuk and Bower, to Dryden and Esposito, through Fuhr and Moog, on to Brodeur and Roy and now to Thomas and Roloson, these men have galvanized the gaze of fans, maybe because their nerve, or nerviness, is outside of the typical Canadian mindset of self-preservation and safety.

The Dilemma of the Canadian Hero

Wayne Gretzky became a hero for Canadians for more than his hockey skills. He taught us about the world we live in and gave us someone we could identify with. He did this through making the most of his talents as a young man and then, when he got older, shifting his role to that of statesman. Along the way, he survived the ultimate Canadian dilemma—what to do when your talent is too big for Canada.

Like the kid who got sand kicked in his face at the beach in the old Charles Atlas muscle building ads, the ones that seemed to be on every back page of *Archie* comic books years ago, all Gretzky needed was the right information, and he could be strong. For Wayne, the magic resided in the secrets his father taught him on the backyard rink, which allowed him to play a new style of hockey. The "innovation," actually, was an idea as plain as the centre line dividing the ice in half—that you went where the puck would be, not where it was. It was like Mr. Miyagi and Daniel-san in *The Karate Kid*. "Wax on, wax off" became the key for Daniel Laruso to defeat the bullies. Gretzky's special knowledge of the game gave him similar powers, but because his success was not built on physical strength, but cunning, he served as a role model for all Canadians.

Before Gretzky, Bobby Clarke was the great icon of the game. Shaggy-haired, all intensity but rough, he epitomized his time. But Gretzky superseded him, and because of his smallish stature and everyman demeanour, he took every Canadian with him. "If he can do it, so could I," the thinking went.

Gretzky served an important function in Canadian culture. The game produced him right around the time the Gen X kids were going through adolescence. He was someone they could cheer for, a model of achievement who, in many people's minds, these kids needed. What do you do when your parents had protested Vietnam, gotten into riots over civil rights, hung out in Haight-Ashbury and practiced free love? Turns out, not much, according to Douglas Coupland's formulation. Here's one definition of the term Gen X: "a group of flannel-wearing, alienated, over-educated, underachieving slackers."

American kids of the time might have been characterized by a lack of meaning, but for a lot of Canadians, there was The Great One. The lessons Gretzky taught were simple, but profound. Start young to become good at something. Keep at it. Never take for granted that you'll be successful. Even when you are, remain humble. What better example could you want? Still, Gretzky faced a lot of pressure living up to the expectations he had created from a young age.

Wayne was famous from the time he was a kid. He had been on the radar of most Canadian hockey fans from the age of 10, when a story in *The Star Weekly* magazine gave him national exposure. He got 378 goals the season of his 10th birthday, and the media tagged him as an heir apparent to NHL royalty. The parents of boys on other teams, and even his own teammates, resented his gifts, believing that he might destroy the league he played in because he scored too many goals. It wasn't fair. But neither would it have been fair—to this kid, to history—to cut his ice time in order to bring his scoring under control, and people had a sense of that, too. The only alternative was to find him a bigger venue, a more accommodating stage, so he moved from Brantford to Toronto to escape the criticism and jealousy. Years later, as an adult, his move from Edmonton to LA also served to free him from scrutiny.

There's a famous picture of Wayne with his idol, Gordie Howe, when Gretzky was 10. I asked Gretzky about it when I was researching my book *Living the Hockey Dream*, and he told me he met his hero that day during a planned lunch program, and he and Howe were both part of it. Maybe the spontaneity of the moment occurred when photo time came around and Howe, instead of just sitting next to the widely smiling kid in the usual pose, grabbed a hockey stick and hooked the boy around the neck with it. In fact, maybe that playfulness is what made Wayne smile so big in the first place. In a life scripted for greatness, it might have been one of his few genuine moments of childhood joy.

Many fans have a similar picture of themselves and their hero. The look on their faces is always the same. The kid can't quite believe that he or she is standing there, and the player is smiling dutifully, happy to be part of the picture but perhaps with one part of his mind on whatever he was doing at that moment when the eager fan approached him.

Why do these pictures mean so much to us? Because for one moment, we were part of that person's life; we had a glimpse of the immortal. In the case of Gretzky, so many Canadians had so much of him that he seemed like he belonged to all of us. But at 27, in the summer of 1988, after a wedding that rivalled that of Charles and Diana, he up and left for Los Angeles. Anyone who becomes a star in Canada eventually comes to a similar crossroads and must decide whether to make it big in the U.S. Canadians love to see this happen, though they also view people who leave with suspicion, and sometimes resentment.

In one sense, the trade was inevitable. Common wisdom maintains that Gretzky was too big for the market he was in. That is, if it's okay to think about a hockey team and a hockey town as a "market" to begin with. If you go along with this premise, you agree with the commonplace claim that The Great One's trade was good for hockey. It took a moribund market (LA) and opened it up. His presence in California made hockey cool, and the stars turned out to see him do his magic. Unfortunately, the other side of the trade, of course, is that a hockey team that *was* a dynasty, and might have continued to be one until the end of the 1980s and into the 1990s, became like all the other teams. Sure, the Oilers won another Cup without Gretzky, but his departure was more than just painful. It was devastating. As Jim Taylor said in *Sports Illustrated* at the time, "Forget the controversy about whether No. 99 jumped or was pushed; the best hockey player in the world was ours, and the Americans flew up from Hollywood in their private jets and bought him. It wasn't the Canadian heart that was torn, it was the Canadian psyche that was ripped by an uppercut to the paranoia."

The calls for government action to void the deal were immediate. In hindsight, that seems so naïve and so perfectly Canadian. "Look, we have a problem, and though we often complain about the government, when things get bad, we expect them to be there for us, to make things right," was the collective cry. It's as if the native son had no control over the workings of his career, though that's not entirely the case, as Brunt points out in *Gretzky's Tears*. He says that there was at least one opportunity to call the whole thing off. As we all know, Gretzky didn't take it.

So after a tumultuous summer (for everyone), Gretzky found himself in California. At once, he became a lost son who had to answer for leaving and an ambassador for a team and a sport that had struggled to gain attention over 20 years since the expansion to 12 teams, and by the time of the trade, 21.

Part of the reason he went, so it was said, was that he wanted to give his wife a chance to further her film career near the heart of the entertainment biz, Hollywood. For that, too, people forgave him, even when it became clear that her career hadn't really taken off.

For Gretzky, the move to LA might have been about expanding the game in an unlikely place, but another way to look at it is that Gretzky, too, grew as man on his own terms, and luckily for him, Canadians were able to understand this.

The ability to disappear in a city of 10 million was exactly what he needed after a life of renown, an idea that Brunt discusses in several sections of *Gretzky's Tears*. Perhaps we forget that Canada, for all of its size, can be too small for some people. In LA, hockey players can live normal lives off the ice, largely unrecognized, whereas in Edmonton, Toronto or Montréal, being an NHLer carries a caché that can never be forgotten. Imagine what it must have been like for the guy to try to shop or go out to dinner in Edmonton. In LA, Gretzky could take comfort in knowing that he was probably not the most famous guy in the room in most upscale restaurants. Maybe he saw California not so much as a place to increase his footprint as lessen it. Living there, when he wasn't "at work," he could be himself, whatever that meant to him.

To this day, Gretzky's off-ice persona has never been revealed. He simply maintains, in any public situation, the politely deferential self that makes him forever the small-town boy with a father who coached him to greatness on their back-yard rink. Is Gretzky still that small-town boy? Canadians want him to be, and need him to be, because that kind of hero reflects the favoured quality of honest virtue that is at the core of the national self-definition, but it's naïve to think that this is possible in the case of a mega-star like Gretzky.

So what did Canadians do when he left? For one thing, they didn't boo, which is what American fans often do when a favourite player deserts them for greener pastures or more money. Witness Daniel Briere's returns to Buffalo, or Rob Blake's to Los Angeles after the two times he left. These guys couldn't touch the puck without igniting the wrath of the locals.

Briere left the Buffalo team that had seen him have his best year, and he signed on with Philadelphia for a boatload of money in 2007. The Sabres were in the smaller market, obvi-ously, and so couldn't afford the kind of monster contract Philly offered, and Briere had to endure the scorn of his former hometown supporters upon his return with his new squad.

Contrast Patrick Roy, who left Montréal in that famous fit of anger after not being pulled against the Red Wings. In that same 1995–96 season, he led Colorado to its first Stanley Cup victory. The Avs' win was doubly hurtful to Habs fans because the team had been the hated Nordiques until the previous summer, when they had relocated to Denver. But Canadiens supporters, after a suitable mourning period, reacted as Canadians so often do when one of their own defects to the U.S. and succeeds. They felt proud of him and were happy for him. By 2008, wounds had healed, and Montréal retired Roy's number in a celebration at the Bell Centre.

The same was true for Gretzky. Stephen Brunt points out that because The Great One was a hockey player and not just any entertainer, our sense of betrayal at his departure was much more intense—we believed that nothing could take one of our own, good at our own game, to the other side of the border, until it happened. He elaborates:

> *Had he been an actor or a comedian or a musician, Gretzky would have been simply the latest in a long line of Canadian talent that has successfully taken its act south.... His departure would have inspired melancholy, but would also have been completely understood. And when he succeeded there, on the big stage, Canadians would have felt a certain pride in his accomplishments, a certain vindication of his talent.*

Of course, he didn't practice any of these professions. He played hockey, the one thing we believe we excel at. Maybe that's why his leaving shocked us so much. We didn't get over the hurt, but we handled it with grace, and we didn't hold it against him.

Think about stars that have crossed the 49th parallel and have done well: Donald Sutherland, John Candy,

Steve Nash, Alanis Morissette. Canadians love to claim their own. "She's Canadian," we say if Morissette's name comes up in conversation, hoping to catch the (American) person unawares by sharing a secret that we alone know. As we make the claim, we are proud that the star has managed to get noticed in a sea of wannabes. But at the same time, there's the slight sense of betrayal. "Wasn't it good enough for them here?" "Don't we have equivalents to those Grammy/Oscar-type awards that they seek?" It's a love–hate tug of war.

With Gretzky, there was no animosity. When he first returned to play in Edmonton, the crowd gave him a four-minute standing ovation. And at the end of that 1988–89 season, the city erected a life-sized statue of him holding the Stanley Cup aloft outside their arena. That's the kind of gesture that might have taken a decade to accomplish in other NHL cities, something that might be done only after sufficient time had elapsed that the leave-taking had been forgotten. This says something about Canadians and their tolerance for a hero who deserts them to make it big in the U.S. To cite a similar incident, when Saku Koivu returned to Montréal as a member of the Anaheim Ducks in 2011, fans gave him the longest standing ovation in recent memory. Though not a native, he had been their captain, and they still felt it right to honour him.

By 2004, Gretzky was voted among the top 10 greatest Canadians, even though he had neither played nor lived in the country for nearly two decades. It didn't matter—he was still one of us, and he *was* hockey. Of the rest of the men (all men!) on the list, including Terry Fox, Lester B. Pearson, David Suzuki and Frederick Banting, none had spent significant time outside Canada. It's also worth noting that the only other hockey person on the list is Don Cherry. Notice that none of the other famous "defectors"—from Mike Meyers to Jim Carrey—were chosen. As a hero, then, Gretzky accomplished two things in his hockey career—he showed us how to succeed while being humble, and he survived the move to the U.S., which seems to go along with making it big in showbiz.

A New Lesson

In the next phase of his life, Gretzky did something that displayed his growing maturity as a hero. When he returned to direct Team Canada's Olympic effort in 2002, the country embraced him once more, and he paid us back by the way he performed his job. In one of the most shrewd off-ice moves by a manager, ever, he responded to the pressure his players were being put under in Salt Lake City by striking out at the media. This from the man who had remained soft-spoken to the point of shyness throughout a two-decade-long professional hockey career. His outburst relieved the pressure his team was feeling, and it is what many people believe allowed the team to prevail to win the gold medal.

What Gretzky was doing, though few thought about it at the time, was teaching Canadians a new lesson. It wasn't about how to appear and disappear magically on the ice, or how to find the perfect spot to thread a pass to a teammate. The lesson was about growing older, and changing. In fact, he had been demonstrating this for some years leading up to that point. As he got older, Gretzky taught us that people do indeed age—more profound than it sounds.

It is true that with players entering and leaving the game more quickly and being ever younger in today's NHL, our attention tends to gravitate toward the older guys, the ones who have survived. Rod Brind'Amour, Joe Sakic, Mike Modano, Teemu Selanne, Johnny Bucyk, Doug Harvey, Dominic Hasek, Mark Recchi—all of them played on after 35, and they thrived. With each successive season, fans not only sensed their awesome abilities but also learned by watching that every day must be taken as a new gift. But at some point, no matter the struggle, nobody can defeat the cruelty of time.

Gretzky never lost his blond good looks. But by his own telling, he found it increasingly hard to play at the level that he needed to as each new season rolled around, and finally, he let hockey go in 1999. Maybe he knew all along that's what he would do, since the number he chose, and the year that his first contract was to expire, was 99. He probably could have put in another campaign or two, celebrating his 40th birthday on a game night. But he didn't. He knew it was over, and he skated off to do something else.

In contrast, Gordie Howe, for anyone who saw him play, seemed ageless. He first retired at 43 and sat out for two years. But when his sons Mark and Marty signed with the World Hockey Association's Houston Aeros, the old man decided to go along for the ride. And it didn't stop there. When the WHA folded and amalgamated four of its teams into the NHL in 1979, Howe was still playing. By this time, he was 52, and his hair was completely grey. Even after that season, in which he potted 15 goals and 26 assists over 80 games, he was probably capable of playing on. His son Mark told me in May 2009 that it was management that suggested Gordie retire. But even then, he was still around, playing a shift in the International Hockey League a few months before he turned 70, in 1998, as if to show that he was never going to get old. Yet for some who saw the game, Howe's presence was a stunt—a sign of the inability to let go.

When Gretzky came back to manage the Olympic squad, he had come full circle, from being the meek but deadly boy who scored at will, to being the NHLer who handled the personal and team pressure with quiet resolve, to being the older player who still had the skills, just not quite like he used to. In Salt Lake City, and comfortably into his 40s, Gretzky was the burden-carrier, but in a different way from when he played. Now, he was one of the adults, so to speak, one of the bosses. Who knows how much he wished to put on the skates, since he was only a handful of years removed from his on-ice career, and put into action what he wanted his team to do. But he, and we, recognized that this was no longer possible. And in allowing Gretzky to take his place on the world stage during those Games, Canada as a country grew up a bit, because we realized, perhaps for the first time, that our heroes are mortal, no matter how magical their hockey exploits, and that they can give us other things after they hang up the skates.

The Enduring Impact of Role Models

Hockey players are oftentimes role models of the best of Canadian virtues. That "aw-shucks, it was my teammates who helped me" attitude isn't just a pose. There are many stories of generosity, though NHL players often come in for their share of criticism because of their salary demands. It's rare that players do not take the Stanley Cup, for instance, to various hospitals during an off-season. Many of those who have made piles of cash in the game also give a lot of money to charities.

The Sedin brothers donated $1.5 million to help build a new children's hospital in BC. Why didn't they send the money to their home in Ornskoldsvik, Sweden? Because the twins "feel very fortunate to live and work in Vancouver and want to give something back that would benefit children and families across the province," they said at the time.

Such generosity is obviously not unique to hockey players, but still, it suggests the core of decency that inhabits the sport. But acts of charity don't have to involve monetary donations. Take the case of Brooks Laich of the Washington Capitals. He was brought up in Saskatchewan, and even though he now scores around 20 goals a season in the NHL, that doesn't keep him from practicing his good prairie values, humbly helping out when he sees someone in need.

Cruising along the expressway the night his team lost to Montréal in the 2010 playoffs to get eliminated, Laich noticed a car parked at the side of the road, with a mom and her teenage daughter trying to fix a flat tire. When he stopped, they recognized him, being fans and having seen the game he'd just played in. However, Laich was not there to be a superstar, but to help, so he rolled up his sleeves, got out the jack and changed the tire. His response when they asked him how to repay him was to the effect of "pay it forward." No big deal, and this on the night that his season had come to an end.

A story like that makes Canadians realize that even the bright lights of fame can't change what matters at the heart of the country—being yourself, having genuine humility and getting things done when needed. It's not that an American wouldn't do the same, or even a Russian (maybe that Washington, DC, road just wasn't the one that Alexander Ovechkin takes home). It has to do with the surplus of good in the Canadian spirit that can't help but emerge at opportune moments.

Of course, Canadians are not unique in worshipping their heroes and wanting a part of their lives. My wife's nephew, who lives in France, idolizes Formula One drivers, or at least he did as a kid, until he approached one multi-time champion for an autograph and was turned down. That's a story you never hear about hockey players. They seem to accept that their job extends to off-ice moments, even if that means that they are sometimes interrupted while shopping or dining.

While in their heyday and after, hockey players seem more willing than athletes of any other sport to give to their fans. And hockey fans show their love for their heroes in ways that are probably unique to the game. Brent Severyn, who was in the league for 300-plus games over eight seasons with a variety of teams, received perogies on every stop of his NHL career from a woman in his hometown of Vegreville, Alberta. Whether he was in Florida, New York, on the west coast or in Dallas (where he won a Cup), he could count on her finding him.

Others have likely done the same for their favourite player, because hockey heroes become archetypal to fans, emblematic of their own struggles in life. We are all, at some time, new at something, a rookie. We make mistakes, or we fail. So when we hear of Steven Stamkos making the Tampa Bay Lightning in the fall of 2008, we're happy for him. When we find out he's scratched for a couple of games, we understand, because we've had a tough time adjusting at work early in our careers, too.

We use the figures in the game to help us understand life. Coaches become analogous to our own bosses, particularly the strictest ones. Sure, we'd all prefer a fatherly Terry Murray or a calm and collected Dave Tippett behind the bench. We might even accept a fiery guy like John Tortorella. But nobody wants a boss like Marc Crawford—you just never know what he's going to do next. How about a fuming, steaming, but silent, Joel Quenneville? Or an uber-controller like Scotty Bowman? And who would ask for a Conn Smythe or Punch Imlach, people that the players absolutely hated? (That doesn't mean these men were bad for their teams—they knew how to win—it just wasn't always fun for the guys who worked for them.)

However, these people appear throughout our lives, and the fact that our hockey heroes have to put up with these hardnosed personalities, too, makes sense to us. Our hope is that somehow, our tenure in the job will outlast that of the head honcho, and that the next person who moves into the corner office will be an inspirational Roger Neilson or an even-tempered Alain Vignault.

NHL players, though they don't know us, become our loyal friends, guys who've played alongside us during our youth and who still hang with us in the senior leagues. For the generation who grew up in the '70s, someone like Guy Lafleur was a hero and almost a buddy. As fans watched him play, his personality came through, especially when he removed his helmet after his third season. His hair flew wildly as he streaked in on goal, and those with hockey dreams could see themselves in him. When he was interviewed by Danny Gallivan or Dick Irvin (for the English-speaking audience) after the game, he felt familiar to us, like an older brother who left home early and was returning for a visit. (That is, if we had an older brother with a few Art Ross trophies, a Conn Smythe, a couple of Hart Memorial trophies and a handful of Stanley Cups.)

After Lafleur called it quits for the second time, in 1991, he didn't just disappear. He was involved in the Habs' organization, and he appeared on TV from time to time. Still, fans felt a sense of loss, which one expressed in these words: "Watching a Canadiens game would never quite feel the same.... Gone was our boyhood idol, and the realization that we were perhaps all getting older started to kick in." He was actually speaking of Lafleur's first retirement, but the words work just the same.

The 100th anniversary of the Habs played itself out over the course of the 2008–09 season, culminating in the commemorative game of December 4, 2009 (the following season). When Lafleur, Dryden and other former Montréal stars took a warmup skate before the game against Boston, it served as a reminder to their admirers that these guys weren't a figment of the imagination but a real presence in the world. Seeing Lafleur again, particularly, allowed memories of the Montréal Stanley Cups of 1976–79 to be rekindled. It was almost as if no time had passed at all.

What other sport has that effect on Canadians? The CFL has its heroes—think of Pinball Clemons in Toronto—and baseball has Joe Carter from the Blue Jays and Gary Carter from the Expos. But they didn't grow up in Canada, and their experiences are not those we share, of going to the arena early on a Saturday to play or fighting off the cold to flood a backyard rink. Only Canadian-born hockey players represent these shared experiences, which is why we look up to them so much, even long after their careers are over.

When Heroes Fail

Heroes shouldn't let us down, but that happens, too. Fans might like to think that every man who makes the NHL has a special, magical touch, some whisper of the gods that makes him invulnerable to the foibles of the rest of us. But, as happens in real life, there are those with substance abuse problems, such as Theo Fleury or the late Bob Probert. These challenges are sometimes overcome, which both of these men did, but sometimes not, and those who flame out form an important part of our worldview, also.

For example, John Kordic made his debut in 1985 with Montréal and won the Stanley Cup the next spring with the Canadiens. He was 20 at the time and known for displaying a rough edge on the ice. Over the next six seasons, he played with three other teams—the Leafs, Capitals and Nordiques—totalling 244 games in his career. He scored a handful of goals, 17, and added 18 assists. But his penalty minutes reveal his strengths. He had three short of 1000 when he found himself out of the NHL at age 27.

During the 1990–91 season, his Washington team ordered him into rehab for alcohol abuse, and he missed the end of the campaign. He was signed by Québec for one more year, and he played in 18 games for the team in 1991–92, notching 115 penalty minutes. The next summer, he was training for another shot at the league in a tryout with Edmonton when he died after an altercation with police. It is thought that a combination of drugs, alcohol and steroids, plus the exertion of trying to keep the cops from restraining him, led to his death.

Other hockey heroes meet ends that we would rather they didn't. Keith Magnuson, who was a staple on the Chicago blueline through the 1970s, including his second season, when his team lost to Montréal in an exciting seven-game Stanley Cup final, was killed when the car he was riding in crashed. The driver, another former NHLer, Rob Ramage, was convicted of impaired driving and served prison time over the matter. But even when a player falls, again, there are big hearts willing to take him back, and perhaps hockey players know this, which explains, in part, why they are so generous with those who buy the tickets that give them the chance to ply their skills.

The stories of these men show us that NHL players live real lives, too. It seems all glory and glamour when you're watching from the stands, and it's easy to imagine that these guys don't have to deal with normal life when they're off the ice. Not so. Kordic's case is a sad one, and he probably caused more disruption on the teams he played for than he had a right to, but it's instructive nonetheless in a culture where heroes are created with the donning of a hockey jersey. For our part as fans, maybe it's time to starting thinking of hockey players as human, as we have learned to do with Wayne Gretzky. But that would demand a major shift in our behaviour and our thinking.

Hopefully in the end, we'll have more Gretzkys, Tony Espositos, Rick Kehoes and Doug Gilmours—honest, personable heroes—than Kordics, and fans can continue to revere the guys in NHL uniforms as gods. If our country is hockey, then like every place that has a grand, enabling myth, the ability to worship a hero allows that myth to function. This, in turn, gives us the strength to deal with the mundane aspects of life, because it's never that long until we can forget ourselves in the action and excitement of the next game.

chapter five

A Touchstone to Look Back On

Do You Remember When?

Certain events stand out as hallmarks in the history of any people. "Do you remember seeing The Beatles on the *Ed Sullivan Show*?" It's a question not as many Americans ask now as might have a decade or two ago, but it still marks a turning point in popular culture. "Where were you when you heard about Kennedy's assassination?" is another familiar memory, from the same time period.

Canada, too, has its memorable moments, but the one that stands above all others concerns hockey. "Where were you when Paul Henderson scored the goal?" is the question we ask each other when the topic of great moments in Canadian history comes up. It's so common a query that the interrogator doesn't even have to specify the context—the September 1972 Summit Series between Canada and the USSR. Henderson himself says that rarely does a day go by that he doesn't talk about the goal. "Almost everyone I meet wants to tell me what he or she was doing when I scored the winning goal in Moscow," he claims about the tally.

To many Canadians, including those not yet born when it happened, the goal matters more than any other event that has taken place since, including Crosby's golden goal to defeat the U.S. in the 2010 Olympics. Why? Because the series showcased a clash of values between an inscrutable enemy (the Soviets) and a bully-turned-underdog (us), who was surprised that it took all we had to finally triumph.

(Too) Certain of Victory

Canadians were confident from the start that their team would dominate the series. Because it was made up of superstars of the NHL, Team Canada was supposed to be invincible. Predictions were that the club would win every game, and while nobody quite said it, most people thought that the Russian team would politely gawk at our stars, like spectators, rather than play them hard on the ice. The Soviets had us believing that they were in Canada to learn our sport, and that winning wasn't even on their radar.

From the moment they got off the plane in Montréal, the Soviets were alien beings to the Canadian eye. Each man had a stiff, military bearing and a rigid, unsmiling face. We believed that for them, hockey was not a joy, but a chore. We thought their approach to the game would reflect their stultifying, systematic approach to life and that our creativity would allow us to prevail over them. After all, our country *was* hockey.

What really did Canada in, and what made the series memorable, was that we forgot that our side might have vulnerabilities, not realizing at the beginning that there was no "us"—no sense of team—with this group of players. Great individuals oftentimes do not add up to a great team. To say it another way, until late in the series when the guys pulled together, they, and the country at large, forgot a primary Canadian value, that the group matters more than the individual, and it nearly cost Team Canada the victory.

Our feeling of superiority was reinforced in the first minute of game one, when Phil Esposito took the puck through centre, went into the Soviet end and worked it around to linemate Yvan Cournoyer, who passed it to a defenseman. The puck was shot on goal, and then Esposito batted it into the net after a touch by his other winger, Frank Mahovlich. Thirty seconds had gone by since the initial drop. "It's going to be 20–0," was the thinking of fans watching in the Montréal Forum and on TV.

But as the period went on, the Soviets cashed in their spectator tickets and started to play. Pretty soon, they were running the Canadian players around like an older brother would a younger one on a backyard rink. The Canadian response, according to team captain Esposito, was to spend the first intermission complaining. "We were dying after the first period," he later recalled. "I remember walking around and everyone's complaining, 'Oh, it's hot. Boy, it's hot, it's hot. Eee, it's hot.'" He smiles as he summarizes the game in a documentary on the series. "Hot—that wasn't the half of it. It was hot in that building, but we were suffering."

Brad Park concurs as he recalls Team Canada's panic. "These guys are in shape. They are coming at us. We're in trouble." Wayne Cashman nails the problem: "This wasn't the Russian amateur team. That's what we kept hearing, 'the Russian amateur team,' and they were more professional than we were, and they were ready."

The home team resorted to cheap-shot tactics, with Cashman (not dressed for the game but a visitor to the team's locker room between periods one and two) suggesting to Esposito, "Let's spear a few of them....We'll see how tough they are. Let's get them in the corners." The Russians were particularly irksome in that they never gave up on a play, instead chasing down a puck carrier who beat them, and taking it back from him. In response, as contemporary observer Jack Ludwig described the events, "Bobby Clarke...was among the first to fall into chippy bush-league tactics." Other players did the same. "Rod Gilbert, looking very bad every time he stepped out [onto the ice] tried to get back at the USSR players with punches, elbows, and other shinny tricks," Ludwig claimed at the time.

The Russians did not let up, and they won the game 7–3. It was reported in the papers the next morning as "a shocking, incredible result" and a "humiliation." Ludwig also explains that the dailies used metaphors taken from World War I and World War II in their discussion of the game—"Ypres was involved. Dieppe. Dunkirk"—and goes on to note that these were all overblown, given that hockey games do not cost people their lives, as battles do. The point was a valid one, but the series did take on a war-like quality, to players and fans alike. Phil Esposito said in 1997, "It scared the hell out of me that I would have killed them to win. That scared me." He wasn't exaggerating, nor could he have over-stated how Canadians felt about him and his fellow players. They were our team. They were "us," and we didn't care to what lengths our players had to go to win. When the first four games saw us gain only one win, the collective Canadian conscious-ness was on edge. What was happening to our superstars?

Superheroes Sometimes Stumble

All kids spend a good deal of their time fantasizing about who they might be. Remember the summer you discov-ered Spiderman or Batman? Your life became a crime-fighting movie; every person who walked by the house was a villain, the backfire of every car that resounded in your neighbour-hood a clue that would lead you to the truth. The truth about what? In real life, nothing—neither murder nor mayhem invaded your home (at least, let's hope not). But thinking you were a world-class superhero gave purpose to those lazy sum-mer mornings when TV was off-limits and it wasn't yet time to go to swimming lessons. As soon as fall arrived and hockey began again, though, all thoughts of heroes, other than those on the ice, vanished.

For many Canadians, no matter what age, hockey provides something to believe in. As you grow to adulthood, your dream of one day winning the Stanley Cup yourself shifts to hoping your favourite team wins it, and when they are out, to picking a "girlfriend team" that you can pull for. But the phenomenon is the same whether you're a kid or an adult: life is lived out with a sense of expectation that your team will be victorious. As such, your hopes become synonymous with those of the players who make up your club's roster. Back in 1972, the Team Canada players were heroes far above our dads or any other male role models in "real" life.

The Team Canada players were, for fans, larger than life that September. After all, they had been assembled by plucking the very best of the NHL rosters, at this point 16 teams strong, with Long Island and Atlanta joining for the upcoming campaign. It wasn't like an All-Star team is now, with even representation for all teams, either. This was more like the Olympic squad, carefully put together to give the greatest balance of strengths. Thirty-five men were invited to the initial camp, though as the series went on, some saw limited action, others none, which led to a few leaving Moscow (where the last four games were played), including Vic Hadfield. Interestingly, Hadfield was tapped for the team with both of his New York

Rangers linemates, Jean Ratelle and Rod Gilbert. The trio was "considered Canada's most Soviet-like for its passing prowess," but they fell flat in game one. Hadfield played in just one more game, in Vancouver (the fourth game), while the other two appeared in six of the eight contests.

Looking at the Team Canada roster, it was obvious then, and still is today, that these guys were the showboats of their teams. Phil Esposito was at centre, his brother Tony in net. Ken Dryden, who had been the unstoppable stopper rookie phenom a year earlier when the Habs beat Chicago to win the Stanley Cup, was the other goalie who played, including in game one. The defense was made up of guys like Serge Savard, Guy Lapointe and Brad Park. Bobby Orr famously did not play because he required knee surgery at the time.

We believed that nobody on the planet, and maybe not on any other, could dominate the Canadian team—until the aforementioned events of games one through four. Coach Harry Sinden was so surprised at the opposition that at one point he exclaimed, "They're all over the place. Are they putting eight guys out there or something? Why the hell is this happening to me?" He also noted, "With [the Russians] every trip up ice is a threat, which isn't so with NHL teams." By the time the two teams left Canada, with our boys headed off to play some exhibition games in Sweden, our side was down 2–1 with one tie. How could this be?

Confronting the Other

Measured by contemporary standards, no place was so foreign to Canada as the Soviet Union was in 1972. Sure, these days, there are countries where hockey doesn't seem to belong. Should the Chinese National men's team win an Olympic hockey gold medal anytime soon, it would be surprising—especially if Canada is on the losing end. Ditto for a team from the Middle East, or India, though who knows if they even play hockey in the latter country. It would be a shock, but it wouldn't threaten our way of life. But 1972 was different, because we projected our entire political system, and the Soviets', onto the games of the Summit Series.

It was freedom versus control. The flowing hair and wide-lapelled jackets many members of the Canadian team wore when they arrived for the first game at the Montréal Forum, for instance, symbolized that these men were allowed to make personal choices, including the way they styled themselves off the ice. They represented our infinite ability to decide how we wanted to live, whereas the Communists' similar, soldier-style haircuts and plain grey dress slacks reflected their lack of choice. (In fact, the Russian players were military officers whose job assignment was to play for the Red Army team.) The games thus took on an importance far beyond themselves in the immediate moment of Cold War politics. The series became mythic, however, because of the way it unfolded, with the Canadians squeaking out a 4–3–1 victory in the last 34 seconds on the goal by Henderson.

Because of the drama of the win over an enemy coded as entirely alien, the series became an event around which future Canadian sporting, political and cultural life would revolve, even down to the present.

The irony is that the great fear of losing the Summit Series and what that would mean for Canada shouldn't have been a concern. The Canadian team made a classic mistake, as explained thousands of years ago by Chinese philosopher Sun Tzu in *The Art of War*: they underestimated their opponent's strengths. The Russians also played this perfectly, as if following the ancient wisdom Sun Tzu offers: "A military operation involves deception. Even though you are competent, appear to be incompetent. Though effective, appear to be ineffective."

Assistant Coach John Ferguson said it simply in the documentary film *Team Canada 1972*: "Did we ever get fooled."

The Soviets had pretended in the initial practices that they could not skate very well. They had crummy, old equipment, antiquated wooden sticks and dated skates with blades that had been sharpened down so far that they were thin wisps. At that time, even a minor league player in Canada was sporting a curved stick, fibreglass reinforcing the blade, with maybe a painted yellow or fluorescent shaft completing the package. The Soviets had none of this.

But poor equipment and seemingly inadequate skating skills were not the only story, nor the true one. The Russians were good for two reasons: they played a style that never gave up the puck unless necessary, and they were in superb condition. The Canadian players were in their preseason form, basically completely out of shape, even when game one began; the Russian players were finely honed machines that played and trained every month of the year.

During the period breaks in the 1972 Summit Series TV broadcasts, video footage showed the Russian players in their living rooms, swinging a "kettlebell" around, their muscles bulging. Ironically, nearly 40 years later, that fitness device is becoming popular in North America. It's a heavy iron weight with a handle moulded into its top, and lifting and swinging it builds muscle. From these video images, Canadians learned two things: these poor Communists lived in tiny, crappy apartments, so their way of life was far inferior to ours; and they were monsters in terms of their fitness level, far surpassing the conditioning of the Canadian players, at any time of the year, let alone before the NHL pre-season.

The Canadians' method of training was donning those old-school thick sweatsuits and doing a few sit-ups in a hallway of the Montréal Forum. Even if the NHL season had been starting, these guys wouldn't have been in condition on day one of training camp. They'd still be carrying their summer beer weight, and they'd go to camp to get in shape. By Christmas, they'd be hitting their stride. September 2, when the series began, was well before they would normally tune up to play and was nowhere near the date they'd be ready to take on an opponent with the kind of physical prowess the Soviets possessed.

The Red Army team also had an odd style of play that didn't allow them to do what the Canadian players did, which was fire the puck high and hard into the zone, then go crash and bang and get it back for a scoring chance. The Soviets, it was later discovered, learned by watching film of the Montréal Canadiens of the 1950s. They kept the puck, carefully passing it back and forth as they crossed the blueline. As Paul Henderson said in astonishment some years after, "They broke all the rules on us. I mean, they come [sic] up and didn't like what it looked like, they turned around and went back—what is, what is this?...It was very unnerving," he explained, "because it was our game."

So neither the Soviet style of play nor the fact that it was working against our heroes made sense on those nights in September 1972, and by game eight, with the series having shifted to Luzhniki Sports Palace for the final four games, the situation looked desperate. The series was 3–3–1. The final game didn't start with a great deal of promise, either, and by the end of the second period, it was 5–3 for the Russians. Years later, Ken Dryden said that at the break between periods two and three, the team wasn't dejected about being behind. "There's no overtime, there's no ninth game, there's no anything else. And so, you know, there's almost a kind of mellow sense…[that] well, let's see what can happen. You know, let's do what we can do and who knows?"

More Than Just Hockey

Teamwork, decency, standing up for something, doing whatever it takes. On the best teams, everyone buys in to these philosophies, but on a team with any hope of winning at all, there's usually one guy who models those values. Peter Mahovlich was that guy during game eight. Midway through the third period, he saw his team's chief executive, Alan Eagleson, being taken away by Russian soldiers after a disagreement about a goal that the Soviet arena officials were seemingly going to disallow. Mahovlich didn't know where Eagleson was going, but he knew that the guys with the guns weren't acting in friendship, so he climbed into the crowd, and, with his hockey stick, defended Eagleson, prying him from the soldiers' grasp and getting him safely back to the Team Canada bench with the help of his teammates.

In a documentary filmed for the 25th anniversary of the series, Mahovlich said, "We were all together, and they weren't going to take Alan away. That's the way it was." Phil Esposito concurred, saying, "I don't think the Russians had any idea what the hell we were doing. I don't think we knew what we were doing. They had guns. We had hockey sticks. I mean, this was really the David and Goliath here." Though Espo's reference is to a man-to-man (more accurately, boy-to-giant) encounter, the "we" he uses tells all. No matter that the dangers of intervening were murky—Eagleson said that if the Russian guards got him out a nearby exit, he knew he would disappear for hours, if not days—action was called for, and together, the team did what it needed to do to keep one of its members safe. Commenting on Eagleson, Bobby Clarke said that the team executive was a big part of the squad's winning the series.

Across Canada, kids were watching the game in schools, and adults slipped out of work to see it on the TVs in Eaton's or Simpson's furniture departments. In those days, there were no VCRs and no replays of games on cable channels, so you either saw the action live or you missed it. Nobody wanted to be the one who missed it. The goal stood, and the game was tied, 5–5, with just over seven minutes to go. The series, had it ended that way, would have been 3–3 with two ties, and that seemed, though nobody could have imagined it 26 days earlier, like a victory of sorts for Canada. Then word got to the Canadian side that the Russians were invoking the international custom in the case of a tied "friendly" and using the tiebreaker of total goals. To that moment, the Canadians had 30, the Russians 32. They would "win."

It wasn't good enough, and the Canadian team pushed during the last several minutes. Once, the puck went past Henderson and wide, while he crashed into the boards behind the Russian net. Then, with about 40 seconds to go, Cournoyer shot the puck from the right point, and it went wide left. The Russian defensemen let it get away from them as it came out of the corner, and Esposito, cruising through the slot right to left, took a shot on goal. Tretiak made the save.

Meanwhile, Henderson had snuck to the front of the net, and with Tretiak lying on the ground, shovelled the rebound under him. "Henderson has scored for Canada!" Foster Hewitt pronounced on TV, the slightly metallic twang in his voice evoking both triumph and irony at the same time. Canada went crazy. People on the street hugged each other. And in the school bus I was travelling on in suburban Montréal, the driver threw his hands in the air. We all screamed and jumped up and down in our seats, breaking the usual decorum that Jack, the driver, made us adhere to. The call had come through on the little radio he had mounted next to his seat, so we didn't see the goal, but it didn't matter. In that moment, we felt like we were there.

The celebrations started all over the country. In the big cities, people poured out of office buildings onto the street. In small towns, vehicles honked their horns. And when the team came back from Moscow, landing at Dorval, a throng 20,000 strong met them, including Prime Minister Trudeau, who, bedecked in a sport coat, open shirt and ascot, had dropped the ceremonial first puck on September 2 to get the series started.

The moment was perfect, given that there was an election campaign going on. Being a part of the victory, naturally, was good politics—maybe the luck would rub off at the end of

October, when Canadians would turn out to vote. More than
that selfish motive, though, Trudeau looks to have had a sense
of history. Not in his tenure had Canadian soldiers gone off to
war, and while he had been old enough to fight in World
War II, he hadn't done so. But this moment he could seize,
and as he greeted the returning heroes, he treated them as
though they'd been to war, not like they'd just won an exhibition hockey tournament. The players, in turn, lauded him,
with Serge Savard picking him up onto his shoulders, then
later giving an emotional speech in which he gave John
Ferguson's autographed hockey stick to the PM.

More Than a Goal

The goal, of course, was more than just the Summit
Series winner. It symbolized to Canada and (we believed) the
world that democracy had won. It was the greatest example
to that time of the triumph of the West over the Soviet
system of repression and state control of the individual. The
win also gave Canadians bragging rights over the Americans,
who hadn't engaged in any sort of diplomatic or sporting
conquest with the Russians since the Cold War had begun
20 years earlier.

As scholar Kelly Hewson explains it,

> [T]*here was a Cold War scenario being
> played out; not only would our "triumph"
> be sporting, it would be political. And as*

always, there was a third character in the romance—the United States. In defeating the Russians, we could show up our mutual neighbours, who were fighting the still evenly matched battle of the Space Race with the Soviets.

Canada had proved that the Western way of life was better, or at least proved it to Canadians. The feeling evoked was that, like at Passchendaele or Vimy Ridge, the country had a role to play on the world stage. The country was coming of age, internationally. As one fan proclaimed on that day, "It's the same thing [as] when the war was over, eh?" (referring to World War II).

The U.S., of course, had used sports games to win political battles as well. They were engaged in an arms race with Russia, but they were also taking part in a diplomatic dance with the world's other great communist power, China. This led to the famous "ping pong diplomacy," in which a U.S. table tennis team travelled to China at the invitation of the Chinese government in 1971. Prior to this, China had been closed to sporting events since 1949, and diplomatically closed as well. This apparent détente, to use a word perhaps better suited to the USSR, made it possible for U.S. President Richard Nixon to visit China in 1972, and for the two countries to restore, or "normalize," their broken relations as a result. But come on—a table tennis tournament against the rough and tumble of hockey? What were the Americans thinking?

Canada, in the months directly following the series, felt as though it could conquer the world, although it was a wise idea not to actually try to do that. It was a perfect moment—the one thing we, the small nation, believed we could succeed in had been challenged. When we prevailed, we were like any underdog team that comes on from behind to win a big game—unstoppable.

The Series Lives On

The series win, and the goal, are part of the fabric of Canadian life, and every September, they can be revisited as a way of measuring who we are and what matters to us. Their continuing presence in our cultural memory helps to form our identity by confirming the crucial role hockey plays in defining our country. In fact, Hewson comments that:

> [I]t *doesn't matter* [if one did not witness the game] *because the magical moment of Paul Henderson scoring that winning goal is so often reproduced, played and replayed that Canadians born well after the fact can still experience the thrill of victory, that fundamental moment of national identity presumably never to be felt again.*

Yet had the Russians not surprised Team Canada by playing so well, the Summit Series wouldn't have mattered the way it does. We would have won, it would have ended and people would have gone back to business as usual. There was, after all, much more pressing news breaking in the hockey world that fall—the WHA was starting up, and many of the best players in the NHL had agreed to play in the new league, including the most notable of all, Bobby Hull.

The fact that Canada almost lost the series explains why "the goal" means so much, and perhaps accounts for the continuing institutionalization of it in this country. For the series' 25th anniversary in 1997, a new set of documentary tapes came out, including game eight in its entirety for the first time. Then came the whole series on DVD in 2002. Bobbleheads, T-shirts, hockey cards and replica sweaters have also appeared in recent years. Books have been written and a feature film produced.

More than just an idealized, nostalgic moment, the series has become a touchstone that we continually return to when subsequent hockey victories seem in doubt. Consider the World Junior Championship in 2003. The Canadians had won five straight gold medals from 1993 to 1997, then lost to Russia in 1999 and 2002. The years in between, Canada had won bronze. Consequently, by 2003, the desire for a victory was acute, and the string of losses was read as a failure of Canadian hockey as a whole, maybe even a collapse of our hockey supremacy in the world, forever. So when it came time to play the Russians for gold for the third time in five years, is it any wonder that people calling in to the Toronto sports talk shows were saying things like, "This is this generation's 1972"?

It's easy to invest huge meaning in something that has such tantalizing parallels with epic events of the past. The problem is, the situation wasn't the same. The Russians were not the Soviets anymore. They weren't alien beings that represented a way of life drastically different from Canada's. They were just a better hockey team than the bunch of kids we put out there, and they won, again.

Fast forward to 2010, by which time the Canadian juniors had won five straight golds (2005–09). The 2010 team lost the gold in OT to the U.S., but attention quickly diverted from that tournament to the Olympics. Yet even with the contexts changed by time—the Russian "threat" having long receded—going into the final game of the Vancouver Olympics, the 1972 series was again the touchstone. The comparison stretched as far as California, in an *Orange County Register* story reminding readers that "Paul Henderson's winning goal in the 1972 Summit Series with the Soviet Union united Canada, providing it with a sense of identity." The article commented that similarly, "the most anticipated Olympic hockey tournament in history is seen as another defining moment for a nation and its game."

But were these comparisons accurate? Two distinct ways of life weren't being challenged in Vancouver, one free and one repressed. Rather, it was the old "us-versus-them" push-pull where polite Canada was trying to defeat its more brash southern neighbour. Had Team Canada lost, it likely would have led to calls for an investigation into the ways that we train our young players, how we nurture our teens as they develop into future pros and how we pick our Olympic teams. The seven losses in a row in the World Junior Championship between 1998 and 2004 certainly prompted such demands. But nobody would have said that the Americans were about to take over our country had they won the Vancouver gold. At least, not more than they already have with their pop culture, consumer goods and retail presence in Canada. Sure, we wanted to beat them, but no, it wouldn't have scared us to death had we not. So while seeing Crosby score that OT winner stunned us into holding that moment in our minds forever and gave us a new "goal" that needs no context or explanation as a conversation starter, it can never measure up to Henderson's goal.

On the flip side, when you win consistently, as Canada did in the World Juniors from 2005 to 2009, memories tend to fade. Unless there's a miraculous Henderson-type late goal or a spectacular come-from-behind victory, winning one year after the other, while expected, becomes a bit monotonous. That does not belittle the accomplishment; rather, it suggests that the reason the goal on September 28, 1972, prompts so many "Where were you when it happened?" questions is that until Henderson did his magic, the outcome of the game and the tournament, not to mention our place in the hockey world, was entirely in doubt.

Had Canada lost, maybe all memories of the series would have been buried, too. This happened with the next great series, the 1974 Summit Series of WHA stars against those same Russians. The DVD set of these games is fittingly titled *Team Canada 1974: The Lost Series*. But because Team Canada 1972 won, and in dramatic fashion, September will always be over-laid with memories of those eight games in a pattern that rings true for Canadians who know the (original) Summit Series.

A Series for Everyone

While the 1972 series is major touchstone in Canada, the irony is that the Canadian population at present is made up of approximately 34 million people, roughly 50 percent of whom could have no first-hand recollection of Henderson's goal. They either weren't born yet or were living elsewhere. But because the series is referred to so often, because it has transcended hockey and become history, and because of the continual references to it in pop culture, they know it anyway. Consider the mention in the Tragically Hip song "Fireworks":

> *If there's a goal that everyone remembers,*
> *it was back in ole '72*
>
> *We all squeezed the stick and we all pulled*
> *the trigger...*

Or there's David Adams Richards' novel, *Nights Below Station Street*, in which the character Terrisov critiques Canadian sporting endeavours. Criticizing Canadians for not putting enough fun in the game, he says that they should train harder and earn less. The narrator says, "He neglected to mention the 1972 series." But another character doesn't forget. Referencing Russians, the narrator tells us that the character named "Adele said she did not like them ever since the 1972 hockey series." To understand our literature, you must be familiar with that tournament. The converse, of course, is that continual reference to the series—Harper even used its imagery in a 2011 campaign commercial, though he failed to pay for the rights to the footage, according to *Maclean's*—makes it hard for anyone living in Canada not to become familiar with it.

If there is any regret, it is that the grand moment may never be repeated, because there probably won't be another time when the stakes are so high—including Vancouver 2010 and its overtime goal. Politics are different today, and thus a hockey tournament could not be so over-invested with meaning as it was back then. But that fact just makes the memory more precious for those who were there, and more to be longed for by those too young to have been, or who were living somewhere outside of the reach of what, to Canadians, seemed like the battle of the universe. It is a memory that reinforces the importance of hockey as central to the Canadian psyche.

chapter six

Icons That Live On

The Beautiful, Glorious Cup

In Shakespeare's *Richard II*, John of Gaunt at one point laments the decline in his homeland, and he utters words that sound out with glory even 400 years later. In Act 2, Scene 1, he calls England:

> *This royal throne of kings, this scept'red isle,*
> *This earth of majesty, this seat of Mars,*
> *This other Eden, demi-paradise,*
> *This fortress built by Nature for herself*
> *Against infection and the hand of war,*
> *This happy breed of men, this little world,*
> *This precious stone set in the silver sea*
> *...Against the envy of less happier lands;*
> *This blessed plot, this earth, this realm, this England.*

Imagine the character's voice rising in volume and intensity as he ends this speech, and you have the tone. Some of it might even be read as an apt description of Canada, though the anti-royalists might object a little to the King stuff.

And hockey people might point in a different direction in accounting for the glory and majesty in this country. To them, the pride of Canada is because of the tradition that is resident in the Stanley Cup.

What would Canada be without that trophy? Just another mid-sized nation struggling to maintain its population in a world of demographic shift? Okay, that's an overstatement. But let's play with Shakespeare's lines a moment to see how, in the Canadian imagination, the beauty and majesty of our country might be seen to coincide with that of the Cup itself.

What if John had said:

> *This sacred gift of the queen's representative, this sceptred*
> *   sphere,*
> *This Cup of majesty, this beacon of victory,*
> *This glorious vessel, demi-paradise,*
> *This monolith, built by history for herself*
> *Against corruption, and the hand of war;*
> *This happy team of men, this little world,*
> *This precious chalice held in the Hall of Fame*
> *Against the envy of less happier fans;*
> *This blessed Cup, this team, this league, this Stanley!*

Read that again, only this time, out loud. Practice a couple of times so that you get louder as you go, ending in a grand crescendo. Probably, you should not do this in public. But as you finish, ask yourself whether those words feel at all odd. My guess is that they do not. Although Canadians as kids don't learn a poem about the Stanley Cup, they might as well, because somehow, they get the idea that this object is grand beyond all but the most glorious words used to describe it, and that it exists as an icon and beacon of Canada, regardless whether a U.S. team holds it at any given moment.

In comparison, the American sporting leagues' top prizes pale. The World Series trophy has a circular base and the replicas of 30 pennants standing up from it. It's silver, gold and shiny. But every year, a new trophy is made and is given to the team that wins. The NFL's Lombardi Trophy is a space-age thing looking very much a product of its time (as is the Stanley Cup, but of a more glorious era), and it goes from shiny to fingerprint-smudged in the 15 seconds after the league's commissioner hands it to the winning owner and QB. The NASCAR Cup—be that Winston, Nextel, Sprint or whoever they're selling its rights to in years to come—well, enough said about that.

But the Stanley Cup, to use an expression that people throw around a lot these days, "is what it is." That usually is said with a shrug and a sigh, like "Oh well, accept it, because you can't change it." But in terms of the great and glorious Stanley Cup, the words mean something more. It is what it has always been and will always be, beautiful and majestic, and we treasure it beyond any other icon in the land.

Every time any player on any team touches that Cup (and everyone knows the superstition that says that you should do that only when you've won it), he is touching the same Cup that the greats have touched. While the fingerprints of Howie Morenz, Lester Patrick or Denis Potvin have long been wiped off it, their remnants are still there, because the Cup has a continuity that stretches back to the original days of hockey. Of course, what Lord Stanley of Preston donated in 1893 wasn't the multi-tiered trophy that has existed in its present form since the 1950s. His gift was the bowl and base at the top of the current version. However, the sense of the trophy's value has resonated since its beginnings.

The magic of the Cup is why a team would travel for nearly a month over 6500 kilometres to challenge for it, as the Dawson City Nuggets did in 1905. It's why a team would risk death during the Spanish influenza epidemic to try to win it, as the Montréal Canadiens did, going to Victoria in 1919 and losing one of their star players to the flu in the process.

This is also the reason players are willing to give up so much to get their names on the Cup. Think of the 2010 playoffs, when Eric Belanger lost several teeth, two of them screw-ins that had replaced the ones lost earlier in his career. He pulled out the stumps on the bench, went to the dressing room for a quick shot of Novocain and got back on the ice. When asked why, he said something like, "It's the playoffs; what are you going to do?" Duncan Keith, same playoff year, gets a puck in the mouth, loses seven teeth, finishes the game and does an interview afterward. He said he'd lose them all if it meant a chance to play for the Stanley Cup. He did get that chance, and he won it, too.

Players who have won the trophy have been known to say that they hurt until the middle of July from all the battering it took to survive the playoffs. But ask Canadians whether they would make a similar sacrifice to see their names engraved on the Cup, and most would say yes. No hesitation.

Of course, the "problem" is that, in many years, an American team wins it. Since 1994, as everyone knows, the Cup has been in U.S. hands. But let's take a few examples and ask whether this is really what it seems to be. The 2007 Ducks (newly non-Mighty) won the Cup, keeping Ottawa from claiming their first one since 1927, when the NHL was just a decade old and had not yet found its Original Six form. The Ducks, to put it another way, kept a "Canadian" team from winning the Stanley Cup and bringing it home.

The demographic profile of the team that won, however, looks like this: of the 25 players on the official finals roster, four are American. Three are from elsewhere (Finland, Russia and Sweden), and the rest—that's 18—are Canadian.

The Senators, the "Canadian" team, had nine players from the rest of the world, including three from the U.S. According to official team statistics, they had a roster of 23 men for the finals, and only 14 of them were Canadians. So who was more Canadian? The Ducks. But both teams were essentially Canadian at their core.

You can't judge a book by its cover, and even this "Canadian team in American disguise" trick has a history.

The first U.S.-based team to win the Cup was the Seattle Metropolitans, in 1917, but the players were all Canadians. However, indignation arises when Canadians perceive that the Americans are impinging on our sacred space because they hold the Cup on their soil.

In 2006, the Oilers lost the finals to Carolina. The Hurricanes are a team that plays deep in NASCAR territory and that brought the indignity of cheerleaders to the NHL. But before Canadian fans get all riled up over that, they should notice something "worse": the 'Canes that year were more "other" than they were "us." Their Cup roster shows 12 Canucks, seven Yanks and six from other parts of the world. Edmonton, on the other hand, had a group that featured 16 Canadians and nine from elsewhere. So there were two reasons to be on their bandwagon.

To zoom ahead to the most recent time a Canadian team had a chance to grab the prize—in game seven in Vancouver in 2011, half of the Canucks' game-time roster were Canadians. Two-thirds of the Boston squad hailed from Canada. You can decide for yourself what that means. I say it means that the Cup is ours, no matter who won it.

If only Canadian teams could win the Cup every year, Canadian fans might not feel so much anxiety over the Cup ownership question. "If only they could reliably win it once a decade!" you might have just thought to yourself, "it would be our trophy."

Well, for a lot of reasons, the Cup actually is ours. Of the year's 365 days, all but a few dozen see the Cup residing on Canadian soil, in the Hockey Hall of Fame (HHOF). Of course, that differs from year to year depending on who wins it. The year the Ducks won, the trophy spent most of the summer going from province to province. The most recent year the Blackhawks won it, ditto, as all but nine of their players were Canadians. After the Cup's touring is done, it comes back to rest in the HHOF, with the odd days out for events like the NHL and AHL All-Star games, the draft, the NHL Awards (sadly, not presently held in Canada) and charity appearances that might take it to another country, most often the U.S.

Canadians thus might need to adjust their thinking about their relationship to the Cup in a couple of ways. We need to realize that even when an "American" team wins the Stanley Cup, probably a good number of the players are Canadians (maybe, at least for the time being, the majority). And even when fans in New Jersey say, "We have the Cup," they really don't. At that exact minute, it's probably at the Toronto-area silversmith for engraving or in the vault in the Hall, waiting for a visit from the latest crop of hockey fans on a school outing or a curious adult who wants, finally, and in defiance of superstition, to touch its hallowed surface. And because that is a possibility on more days of the year than not, Canadians' goals and dreams are motivated by this trophy. Think of Canada, and what hangs over any mental picture you might conjure up is a magic, spectral image, "this blessed Cup."

The Stick

The "problem" with the Cup, if you can call it that, is that there is only one. (Actually, the HHOF has a replica that is displayed when the original is on the road, but that's not the point here). However, other icons of the game are more tangible and immediate. The hockey stick connects Canadians to the game, evoking memories of our own playing days and reminding us of the NHLers, both past and present, we admire. The stick has changed over the years, though, going from a familiar, handmade object to a complicated, hi-tech device in a series of shifts that have taken the game away from its natural roots.

Scrutinize the photos of the great players of the past, and you'll see one thing in common—each is carrying a heavy-looking wooden stick, with black tape wrapped securely along the length of the blade and a knob of tape at the top end forming a ball for grip. That simple stick represents the game itself, since it's the scoring instrument. Simple maybe, except that it has a million nicknames and as many iterations. The twig. The beam. The toothpick—a prized wooden-bladed stick that has been relegated to street use and is filed down through play so that its blade is long and skinny. These and other names are the ways that the hockey stick gets coded into the language and experience of the hockey devotee.

Why is the stick so special? Because, at least until recently when machine-made composites came to be favoured, to hold a hockey stick was to own a handmade product, natural in its materials and execution. This stick wasn't all that far removed from the Mi'kmaq version of the 19th and early 20th centuries. Michael McKinley explains: "the aboriginal Mi'kmaq craftsmen of Nova Scotia...perfected their art of stick-building courtesy of the hornbeam tree, a tree so strong it was nicknamed 'ironwood.'" They nearly wiped out the population of the old-growth hornbeam forest because their sticks were so popular. In later generations, names like Victoriaville, Sher-Wood and CCM became synonymous with Orr, Howe and Béliveau, and even now, the look of the plain wooden shaft as seen in old photos—though the blades started to bend in the 1960s—is a throwback to history and a reminder of a day when the products we used, on the ice and off, were proudly stamped "Made in Canada." (CCM, nicknamed in my schoolyard as "Crappy Crate Makers," actually stood for "Canadian Cycle & Motor company." The firm shifted its production to hockey skates and equipment early in the 20th century.)

Things started to change about 40 years ago, when fibreglass-covered blades, their dimpled goodness silently promising that they would live forever, invaded the dreams of kids looking for a new stick on Christmas morning. And in recent days, as the American brands Easton and Nike popularized the use of artificial materials such as aluminium and carbon fibre, the natural wood models, which many consider the true iteration of the stick, have passed largely into history, though they are still available for those who prefer them.

The stick, pre-carbon, had a kind of purity that has been lost with the advent of hi-tech sports equipment. In just a few decades, $10 sticks have evolved into super-techie inventions of engineers costing hundreds of dollars. And along the way, they've become much less reliable than the old ones, though they do offer a series of advantages not seen or imagined in the past, namely light weight and super flexibility that allows players to make whip-like shots.

But as an icon, an almost sacred object that will live on past the time of its useful life, the contemporary stick has lost something to its older counterpart. The simple, homespun, accessible-to-anyone game is being shouldered out by inventions that players at a certain level (read: NHL) can't seem to resist, and that, at least in one way of thinking, don't have the charm of the old sticks. Interesting to note is that NHL commissioner Bettman has said on his radio show that the league needs to address the matter of composite sticks. Among other things, they're just too expensive, with teams' stick budgets running into the hundreds of thousands of dollars each year.

We've strayed from the simplicity of hockey as it was always played. Gone is the steadiness of the old game, when the term "special teams" was unheard of, something that football players talked about, not rough-tough hockey guys. The other irony is that abandoning the wooden models has cost us the connection to the land itself, the origins of the game.

Compare this change to the situation with the bats in American baseball. Amateur and college players use aluminium bats, which give off a loud "ping" when the ball is hit. Players in the big leagues and the ones that feed them use wooden models, similar to the ones that Babe Ruth, Hank Aaron and other greats used, and when the ball and bat make good contact, the sound is a healthy "crack" as the ball rebounds over the pitcher's head and sails toward the fence. MLB mandates the use of wooden bats, ensuring that the so-called "boys of summer" will continue to play the game as they have been doing for 100 and more years, thank you very much, and the sport is the richer for it.

As hard as it is to admit, the Americans may be winning the day on this issue. The iconic sound of the bat—a crack versus a ping—remains what it has always been. Hockey might do well to take a lesson and return to the way things were for the first 100-plus years of play. The composite hockey stick is a reminder to Canadians, when they get too smug about their ownership of hockey, that the history and spirit of the game require effort to maintain in an increasingly complicated world.

Hockey Night in Canada

The name says more than it appears to, considering the way the game replicates the nation. Scholar Jason Blake (not the hockey player of the same name) explains it best as he discusses why so much hockey literature uses or puns on the name of the Saturday night staple:

> *Hockey's omnipresence in Canada goes beyond active participation, and there is no segment of society shielded from the national affinity and addiction. The dominant hockey reference is* Hockey Night in Canada, *the wildly successful CBC show that began on radio in 1931 and moved to television in 1952.*

The game is played on a surface that brings to mind the seemingly eternal push-pull of the country we occupy, stretched out on a line that extends from ocean to ocean just like the airwaves that, at least in the days of antenna TV, stretched over the country to bring us the broadcast. The rink is narrow and long, like Canada, and when a fan turns on the TV to watch, there's the sense of being a part of something that is at once huge and intimate. This is our game in two senses—ours as a nation and ours as individuals who feel a stake in the match being played that night, no matter if it comes from Montréal, Vancouver or someplace in the USA. As Blake states, "*Hockey Night in Canada* [brings] the country together, if only for the length of the game, by eradicating isolation through technology." Watching the game, he says, is a ritual, and our participation in it "suffices to make [us] Canadian." The games as broadcast on TV "can be interpreted many ways, but the common denominator is an acting-out of being Canadian."

This leads to a question: Is it the game itself or the shared ritual of watching that matters so much? *HNIC* over the past few years has expanded its Saturday coverage from one game to two, plus a pre-show and *After Hours*. Those on the West Coast can enjoy the extravaganza from mid-afternoon until midnight, sometimes later. And there are some that take their devotion to extremes. In one neighbourhood near Oshawa, Ontario, driving down the streets any Saturday night of the season will show you a glow emanating from garages as guys (mostly) gather in small groups, even in the coldest part of wintertime, to watch a game together.

Why the garage? Maybe because it's okay to smoke out there. Maybe because it's easier to conceal from other members of the household the number of beer cans being emptied. No matter, the point is the ritual, the comfort that can be found in a group of guys who gather for a common purpose. Maybe this is a habit easier to enact in Ontario than elsewhere, where the mythical "Leafs Nation" is the most prevalent form of hockey community. Maybe it would be simply too cold to hang out in a garage on the Prairies, but the bonding rituals surrounding the game give meaning to Saturday nights in every part of the country.

The *Hockey Night in Canada* theme as it used to ring out of our TV sets on Wednesday and Saturday had an incredible power over Canadians. Just hearing it, no matter whether you were reading the paper, washing the dishes or talking on the phone, was the sign to drop everything. The game was about to come on, and nothing could be more important.

We sang the song on the street when we played our imaginary Stanley Cup finals, and who knows how many times we hummed it while walking to school or waiting for Mom or Dad to pick us up after a music lesson or dentist appointment. Having that tune in our heads connected us to the game that was coming that night or on the weekend, even if we weren't going to the arena to see it live, and even for those who lived far from the centre of the hockey world.

The way the song resonated within us is part of the reason an uproar occurred when the CBC decided not to pay up for the rights to the tune in 2008. How could it be that the song that we thought of as our second national anthem was going to disappear (albeit not completely, but to a rival network)?

The head of Copyright Music and Visuals, which held the song's copyright, said that the CBC was going in a new direction and would not renew their licensing agreement with the company. The explanation sounded reasonable, but it didn't fool anyone, and the most disappointing part about the whole episode was that it all had to do with money.

Most people had no idea a licensing agreement had been in place at all, nor that the theme song had originated as recently as it had, which was 1968, when Dolores Claman wrote it as a promotional tune for the show. Had fans been polled in the spring of 2008 about the matter, they would likely have recalled that the anthem, er, theme song, went back to "sometime before expansion," or maybe "back to *Hockey Night*'s early television days—the 1950s." Such is the power of memory; it can deceive you into inventing a more glorious past for something than is real. The fact is, however, that for everyone under about 45 at the time of the controversy, *HNIC* had never been without the theme, and so its history might as well have stretched back to the beginnings of the show, to the start of the NHL on radio or to someplace else in the distant, irretrievable past.

In the end, the song was sold to the CTV/TSN people, to continue there when hockey came on. But that left the most-watched show on Canadian TV without a theme. What to do? In this age of reality TV, the perfect answer presented itself in the form of a contest that would allow average Joes or Janes to have a crack at becoming famous by writing a new tune. Did they have any idea, these average folks, how close they were coming to the realm of the immortals? And did any of them consider how dangerous it has always been to meddle in the gods' affairs?

People of all ages, from kids to the elderly, and from all regions, English and French, sent in songs. The final five songs were morphed into useable versions by Canadian producer

Bob Rock. He appeared on the screen looking very much like his 1980s self, with hair that made him fit a time not quite in the now. His production credits on past projects, in part, told the tale: Metallica, Bon Jovi, Mötley Crüe and other hair-band era acts were his claim to fame.

Canadians asked themselves why Rock was chosen, but the answer was obvious from the get-go—he has made the great Canadian move—he made it here, then went to the U.S. and made it there. So what if he looked a little bit stuck in the past?

The songs he produced all ended up sounding slightly like they belonged to another time, too, though the one that won, by Albertan Colin Oberst, clearly works to grab the attention when it is heard on a Saturday evening, with a rousing bagpipe undertone and a crescendo that may, in time, displace the old song. *Hockey Night in Canada* in all its glory was saved, and a new generation of fans had something to whistle on their way to the corner rink. With the passing of years, they will forget that this new song has a history, and it will become synonymous with the great game, a second national anthem (or perhaps a third), albeit with a tiny asterisk.

The Game Ticket

Of course, if watching hockey on TV is good, then going to a game yields a shared experience that binds hockey fans together and becomes lodged in each of their memories. For most, having a ticket to an NHL game is rare, and the experience is treasured forever. This seems to be more true in Canada than in most of the U.S. cities with NHL teams, because at home, tickets are so valuable—not only in terms of cost but also demand. With rare exceptions, you can't just walk up to the box office and get seats at the last minute, and as a result, going to a game becomes something planned for and anticipated for days, weeks, perhaps months, or in the case of a forthcoming World Junior tournament, a year. This is why a kid in Toronto or Calgary doesn't get to a half dozen games a year but a precious one or two, if she or he is lucky. For many, it's one or two over the course of an entire childhood. For those with some foresight, the ticket stubs are saved, maybe put inside the game program brought home as a souvenir of the experience.

Perhaps the greatest moment in the history of Canadian spectating was in 1972, in Russia. The games became a test of national will, nation against nation being submerged under a larger rhetoric—the contrast of one way of life with another. Canadian fans, in the Summit Series, created a cheer: "Da, da, Canada; Nyet, nyet Soviet," they screamed in the Luzhniki Sports Palace. It was a clear reflection of their belief that their team was better and would win, and as the series went along, it grew in rancour because the series itself became a life-or-death struggle. For the few thousand Canadians who had the privilege of going to Moscow to attend the four games there, life was probably never the same afterward.

For those who get to attend only an occasional NHL game, the law of scarcity heightens the arena experience, making it necessary for the keen youngster to watch every little piece of action with wide-eyed wonder. The hugeness of the place, the immensity of the scoreboard, the loud noises—all are super-sized, and everything is committed to memory for careful retelling at school the next day, or Monday morning. It's like having been to a famous cathedral or a site like Stonehenge—there's no way you can be the same person after.

There's a slightly different quality when it's a game below the NHL level. The experience is no less precious to those who attend, but perhaps the scene is more familiar because it is more often enjoyed. For kids who play minor hockey, or for their parents or those who follow a local junior team, the arena becomes a recurring icon of Canadian life. While standing in a dressing room or pressing up against the glass watching a game, we meet other people. Some are like us, and these days, some are not. That's great, because everyone is welcome at the rink, which becomes our community.

As the game proceeds, the crowd watches, mesmerized, yelling in unison, so that they too, might as well be one entity and not a bunch of individuals. And then someone blows an air horn. You know the person. He or she is a fixture at most small-town arenas, an annoyance happily tolerated as long as he is judicious in choosing moments to offset the crowd's enthusiasm with a blast that shatters the eardrums of those in the surrounding rows and momentarily cracks the spell of the unified chant that the home crowd had been enjoying. In the moment of that sonic eruption, the east-west flow of the game is broken, and the geography of the place shifts. The rink embraces everyone, and the field of play, so to speak, extends past the boards and into the crowd. No matter what ticket price you paid, you're getting more than your money's worth.

The arena experience, however, isn't what it used to be. In the modern way of game presentation, at many levels of hockey, fans don't get to express their energetic support of their heroes on their own terms. Instead, the house music takes over, booming out its beat in an attempt to engineer what might come naturally if fans were left to their own devices.

A few years ago, I wrote an academic essay entitled, "What Ever Happened to the Organ and the Portrait of Her Majesty?" It discussed hockey game presentation and argued that we've lost something because the majestic organ has been shoved aside in favour of stadium rock, and the dignity of the never-aging queen looking out at us from the portrait that hung on the end wall has been upstaged by fancy graphics and ads on giant suspended scoreboards.

Pictures of Queen Elizabeth II were in every elementary school, and still are. The one at Queen Mary in Peterborough, where I attended grades seven and eight, was anchored to the wall at the front of the auditorium where we went from time to time for a movie or a music recital. With her watching, we behaved, but out on the playground, we could forget Elizabeth and do what we wanted. Not so in the hockey arena (in Peterborough, the hallowed Memorial Centre), where we sensed her presence, emitting a message that we unconsciously absorbed. It was one that some of our grandmothers reinforced when they made us watch the queen's address on TV Christmas mornings: we are still subjects of the Crown. Her image bound us together, proving the old maxim that a picture speaks a thousand words. Maybe it's no coincidence that one popular synonym for "picture" these days is "icon." And perhaps part of the excitement of the NHL's return to Winnipeg is the promise that the giant portrait of the queen that hung in the arena there for two decades might make a return.

In the new millennium, crowds at games have become so homogenized that the way fans experience the game isn't pure anymore. The sweetness and innocence (and tobacco-smoky goodness) of the old arena has become antiseptic because the music and advertising package presented whenever play halts is completely pre-formed. The game has become secondary to the marketing of the brand that is the team and its sponsors, and sometimes it feels as if the whole point of the experience is to rush to the next TV timeout so the in-arena sideshow can recommence. How different from that time when the queen mutely watched the proceedings, and you, as a player or fan, somehow knew that you had to keep a wary eye on her when you yelled a bit too loud or did something that you shouldn't have to another player.

Some might ascribe this change to hockey's having made its way to places where it was never played before. Texas, Tennessee and other southern states with teams often take the blame for corrupting the game by making the time in the breaks as emotionally charged as the action on the ice. An audience in the U.S. south, some argue, needs the prompts and cues coming from the loudspeakers, but a Canadian crowd, schooled in the game because they've played and watched it all their lives, doesn't need to be insulted with "Make Some Noise!" in that annoying but familiar voice that seems somehow to invade every NHL arena.

One aspect of the arena experience that has not lost its iconic quality, however, is the national anthem, which figures into our imagination of what a hockey game should be just as it always did. In the old days in Montréal, Roget Doucet (who died in 1981) changed the game, literally, by how he sang the anthem. His version built to a climax as he rose to the top of his vocal range in the final phrase, so that by the time he was hitting the final notes, you knew he had given all he had. You could almost feel your own breath leave you as a combination of exhilaration and exhaustion hit you as it might have hit him.

The other thing you might have noticed if you heard Mr. Doucet sing was that his tempo was quick. There was no "Let's make this a contest to see how long I can stay out here," which is what some of today's anthem singers seem most intent on doing. The organ beat out the rhythm, and old Roget sang as if he was in a hurry to get off the ice. It's not that he was being disrespectful to the song, or the country. Quite the opposite, since he raised it to a new form of majestic art. But maybe his message was more subtle: no matter how important the anthem is, the game matters more. The puck has to be dropped, and nothing—not queen nor country—should get in the way of these sacred proceedings.

In Ottawa, this tradition is carried on by the Senators, who have police officer Lyndon Slewidge sing the anthem. His fancy uniform and white gloves suggest the solemnity of the task. He belts out the song in a voice rich in operatic depth, the tempo fast. And when he implores "God, keep our land, glorious and free," there's no way we could believe that anything else could happen. Similarly, when he pledges on our behalf that "O Canada, we stand on guard for thee," his voice rising in pitch and volume as he gets to the end, it's like you want to ditch your job and join, well, something that would let you do your part. But then it's time for the opening faceoff, and everything else is temporarily suspended in the excitement of the game's beginning.

Stuff to Have and to Hold

Perhaps the most common icons of the game are the items that kids (and many adults) collect as fans. Not necessarily valuable, the cards, stickers and other goodies that fill drawers and sit on shelves are nonetheless treasured for the ways that they connect us to hockey. Douglas Coupland knows this, and in his book, *Souvenir of Canada*, he hits readers with an image that every Canadian kid growing up in the 1970s recognizes, and anyone born earlier or later has an equivalent to—the Esso Power Players album.

For those unfamiliar, this was a sticker book (though to describe it like that sounds so unglamorous; it was more than just a sticker book) that kids tried to fill by getting their parents to buy Esso gas. Along with a fill-up came a packet of stickers. Your goal was to fill the album's 252 blank spaces for all 14 teams (18 per team). Nobody in my school ever accomplished that feat, but eBay has healed that wound for me, and now, 40 years later, I still have my incomplete original book as well as a perfect version, full of stickers. What's even better is that the album I recently bought is the hardcover "Deluxe" edition. Turning its pages, I can only imagine the lucky kid who pasted in all of the players and took the album to school back in the day.

On the other hand, maybe he wasn't so lucky. Maybe everyone hated him because he was the only kid in his school who had the whole book completed. Back then, there were no card stores, no place a rich kid could walk into, plunk down a wad of cash and come out with a box of the packets. You couldn't get the stickers anywhere other than an Esso gas station. Maybe the kid who filled the book was the son of a family who owned such a place. But how many of those could there be? And how much fun is it when the book is complete? The excitement was in not knowing what you'd get with your dad's next fill-up, nor how close you would come to completing the set before the promotion ended. The "Power Players Album," as we called it (the proper name on the cover was NHL *Power Player Saver* and in French, NHL *Les Grands Du Hockey Album*), is a reminder of something that hockey used to teach kids—that what you have, you should value and hold on to.

The same was true of hockey cards. Back then, cards weren't bought in boxes; they were acquired in packs, usually bought one or two at a time with your allowance or snow-shovelling money. One pack contained 10 cards, and you hoped against hope that you got the card you needed when you peeled back the waxy paper. If your pack was full of "got-its," you figured out how to trade. These negotiations were the first lesson in exchange a kid learned, and while collecting and trading are not exclusively Canadian pursuits, the experience, certainly as it pertains to hockey cards, is nearly universal in the country, among the boys if not girls.

Hockey cards were an early version of training in the economy of money. Everyone knew the value of a given card and what would be a fair trade for it. Getting the ones you wanted was a matter of luck, when packs were bought a week apart, and shrewd dealing. You learned to ask around when you wanted something or needed a particular player to complete a team set. But you never gave away how valuable the card might be to you. That would drive the price up even more.

The smartest kids ended up with the cards the rest of us on the playground envied. Again, the exception to this rule was the one kid in the class whose dad bought him cards by the bucketful, and his position was precarious. On the one hand, everyone wanted to be him. Why go through the agony of buying a pack a week with your allowance money only to have to trade or try to win the cards you really wanted, when you could just buy handfuls of packs and (it was assumed) get everything you "needed" all at once? On the other hand, the fun in collecting was in not knowing if you were going to get all the cards you wanted, just as with the Power Players.

Kids enjoyed the slow but sure method of accumulating hockey cards for the same reason hockey teams play the regular season. Sure, it's a lot of games, and some of them seem quite meaningless. Play an out-of-conference foe that is at the bottom of the standings and on the other side of the country, and the thought is, "We need the two points, but this isn't exactly a game that's going down in history." But still, every game, or card, does count, and you never know what might happen that will make the record books or will live on for some other reason.

The alternative, shortening the whole season, is like getting all your hockey cards at once—it's just no fun. Think about the abbreviated season in 1994. Consider the possibility that we could double the excitement of the NHL by playing for the Stanley Cup twice a year (don't laugh—back when it was a challenge trophy, it was contested irregularly. Once, it was awarded four times within a 15-month span, from January 1902 to March 1903). That way, you could cut the regular season down to a couple of dozen games and go right to the playoffs. Maybe have one mini-season before Christmas, and one after. Get the whole thing over with in April, while it's still cold in some parts of the country.

Crazy? Sure, but so is buying a box of cards and thus ensuring yourself that you'll get every player in the set. Where's the challenge?

A year or so after a kid started collecting cards, he or she realized that every year, it all started again. That meant a new set of challenges to assemble the best collection possible, but it also increased the value of the cards from last season that were no longer available. The lesson was that rarity had something to do with the passage of time as well as how good the player had been in the old days. One historic rare card was worth many "commons," and kids got to know their values and to appreciate these now-departed players. Each image, as an icon similar to the portrait of the queen, remained in your mind, the player fixed in the exact pose as on his card.

As time passed, the new generation wasn't familiar with the faces on the old cards. Maybe someone raided an older

brother's bedroom for his cards and came across a Bobby Orr
and an Orland Kurtenbach. Who were these guys? And which
one had the more sterling career? Such names didn't mean
anything to eight-year-olds who weren't even born when these
guys were playing. But research yielded the truth and put the
kid in touch with a generation of players who had passed on
the game to the players he now knew. It was a lesson in the
meaning of history.

In the old days, value cut the other way, too. Cards were
commodities. They were bought and traded. But they were also
used. They didn't go into albums. They went into pockets,
bound by an elastic band. When they came out, the elastic came
off carefully, the kid always wary that someone was going to
reach around behind him and smack the cards out of his
hand in what we in my Montréal elementary school called
a "scramble." You learned to take care of something when
you had a hockey card collection. You also learned a lesson
that too many of us these days don't, which is that collecting
items for their own sake is pointless. In fact, there is a word for
it now—hoarding. But having the right collection of cards made
you someone because it was by your own ingenuity, mixed of
course with a little luck, that a collection was assembled.

And, as an irreplaceable part of Canadian childhood,
hockey cards became the tools for the games kids played at
recess, setting them up and knocking them down in order
to win the best ones from each other. They became fodder

for trades, as mentioned earlier. And finally, in a grand tradition that should not be forgotten, they could make a regular bicycle into a motorcycle with the simple engineering assistance of a clothespin.

Things that Last

Ancillaries to the game, such as hockey cards and Power Players albums, serve as more than icons. They teach the important lessons of patience and persistence. If you can stand to wait while the season plays out its drama or while your collection is completed one careful trade at a time, you learn a kind of patience that might just make the mundane activities demanded by Canadian winters easier to endure, like shovelling out the driveway every few days for months. Meanwhile, the typical hockey fan in Florida or North Carolina or California steps outside into sunshine, with no worry about what the weather might hold.

Simple pleasures. Hockey might be a complicated game, its professional leagues more business-minded than ever. But the stuff surrounding the game—from the Stanley Cup to the hockey card—still has the potential to create a world that reduces the complexities of life to a series of simple joys for fans of any age. Is this a distinctly Canadian phenomenon? Probably not, but perhaps nowhere else is hockey—and all the goodies that go with it—so widely enjoyed, nor so deeply embedded in everyday life.

Values to Live By

The Masters of Winter

To many fans, the NHL is the epitome of hockey because the league employs the most skilled players in the world. The game is far more than its professional manifestation, though. The experience of playing hockey runs through many Canadian childhoods and hangs on well into adulthood as a source of joy and comfort, a teacher of values and an antidote to a cold Canadian winter. The game soothes us and redirects our attention onto something other than surviving nature's onslaughts.

One of our outstanding cultural critics, Douglas Coupland, discusses the place of the game in Canadian life in *Souvenir of Canada*. "The thing about hockey in Canada as opposed to hockey in other countries is that the sport percolates far deeper into our national soil and thus affects everything that grows in it," he says. He then goes into a charming anecdote about how his mother had seen a table hockey game in his studio and commented that she had had a set like it back in the 1940s. This is somewhat surprising since she was one of three sisters and had no brothers.

Coupland also relates a discussion he was having with his dad about an unnamed Russian player when his mom interjects and says that the player hadn't ever made much money in hockey because he had suffered too many concussions. "This, from a woman who has honestly never watched a game of hockey in her life," the writer marvels, then asks rhetorically how she could know this story. He concludes that familiarity with the game is in the water.

The language he uses all works together: "In the water…percolates into the soil…grows…," but it misses something. These metaphors are spring-summer ones, and hockey takes place, in the ideal imagination of the game, in the dead of winter. In the cold, dark and deeply still time of the year. The time of the year when many Canadians can go outside and estimate the temperature by observing how the air looks when they exhale their first breath.

Hockey isn't in the soil. Summer comes, and hockey vanishes. Though street hockey goes on—and, these days, fans can use the Internet to follow the activities of their favourite teams as they move from the draft in June to free agency day (Canada Day) to rookie camp to training camp to the preseason—hockey players are famously "at the cottage" during the summer months, and the rest of the country is in short pants, tending the garden. What they find growing there are probably not pucks. Maybe the language that best describes the magic of the game comes from the silence of a snowy day.

Let that first tiny nip creep into the air or the frost show up on the lawn one morning, and whether a person, like Coupland's mom, is aware of the coming of a new season or not, it reaches out to her. As fall arrives, and Halloween costumes appear in stores, what really strikes Canadians is that, suddenly, the TV is alive once more with images of the hits, goals and spectacular saves that make the game what it is. And, if we use a term coined from the old-fashioned way of broadcasting television, the game is in the air too, that is, in the airwaves.

That first feel of winter usually brings a flurry of preparation. Snow tires need to be put on. Bags of sand and salt need to be bought for walkways and as an emergency supply to get a car out of a snowdrift. Winter coats need to come out of closets and get cleaned in preparation for the time when it's impossible to step outside without taking all the proper precautions against the temperature. And if there are kids in the family, the hockey equipment must be assessed for size and fitness for the upcoming season.

The time of year when the air screams "cold" forces Canadians to ask certain questions: "What if I can't get to work on time? Will my car succumb to the demon of road salt this winter? How am I going to avoid cabin fever and the accompanying 10 pounds of hibernation weight?" All of these are appropriate responses to the conditions.

But for us, the approach of winter sees these concerns overtaken by others, often connected with the national obsession. For kids, it's, "Will I make the select team this season?" Or, "Who will be our goalie this year?" For adults and kids alike it might be, "Will Toronto make it to the playoffs? Will those trades make my team better?" And the greatest question of all, "Who will hoist the Stanley Cup next spring?"

Winter is tough, the harshness of it something that you either learn to cope with or hide from. Being outside on the mornings when the car will barely crank over is enough to make adults envy the life of the Floridian. But hockey makes the winter better. Think about it—once in a while now, the Rideau Canal does not freeze over to the point where people can skate on it. In a way, that seems like a blessing, but it's really a curse, because what could be more freeing than tossing a puck in front of you and stickhandling it through hundreds of imaginary defensemen all the way from the Parliament to Carleton University?

Playing outdoor hockey makes Canadians more robust and helps us to clarify our relationship to nature, which is often fractured in a safe suburb. Try a simple exercise: next time there's a long, cold winter's night, drive to the edge of town, get out of the car and face away from the city lights. Look out over the fields or woods or whatever is in front of you, and wait. Wait until the silence starts to soak into your soul and you begin to feel the frightening sense of being the only person alive. Think about the atmosphere—the cold can literally kill you. But the opposite is that your awareness of it can remind you that you must fight to stay alive.

Then think about the times you've been on an outdoor rink, alone, the snow falling in big flakes while you skate back and forth, turn and carry the puck as if it's magically attached to your stick. In those moments, you are at your most robust. You are the master of winter. It obeys you. And you need it, because being out on an empty parking lot on roller blades, like you might be if you were experiencing a similar moment in California, does not have the same power. The warm air might feel good, but the cold embrace of winter would be missing.

Coupland does get it right in the end, despite starting off by using language more suited to baseball, maybe, or soccer—the true summer sports. He concludes by saying "Canadian winters are long. Life is hard and so is ice," properly showing how the Canadian spirit of striving is created through the battle with the cold.

The Value of Spontaneous Play

Hockey as an antidote to the cold of a northern winter is just as alive on the local park rink as it is in the 20,000-seat arenas that a lot of fans get to only sparingly. And so, while it's surprising that someone like Coupland's mom would know about the medical history of a player she has never seen, it would be less surprising to learn that she knew all the kids on her block and could identify them by their positions on the rink where they passed their afternoons as she watched, like so many moms did back in the stay-at-home era, from her kitchen window. That's because a generation ago, the air in any Canadian neighbourhood was thick with the shouts of kids working on their game.

Of course, it didn't look like that's what they were doing. It looked like a scrabble of arms and legs, everyone for him- or herself. If there was any sense of rough organization, it was often a shifting set of alliances made and broken as kids came and went for meals or hopped into the family car to go to a "real" game or a piano lesson.

The values of sportsmanship and compromise learned in these pickup games were vital. The problem is that nowadays, the spontaneous game is being overtaken by organized hockey, robbing kids of the joy of youth and the freedom to play without strictures. A 2008 documentary called *Pond Hockey* (focusing, as it turns out, on the American Midwest, Minnesota to be precise) laments that kids these days don't spend enough time on corner rinks and ponds.

Filmmaker Brett Kashmere, whose 2006 documentary *Valery's Ankle* diagnoses the violence in hockey, echoes this same idea. "In every town and city across Canada," he says, "hockey is more than a hobby or an interest. It's an expectation…. [But] corporate monoliths now control the game. Kids no longer learn to skate on frozen ponds, to improvise in an unstructured, casual manner." Instead, they are groomed to "make it" in hockey from a young age, and they learn early to play the game in a way that denies their individuality. They are commercial assets.

Is anything accomplished in a leisurely afternoon of skating around on a pond or playing pickup games on the road? No, and yes. Nothing about the history of the world changes. But those who partake in such spontaneous play learn to value their own inventiveness, and they share something with others who participate alongside them. Roy MacGregor succinctly describes the street game by suggesting that it is "where the first taste [for hockey] is developed and where drama and comedy play out on small stages from one end of the country to the other. Each version of the game has its own ethos, and yet is recognizable by all as one and the same."

Well-known hockey writer Andrew Podnieks says that "the road variety of hockey is to that sport what soccer is to the rest of the world—simple game, simple rules, inexpensive to play, accessible to all," and if those aren't good, core Canadian ideals, then what are?

When you were a kid, your mission in life was simple—to get home from school as fast as possible, grab your skates and stick and get to the rink. The first kids to arrive got in the game the quickest, and if you were a straggler, you had to wait a while, especially if the two squads were equally matched, numbers-wise. No one wanted to stand on the sidelines, in the snowbank, while everyone else had all the fun.

Sadly, these days, kids are often denied this pleasure and forced to live a structured existence. They have calendars, and even their leisure time is programmed. To prove the point, name one kid you know who isn't at least a two-sport athlete, and maybe takes music lessons on the side. If you can think of one, you've got an unusual child in mind. Peek into the closet of the average 12-year-old and you'll find a karate gi, a soccer jersey, a baseball uniform and maybe some reminder of the hockey season just over or to come.

There's nothing wrong with playing more than one sport. The problem occurs when kids are involved in organized activities all the time, at the cost of the unstructured play that would otherwise take place on corner rinks and empty lots, or, in the case of a lot of Canadian kids, out on the street in front of someone's house. Being free to play without adults around gives kids the chance to learn to work out their differences. It allows them to understand that competition is a part of life. And it shows them the joy of letting loose. These days, kids are often denied this freedom because they have to be watched wherever they go, for safety reasons, and because even house-league hockey is a serious endeavour, with rigid practice routines enforced on children to improve their skills.

A Canadian psychologist who weighed in on the matter of free play and street hockey says that adults do kids a disservice when they structure all of their play in places that are adult-controlled and measured for safety. "Genuine compassion gives children what they really need, not what makes those raising them feel safe and secure," says Dr. Michael Ungar. He points out that the game teaches kids social organization, conflict resolution and rule-making. It also gives them exercise and forces them to practice inclusivity.

Ungar ponders what happens when kids don't get an equal opportunity to play. Will this damage their self-esteem? "I say, let it be so. Let the children figure this [fairness] out themselves," he suggests. His idea is that kids will do the right thing on their own when there's something unfair happening on the playground or street. He says that if things get really out of hand, then a parent can go outside and intervene, but even that action should give the kids back the control. "[A] little nudge from a concerned adult," Ungar claims, "is all it takes to shame kids into being more inclusive."

Such no-adults free play does something else for kids—it lets them develop the hockey skills and the moves that evolve from the spontaneity of the situation. No coach is yelling to play the system, and no parents are eagerly eyeing their son or daughter to make sure the kid is following orders and conforming to the wishes of the person who doles out the ice time. (And parents don't have to worry about how much ice time junior is getting, either.)

Parents today are so invested in their kids' progression to the NHL that they often don't see the value of unstructured hockey. "How will they learn the game?" is the fear, expressed aloud or felt in the adult's heart. Those who hold such thoughts might wish to know that when Taylor Hall was about to be drafted in 2010, he was answering questions at a press luncheon in LA, and a local reporter asked him, "Do you have a moves coach?"

Hall looked at her and said, "No, I don't. In fact, I've never even heard of a moves coach." When asked where he came up with his puck dangles, the young man replied, "I just figure those out on my own." The reporter went away not quite comprehending how this could be true. I know this because I was there to witness the encounter.

What she didn't realize was that Hall, and anyone else who plays hockey with intensity blended with creativity, doesn't need someone to tell him (or her) how to do things. He can invent ideas on his own, but he has to be given the chance to do that. The playground, street or corner rink allows that opportunity, with no penalty when a move fails, except to see the other gang of kids steal the puck and get a goal.

Talent like Hall's thrives in places like the backyard rink and the street, and if parents take these venues away

from kids by over-programming them through constant formal practices, children will lose their love for hockey. Most of
them won't grow up to be professional players anyway, and
then what will they be left with? Memories of one too many
clinics where all the fun was sucked out of the sport.

If hockey becomes all about technical perfection, the
result is the robo-player. That is, a guy who is coached so
well that he almost can't help but make the NHL, but who,
conversely, is coached so well that he has lost all of his spontaneity. Obviously, a degree of talent has to be present to
make the pros, and determination as well, but when these
are over-balanced by coaching, something is lost. The solution is as simple and present as tossing a ball or puck into the
middle of a scrum of eight-year-olds and telling them that
the side that scores the most goals wins.

Aside from what street (or pond) hockey does for the
individual, it has a group effect too, by forging a sense of community. As sportswriter Stephen Brunt commented in Roy
MacGregor's article:

> It is a game ordered not so much by offi-
> cials enforcing a code of conduct, but by
> self-imposed etiquette. To keep playing,
> rather than taking your stick and going
> home...requires learning how to function
> co-operatively with others and acknowledge
> a few simple rights and wrongs.

The recurring theme that surfaces with Brunt, MacGregor and Podnieks is clear—hockey played spontaneously creates values that transcend the street or rink.

The simple code of ethics that kids learn operates not just among themselves but in how they relate to their environment. The kids at play own the street, but they also know their place on it. They all defer to a vehicle with the yell of "Car!" Law and order are always allowed to prevail in these moments, and most kids don't even question the order of importance that places the car before hockey, because the players realize that they don't own the street—they're just borrowing it for a while.

The War Against Spontaneity

Andrew Podnieks claims, "There is no word more fundamentally important to hockey than the word 'car'.... For that is the word every kid has screamed a thousand times during his formative years during a road hockey game." He goes on to describe the scene:

> The road hockey rule is a simple one. With that word "car!" the ball carrier stops exactly where he is, as does everyone else except the goalie, who hunches down a bit, lifts the net onto a shoulder, and moves it to the side of the road. They all then watch as a neighbourhood car drives by.

Suspending the game for these brief moments is harder to do than it looks, because it makes kids put their fantasies of being Dion Phaneuf or Matt Duchene on hold while they wait for the car to pass.

The simplicity and regularity with which this deferral to the automobile occurs makes it difficult to understand the attempts to regulate street hockey, but the move to do so goes back much further than most people think. In fact, hockey historians report that, "At Montréal in 1842, shinty [sic] players were prevented by law from playing their game on city streets."

According to Podnieks, "Most Canadians have no idea that road hockey has been illegal since the early 1970s." Regulations came onto the books as cities became worried that an accident could leave them legally liable. He points out that in places like Kingston, Ontario, and Dollard-des-Ormeaux, Québec, anti-street-hockey ordinances have been debated or enacted. In Toronto, a debate rages about whether to change the law that levies a fine of $55 for playing any ball sport on the street.

Journalist John Lorinc put the problem into an almost mythical context when he said, "With the memory of the two [2010] hockey golds still vivid in the minds of many Canadians, the question now is whether those curmudgeonly by-laws prove to be more formidable opponents than the Americans." It's a sad day when a kid can't go outside and recreate the goal he's just seen Crosby score to defeat the U.S. and win the gold medal.

The problem with legislating street hockey is not its heavy-handedness, but that it ignores a simple fact—kids know they have to move over for oncoming traffic. Sure, there is the sense that they own the street, and that the cars are the interlopers, but as one supporter of striking down Listowel, Ontario's, anti-street-hockey regulations put it, "If anything, I think it teaches the kids to be even more aware of traffic."

Dr. Ungar admits that on occasion, kids at play in a street hockey game get rude to passing motorists, but he says, "if we want this next generation to feel a part of their society and behave appropriately, we'd be wise to make sure they know we like them and that they belong." Two hockey players a generation apart recognize this, and each has concerned himself with the fight to keep street hockey legal. Sidney Crosby got involved in trying to make the streets okay for kids to use when he urged Halifax mayor Peter Kelly to rethink a law that might have been used against the game. Bobby Orr also spoke up about the matter when a ban was proposed in Rothesay, New Brunswick.

Hopefully the intervention of two icons of the game will allow one more aspect of Canadian childhood under fire from the twin forces of government control and parental fretting to survive into the next generation. Roy MacGregor expressed these hopes when he said that it would be best if judges realized that "there are better uses for the law than putting a damper on children 'hollerin' and whoopin' like mad with pleasure'"—those last words out of the mouth of someone who had filed a complaint about street hockey being played in Hamilton, Ontario.

Lessons Learned by Losing

Don Cherry espouses the gritty values of the third-line mucker on a weekly basis on his "Coach's Corner" segment. True, when he shows pictures of lost Canadian soldiers and talks about them during *Hockey Night in Canada* broadcasts, Cherry's language is often over-the-top emotional (to draw on a World War I expression). "What a beautiful boy, look at that," he'll say as he stands there in a flowered blazer and wild tie. The first question many fans, or perhaps those unfamiliar with the approach he uses, might ask is, "Who's that gentle eccentric who has made his way into the *HNIC* studios?" But it's exactly because Cherry doesn't worry that the audience may think he's soft that he can let his heart bleed all over Ron MacLean's suit. And to balance his segment on the soldiers, he hits hard on issues going on in the game.

Cherry knows that he's tough enough to take you, and this explains why he can praise a kid using weepy language one minute and the next describe the repeated fights of an enforcer like Matt Carkner of the Ottawa Senators using words that focus on how Carkner is out there to do what's needed. Cherry might not have been a great NHLer (one game is hardly a test, after all), but he gets hockey, and his sensibilities have been forged on the rink. That's perhaps why he focuses on the grinders, the guys who do the most sacrificing, rather than showcasing only the superstars. The lessons learned from watching the marginal players, he believes, are more valuable, and their contributions to the team make the difference between winning and losing. Yet sometimes, you have to wonder if the young generation of Canadians is hearing his message.

Ideally, young people—women and men both—learn through hockey to channel and discipline their aggressions, or in situations where the spirit is lacking, to pump it up. They learn to take orders, to submit to a system and to pursue victory, sometimes at all costs. They figure out that they are not the be-all, end-all of life, but that what they accomplish contributes to something larger than they are—the team. The hardness, duty and team spirit inspired by the great game and reinforced as kids play it all fit together. But fewer kids today seem to get this because contemporary childhood has been constructed to feature an almost endless series of congratulatory celebrations that leave out the lessons that life can be hard, that often you have to lose before you win and that losing hurts.

Many times in the history of the NHL, teams have learned something from the pain of losing. Think about the Islanders of the old days. From 1980 to 1983, they won the

Stanley Cup. Just a few years earlier, they had been the worst
expansion team at that time, with a record of 12–60–6 in their
first season (1972–73). Or what about Pittsburgh? In the 1980s,
it was a dreary failed steel town with a team and a dream, and
one star—Mario Lemieux. The Penguins made the playoffs
only once in his first six years in the league (1984–90). But then
they won consecutive Stanley Cups in 1990–91 and 1991–92.
They were a team, but they, like the Islanders, had to lose
before they could win. Most adults shrug at this fact—yeah,
so what? But today, kids are being shielded from the valuable
knowledge that losing affords.

There's a funny cartoon from the *New Yorker* that
sums up contemporary childhood and sports. A kid in soccer
gear is standing in his living room with a huge trophy next to
him. He says to his father, who sits on the easy chair nearby,
"Yup, we lost."

These days, almost everyone gets a trophy, for everything. In kids' leagues, there might be eight teams, and at the
end of the season, there are four finals. In each, there is obviously a winner and a loser. And even the loser ends up with
a trophy. One year, my then seven-year-old nephew got one.
"D Finalist," it said. It meant that out of the eight teams, his
was in the bottom two ("D" group). And of those two, his lost.

In other words, his Timbits Black team was the worst
in the league. But it didn't matter, because in the end, he still
got the hardware. What kind of a message are we sending

to kids who don't get eliminated from the playoffs and don't "lose" even when the other team beats them?

In the old days, losing at hockey taught kids something. Put in the most obvious terms, it taught them that not everyone wins. Sometimes, you lose on bad luck. Sometimes, you lose because the other team got its game together in some mysterious way and beat you. Sometimes, they won because they were just better. In any event, at the end of those contests (remember the old two-games, total-goals format?), you shook hands, and if you were the team that came out on the bottom end, you watched while the other players received their trophies. You got nothing. It hurt, and kids cried. But you knew that whatever the reason you lost, you lost, and you vowed to play better next year. Dads may have taken their kids aside after and offered them a lesson: life doesn't just hand you what you want; you have to work for it. Sometimes, you get a raw deal, and that's part of life, too. It's a tough place, this Canada. If the weather doesn't get you, the Americans might swallow you up. But you persist. You resist. You learn to find a way to do better next time. It makes for a nation of strivers.

Not so much anymore. Consider the story of the two boys whose parents sued their Midget Junior A squad after their kids failed to make the team. Note at the outset that there was no requirement that they try out. It was their decision, and the risks were obvious from the beginning. The numbers are plain: more than 65 percent of the kids who tried out for the team would not make it. A few would, but everyone took the same risk—and the result was either joy or disappointment, and no possibility of a consolation prize.

Most of us, as kids, never got as far as a tryout for a travelling team. We were happy on the local house league team, or not playing at all, especially after a certain age, when size differences and the toughness of the game started to take a toll. For those who were better than average, the prospect of being on a select team tantalized. And not just the kids. Parents knew then as they do now that the NHL wouldn't even be a possibility unless their kid started climbing the ladder young.

Trying out teaches you something, if you're paying attention. It teaches you that you have to go all out on the day that it counts, with no excuses. It teaches you that there's a risk in whatever you do. Try applying for a high-level job. If you get it, and you're later privy to the details of the campaign the company waged to fill the post, you'll probably find out that 10, 50 or 100 other people applied. Probably a few of them were interviewed. All except you ended up disappointed, though it is likely that many had outstanding credentials. But that's how it goes. There's only one slice of pie, and it can't be divided. When someone gets the spot, others don't.

That's the way it is in life. But the two Toronto boys did not just absorb the disappointment and move on. News reports say that part of the damages the parents sought compensation for stemmed from the psychological harm the boys suffered and would continue to suffer from having been cut.

No argument there. Hockey is not just a game on the ice but is a social construct as well. The kids who play in the higher leagues are looked up to. If a youngster, boy or girl, has a history of playing at an elite level and then suddenly one season doesn't make the grade, it's hard. Friendships get stretched, maybe broken. But that's just how it is, and kids have to learn how to deal with it. (Of course, nobody condones discrimination, if that's what happened in the Toronto case. One assumes, however, that those who picked the team were focused on getting the best players, no matter who they were.)

Here are a couple of core Canadian truths to counteract the notion that the harm of not making the cut is lifelong. First, if every kid who misses out on the chance to make a team suffers psychological damage because of it, then a lot of Canadians need therapy. It's not just those who get cut, in fact, who probably need help. What about the vast majority of others who didn't even try out in the first place because they knew that they wouldn't stand a chance? What kind of damage are they carrying around? Actually, probably none, but they do understand the lesson that sometimes we must face disappointment and redefine our goals when we don't get what we want.

Second, if these two boys could have learned anything from their experience, it's that life isn't fair (though maybe they just weren't among the best players who went out), and that one way to get revenge is to spend a summer in the weight room, work with a skating coach, fire a couple of thousand pucks a day in an attempt to cave in the garage door and go back and give it another go next year. In fact, the sooner they turn their backs on this failure and make it a motivation for success, the sooner they'll be where they want to be, hockey-wise. The longer they dwell on the disappointment, the harder it will be to move on to the job of making themselves better players.

Perhaps nowhere are disappointments more evident than in the NHL draft. Every year, guys show up slated to be first-rounders. Theirs will be the glory of stepping onto the stage, putting on the sweater and being, for a moment at least, an NHLer. But with agents present and families at the ready with cameras, top prospects sometimes sit through picks one, two, three…29 and 30, and don't hear their names. It happened to Landon Ferraro in 2009, despite his great hopes and the fact that his dad, Ray, had such an outstanding NHL career. What did Landon do? He went back to the hotel, slept on it and came back the next morning. There, the Detroit Red Wings made him the first pick of the second round and their first overall pick. It wasn't the story the Ferraros had hoped for, but it worked to get the kid his foothold in the game, and the family responded with excitement and enthusiasm, the way things should be.

Even first-round draftees aren't guaranteed that their dreams will be fulfilled. Think about Hugh Jessiman. He was picked 12th overall in 2003, but at the end of the 2009–10 season, he hadn't played a single NHL game, though he went above Dustin Brown, Brent Seabrook, Zach Parise, Ryan Getzlaf, Ryan Kesler, Mike Richards and other notable names in that year's selection process. He finally got a crack with the Florida Panthers in 2010–11, playing in only two games.

How about the late-round draftee or the kid who goes to one training camp after another and doesn't make a dent? Think about Dustin Penner, Dan Girardi, Brian Rafalski, Jason Blake and Martin St. Louis. None of these players were picked in the NHL draft, but they didn't sue. They just worked harder, and eventually, they made it to the big league because they didn't give up.

To put this perseverance into a Canadian context, it's the hearty soul who could move to BC in the early part of the 20th century and endure the rigours of digging tree stumps out of the ground to clear the land and farm it, but that's exactly what Jack Hodgins describes World War I vets doing in his novel, *Broken Ground*. The novel's main character comments on the conditions the vets faced in BC:

> *This was the sort of reward they gave you for*
> *spending three or four years of your life being*

shot at for the King. This was your recom-
pense and thanks. We were farmers who'd
never farmed land like this before, or cleared
land like this before, or for that matter even
seen land like this before the War.

But as the novel proceeds, the vets persevere, making something of the land even when their efforts are threatened by fire.

Or how about the first of the Hudson's Bay fur traders? For the fashionable of Europe, they risked their lives to bring back beaver pelts for hats. What protection did they have from the elements or from failure? Animal-skin coats, and nothing at all, respectively. They just did it.

Think also about the people described by Elizabeth Hay in *Late Nights On Air*. She tells the story of a young woman who spends a year in Yellowknife, working in radio. As autumn progresses, the character, Gwen, can feel the threat of the place. "Now winter closed in again with frigid winds, icy roads, longer nights, and, yes, she was inside a place gripped by the cold," the story's narrator reports. A woman in town freezes to death in the winter and is not found until May. The event reinforces the notion that the place can kill you. One character says that she had been in nearby Igloolik once and "started to walk back to the hotel and thought if she turned right instead of left, she'd never be found. 'The vastness really hit me,' she said with feeling." Still, when people stay "the magic five years" in the North, it is thought that they will be there for decades, if not forever.

Both of these novels represent experiences shared by many immigrants who decide to make Canada their home, up to the present day. In every case, those who succeed are those who struggle, taking on the challenges of an alien place the way others did before them.

Compared to the danger that Canada's early settlers faced, or those living in the north, modern suburban living is a cakewalk. Maybe the most savage aspect about life in most of this country today is the competition for spots on the elite hockey teams that pave the way to the NHL. It's tough. Disappointments are a part of it. But if there's anything left of the pioneering set of values that tamed the wild of this country, it comes out in Canadians' willingness to give it their all and then live with the results. Sadly, kids don't always get this message—and especially the house league player who carts home a trophy regardless of the real outcome of the game.

Canadians aren't the only people who approach life with the values of perseverance, grit and spontaneity, but for us, hockey is the vehicle that gives us these qualities. For the sake of our ongoing success at taming the land we call home, here's hoping we can shake off the forces that would dull our sensibilities as we continue to forge a worldview of striving.

chapter eight

Niceness and Its Opposite

The Quality of Niceness

Canadians, according to pundit Will Ferguson, share an overriding quality: niceness. "You can whack a Canadian on the head, you can scramble his brain and erase his memory, but he—or she—will still be nice," he claims. The lesson is learned early. Being a part of a house league hockey team, a common experience for kids, teaches a set of values, including toughness and sacrifice, but also fairness and sharing. Remember when the buzzer used to signal the end of your three minutes on the ice? You hated to skate back to the bench, but you knew that it was only right that the other kids should have their turn.

Canada is built on an all-for-one and one-for-all ideal. The country has far more social democracy than its neighbour to the south likely ever will. Witness the negative reaction to healthcare change in the U.S. as an example. In Canada, as much as people loathe taxation, they pay their taxes with the understanding that part of the money will be used for the greater good of universal medical care and spread throughout the country in the form of equalization payments. In the U.S., taxes are often more focused on local improvements. Even towns next to each other may have different and unequal ways of levying property taxes for schools. Sharing is not the primary value.

In Canada, despite some griping, it's probably true that most citizens believe that we should pay sufficient taxes to provide benefits such as adequate education for all, not just the kids who live in our local enclave. By contrast, schools in the U.S. can vary incredibly one from another even when they are within walking distance. For example, one will be a 10-rated "School of Distinction." A couple of neighbourhoods away, the elementary school will have few books and no extracurricular activities. Americans accept this as fact, so ingrained is the idea that socio-economic inequality is the norm, and that it's okay for the "haves" to live right next door to the "have nots," as long as the latter don't come over to borrow a cup of sugar.

North of the border, at least in theory, socio-economic differences are not so vast, and the "other" is not considered such a threat. This Canadian ethos of fairness has a history that can be traced clearly back to hockey. Through the disputes between labour (the players) and management in the 1950s and '60s, a set of fair-minded values was codified and subsequently spread beyond hockey to the larger culture. But whatever positive ideals this game offers, it is problematic to see hockey as a complete reflection of the virtue of niceness, because the good things one learns from hockey are miti-gated by other factors, including the selfishness and rivalry inherent in the game, especially at the higher levels.

Playing, and Paying, Nice

One aspect of niceness in Canada is a relatively rich labour market where workers are treated well and rewarded fairly. Statistics show that many more Canadians than Americans work in union jobs—more than double the number in private-sector jobs, nearly two-and-a-half times in the public sector. What few may realize today is that the struggle between players and owners in the NHL paved the way for this situation where relative equity between boss and employee can prevail.

Most hockey fans claim that given the chance, they would play in the NHL for free. Sometimes, players even voice such an idea in interviews. Of course, that's easy to say when you're making, minimum, half a million bucks, and probably a whole lot more. But it was only two decades ago that most players weren't making such fortunes—and a generation before that, they were downright exploited. Their struggle for a fair share of the hockey revenue pie is instruc-tive as a lesson in the virtue of fairness, a core Canadian value.

Growing up in the 1970s, I imagined that my hockey idols would enjoy lifelong financial security as a reward for their exploits on the ice. Talking to one of them a couple of years ago, I learned otherwise. Peter Mahovlich was a hero of mine when I was a kid. He might have scored the most beautiful goal of all time. Go back and watch the second game of the 1972 Summit Series, and you'll see it for yourself. I described it this way after I interviewed Mahovlich for a profile piece I was doing for *Inside Hockey*:

> *Shorthanded, he scooped up a clearing pass out of his own zone, and motored through center ice, his long, strong stride taking him to the opposing blue line far more quickly than it appeared to. At the line, he paused, faking a slapshot, which caused the defenseman he was bearing down upon to close his legs for a block, freezing him momentarily. Mahovlich carried the puck around him and then fought off a hook with his left hand while protecting it. He moved in on the goalie, coming from the right side of the rink, and deked toward the left. At the last second, almost in the crease, he shifted back and stuffed the puck past the goalie on the right side before tumbling over the netminder into the left goalpost.*

The goal was a thing of beauty, and a hallmark of the graceful and gracious player, and person, Mahovlich was and is. He almost floated as he scored that goal, more a god than a man. But if contemporary fans imagine that the lives of players of his era were untouched by mortal—as in, financial—concerns, they would be wrong.

At the time I spoke with him in 2007, Mahovlich was working as a professional scout for the Atlanta Thrashers. When I asked him why he took the job, he told me that he loved the game and wanted to be around it. He also said that his hockey-playing days (he was in the NHL from 1965 to 1981) hadn't made him rich. He still had to work, even as he was nearing retirement age. (He was born in 1946.)

Bob Berry, former Canadiens and Kings player and later coach of several NHL teams, said the same thing when I interviewed him in November 2009. In his day (he played from 1968 to 1977), you didn't expect to finish up your on-ice career and never have to work again. Heck, most players didn't expect to finish up a season to go home and do nothing. They got jobs or worked on family farms. Granted, some of the jobs were cushy—really excuses to stay on the payroll for the summer. Montréal Canadiens players often worked through the off-season in the Molson beer promotions department. Their task? Golf and glad-hand with corporate types and the public eager for a touch of their hero's magic.

One of the most prolific scorers in the history of the game, and certainly a rookie most would have touted as a future superstar, Bobby Hull, went home after his first summer with the Blackhawks and worked in the local Coca-Cola bottling plant. How would that feel to a player today?

Even a third-liner can expect to make enough money to take the summer off, and of course, given the pressures of the modern game in terms of conditioning, there really is no summer "off." Players have to train over the break to be at their best the first day of camp in September.

Even as recently as the early 1990s, players weren't rolling in the bucks. One decent winger in the NHL, who will remain nameless, had a career that spanned the 10 years just before the Gretzky era in LA. His top salary? About $180,000 per year. If he'd had his same career today, he believes that he would have made enough money to have retired with a couple of million dollars in the bank. The fact that he's still working suggests that he hasn't been quite that fortunate. Today, by contrast, payrolls top out around $65 million, most teams have a handful of guys in the $4- to $5-million-per-year range and a 20-goal scorer can easily pull in $2 or $3 million a season.

The financial wealth of today's players has made this generation of NHLers something other than regular guys to fans. But their recent ascent to riches was built on the backs of a generation who stuck their necks out to gain respect from owners with little need to spare anyone's feelings. Stories of management's mistreatment of players in the Original Six era abound. The owners had all the power, and they were perfectly willing to kill a guy's career if he got out of line. Most players from that time tell similar tales: they could not negotiate their salaries, and so they were underpaid. When the players first tried to unionize in 1957, there was fear, mistrust and payback.

At times, players took one another's well-being into their own hands, helping out a fallen comrade, as was the case when Ace Bailey was injured by Eddie Shore in a game in 1933. Unable to play again, Bailey saw his livelihood disappear with one swift charge, but the players managed to raise $20,000 in an exhibition between the Maple Leafs and NHL All-Stars, money they gave to Bailey and his family. However, short of such an occurrence, there was little security for the men who put their bodies on the line to play the game. The pensions were never all that good, and even as the modern era started in 1967, players remained concerned about their futures. The Summit Series, it should be remembered, was sold to the players partially because the revenues earned were supposed to be used to boost the pension fund.

Ted Lindsay was one of the most vocal proponents demanding that the players organize in the mid-1950s as a way to start a conversation about change. Michael McKinley explains that, in this era, players did not discuss money matters with each other, but that Lindsay tried to remedy the situation by approaching Montréal's Doug Harvey with the idea of forming a players' association. Soon, the entire league had signed on. When the owners got wind of it, they panicked. Conn Smythe even saw the effort as vaguely communist. For his efforts, Lindsay was dumped by his

Detroit Red Wings, a powerhouse at the time, and traded to Chicago, a perennial loser, in the summer of 1957. The union idea was quickly abandoned.

For the average Canadian, the poor treatment of the day's hockey heroes revealed the ugly side of the business, but it also demonstrated that players need what any worker in any industry needs: protection, a way to ensure equity when it comes time to negotiate with management. A decade after the Lindsay debacle, the players did manage to organize, and their plight and fight to become valued for their labour taught the working Canadian a lot about the process and structure of workers' rights, instilling a sense of fairness that is now firmly rooted in the Canadian psyche.

The Battle for Safety

NHL ownership before 1967 had other means of exercising absurd levels of power over players besides withholding fair compensation for services. One succinct description of the situation is provided by Todd Denault in his book, *Jacques Plante: The Man Who Changed the Face of Hockey*: "[I]n a league of only six teams, and with an abundance of players eagerly waiting in the minors, it was understandable that players were reluctant to challenge the unspoken code of the game." He is speaking about player safety, and the use of the goalie mask particularly, which management forbade netminders from wearing, citing the twin factors of poor vision and the loss of courage that would

result if the keeper donned facial protection. Plante successfully challenged this dictum in 1959, and his battle to control
his own well-being reflects the political reality of the time.

It was only three years removed from Plante's brave
stand that Saskatchewan premier Tommy Douglas created the
legislation that would ensure medical care for all, a model that
quickly swept across the country. Douglas may not have been
thinking particularly about the parallels of his actions to the
struggles going on between NHL players and owners, but
the "niceness" of his move reflects the decentralization of
power happening in the game at the same time as players
began to voice their concerns for their own safety.

Think about the safety issues related to employment as
a hockey player. Is there a factory in the developed world
where things fly around at 160 kilometres per hour, people
smash into each other on the way to their workstations, everyone carries a tool capable of inflicting injury on the others and
each has permission to swing away almost at will? It would
be a CanOSH nightmare, but that's exactly what happens in
a hockey game. But things are better than they used to be.

Players, these days, have no choice but to take some
protective measures while on the ice. Helmets are no longer
an option. If some people around the NHL had their way,
visors would be mandatory too, like they are in the other
North American professional leagues. In addition, because
of the spate of concussions suffered in the last few seasons,

changes are being implemented to make the game safer at the NHL level. All of this might have been unimaginable a few decades ago, when the attitude was that if a player didn't like it, he could hit the road; there was always someone else who would play without complaining.

November 1, 1959, marked the turning point in the power struggle between players and those who employed them. The saga is familiar but worth recounting. The combatants were Jacques Plante, Montréal's star goalie and a mercurial figure if ever there was one, and Toe Blake, his coach. By the fall of 1959, Plante was wearing a mask in practice, but he was forbidden to do so during games. According to Denault, Blake feared that "the fans and players on the opposing team would openly ridicule Plante for his decision and use the mask as evidence of Plante's becoming puck shy."

Plante was an odd figure, a student of the game and a nervous man who could often be found knitting in the dressing room or on the team bus. He likely didn't care what fans of opposing teams thought, and it's also likely that he had heard it all anyway, since ridiculing the dominant Montréal teams of the era was stock-in-trade in the five other arenas in the league.

The question was settled one night when Plante's nose was almost detached from his face in a game in New York. At the time, teams carried just one goalie, and when he got hurt, the crowd waited for him to get medical attention, then the game resumed. Poet Randy Maggs remembers that era as a hockey spectator on TV. "They'd cut away from the game and play music until the guy was ready to go back in, then the game would come back on," he told me during an interview in May 2009. The alternative was to grab the backup "house goalie," from the stands—on the night of Plante's injury, an usher who used to play in a local New York league.

Blake thought the best course of action was to get Plante stitched up and have him go out again, but the goalie saw this as his chance to get that mask into an NHL game, and when he returned to the ice, he told Blake he wouldn't go back on without it. Blake for his part "realized that without Plante in the net his team's chances of success were severely weakened for that night and perhaps beyond." He had no choice, and Plante went back to work with his face protected.

That November night marked a turning point in the history of the game as increasingly, goalies used facial protection. It is worth noting, however, that the change was not so immediate as one might think. Rogie Vachon began his career with Montréal in the 1966–67 season, and he played without a mask at that time. Gump Worsley played until 1974, only donning a mask in the last days of his career, and that same year, Andy Brown played the last NHL game without one.

Interestingly, it was not the last NHL shift played without a goaltender wearing a mask, because to this day, the NHL rulebook says that a "[p]rotective mask of a design approved by the league *may be worn* [my emphasis] by goalkeepers."

That's why from time to time when the mask is lost, play continues until the defensive team gets the puck back, if it's in their zone. A throwback to the spirit of Toe Blake? The official reason is that the offensive team should not be disadvantaged by the loss of the mask caused by a player on the goaltender's team (or the goalie himself), as they would be if the play were to be blown dead immediately.

Plante serves as a kind of counterpoint to Ted Lindsay. Whereas the latter was looking out for players off the ice by trying to make salaries fair considering league revenues, Plante had player welfare on the ice—starting, of course, with his own—topmost in his mind. His struggle to get the mask approved by his coach was similar to Lindsay's attempts to form a union, in that both showed the spirit of the little guy organizing to make things better for the worker while facing the resistance of those in control.

The Politics of Money

If hockey was becoming more "nice" in certain respects as players gained power starting in the 1950s, that's not to say that the game didn't have elements of ugliness as, later, players forgot their reverence for it in their desire to get all they could in terms of salary. Money disputes came into focus again in the 1990s, but this time because players were getting more than owners could afford, not less. The Canadian dollar was at a low point, and yet hockey teams, including those based in Canada, had to pay their players in U.S. currency. The result was the loss of Québec's franchise and that of Winnipeg to the U.S., moves that most Canadians read as owing to the misguided thinking of the Americans who ran the league.

In fact, some elements of the bust-boom cycle can't be blamed on the Yanks, but come back to the players themselves, who forgot the core (Canadian) ethos of sharing resources, accepting what's fair and not asking for more. Why was the U.S. dollar the standard to start with? Because the players wouldn't take a 30-percent cut to their salaries when they played on a Canadian team. (Never mind that by living in Canada, they were buying houses and cars in Canadian dollars, not American.)

The average person who works hard for a living wage might wonder what happened to the dream these guys had as kids. Wouldn't it be better, the logic goes, to play in Canada, where you know fans care about the game and its history, and where they understand it, not least because many have themselves played it, than in an American market where hockey is just another "entertainment option" (not to say that that's true for all U.S.-based teams)?

And wasn't it enough to play in the NHL, and for hundreds of thousands, if not millions, of dollars? Isn't there a point where you just can't spend the money anymore? So why not take the Canadian market discount by accepting your salary in loonies and toonies, and keep your team fiscally healthy?

Players (and their agents) didn't see things that way. Then again, most of us regular folks have never refused a raise or gone into a salary discussion with the attitude that we'd take the cheapest deal offered to us either. But it just seems that when it comes to hockey, there should be some kind of Canadian exception clause. None was forthcoming, and as the calendar turned to 2000, another ugly time in hockey history approached, but one when an American, no matter how hard it is to accept, came to our aid.

As Canadians observed a new crop of problems emerging, namely financial crises in Ottawa and Buffalo, most of them saw a value in play that they repudiated—greed for more and more money. However, the irony was that they didn't blame the players, nor the weak Canadian dollar, but the league and its American Commissioner, Gary Bettman. The only trouble was, the notion that he was responsible for the financial mess resulting from salary escalation was far from true.

In the early part of the new millennium, the Ottawa Senators and Buffalo Sabres neared bankruptcy, but Bettman was determined to fix the problems and keep the teams intact. For Ottawa, which had entered the league only in 1992, the problem wasn't mismanagement of money—it was because of the city's small 10,500-seat arena. When a new rink was opened in 1996, it didn't always sell out. According to John Kreiser, "[T]he team was in debt up to its ears, even as it became one of the NHL's best-run franchises, with a horde of young talent and a $30 million payroll."

The challenge went out to fans to fill the new arena, and they responded. But it took further efforts to save the situation, including the NHL kicking in some last-minute money. The team survived when new owner Eugene Melnyk came up with the cash to buy it and the arena, but for several months, fans were hanging on every word from the club, thinking that the team might move or fold.

One impulse a lot of Canadians gave vent to during this time was to criticize the U.S.-based business people who ran the league. It was convenient to blame a non-hockey-playing American for Canada having already lost two teams (the Nordiques and Jets) and the possibility of another one going south. The truth was somewhere else, and the NHL might well have lost another one, or two or three teams, but for Bettman's efforts. When the crisis hit, he was clear in his position: "We want [the Senators franchise] to stay put where it is. We don't have complete, unfettered control, but we have a fair amount of influence, all of which we intend to use."

A few years later, the Senators were thriving under their new ownership. As *Sports Business Journal* said in 2007, with the team about to go to the Stanley Cup final, "If not for the dogged determination of NHL commissioner Gary Bettman...both the Sabres and the Senators would either

be playing in another city or might even have even folded."
By contrast, during the crisis at the turn of the millennium,

> *Many believed the prudent business decision*
> *would have been to let both teams' [sic] fold,*
> *hold a dispersal draft and send an unforget-*
> *table message to the National Hockey League*
> *Players Association. The chance to contract*
> *two franchises would have scared the*
> *NHLPA straight, when it came to under-*
> *standing how broken the NHL's economic*
> *system was at the time.*

Nobody ever thought to simply remind them that
hockey players should operate on an ethic that privileges
fairness, at least off the ice.

By 2007, Randy Turner of the *Winnipeg Free Press* was
reporting the exact opposite state of affairs to that of the
mid-1990s to early in the 2000s. Whereas "10 years ago, it was
like Whack-a-Mole, with dire news popping up here, there,
everywhere…," a decade later, things had changed. Back then,
it was "[s]tar players leaving for big money in the States.
Teams begging for government assistance. It was a vicious
circle of mediocrity or—in burgs like Québec City and
Winnipeg—even worse."

In the 1990s, it had seemed like Canada's economy
couldn't sustain our game anymore, but then the loonie
soared, and the game was again on sound footing north of the

border. Turner commented, "[E]ven the most pie-eyed optimist could never have foreseen such a scenario in the darkest days of the NHL in this country, when the dollar was hovering around 70 cents U.S...." Reviewing the condition of the league in 2007, he pointed out that by that time, the Sens were well clear of trouble. In addition, "The Canucks actually make money. The Canadiens are proud once again. And the Flames and Oilers, well, they're not only still here, they're helping to financially assist the struggling U.S. small-market teams." The ugly time was over, and everything seemed nice again, but Canadians had a hard time absorbing two facts—an American had been the one to make things better, and a season had been lost in the conflict.

There Will Be No Hockey

Canada is a nation of people who like to share resources, but one of the things that the troubles in Ottawa and Buffalo, and elsewhere, pointed to was that players' demands were causing salaries to get out of hand. And even more, the owners were in an ever-escalating war to buy the best team—using the Steinbrenner method to win. This, to Bettman's way of thinking, had to be stopped. The owners concurred, despite being the ones whose loose purse strings were the cause of the problem. This resulted in a delay in the start of the 2004–05 season while a new collective bargaining agreement was sought. Or at least, that's what it looked like in October 2004.

Time went on, and fans learned otherwise. Canadians realized that they might as well get used to those special feature movies on the CBC on Saturday night because hockey wasn't likely to come back. Their anger peaked when it was clear that there would be no Stanley Cup champion because there would be no hockey season. It was unthinkable that the country could carry on without the game that had been played in NHL form for nearly 100 years.

The lockout of 2004–05 was perhaps most infuriating to fans because neither labour nor management could really be seen as the good guys. Sure, the owners called off the season, through the Commissioner's office. And that frustrated a lot of people who were, as I was, watching the Internet minute-by-minute over the final weekend when the countdown was on to see whether a shortened season could be salvaged. When it became clear that wasn't going to happen, spirits fell, and managers—those greedy owners—were blamed initially.

But then a different sort of logic took over, and fans began asking themselves how much sympathy they felt for men making millions of dollars per year to play a game. Sure, we believed they deserved special treatment, but at what point did adequate compensation to create a comfortable post-NHL life turn into greed for too much? The feeling was magnified when it was noted that, in the 1980s, several hundred thousand dollars was considered big money for the top players. Back then, an NHL salary was maybe six times what the average working person earned, and although it seemed like a lot of money, it was somehow warranted. But when people did the math in 2005 and realized that many players made in a year what an average Canadian makes in his or her entire working life, sympathies waned.

Two responses sprang from this realization. First, fans started to ask themselves whether all of hockey was centred in the NHL. Why was it that Canadians saw their worldview so intricately wound around a league whose values hardly reflected the national ethos of sharing? What if the NHL could be replaced with a purer, less corrupt version of the game? The Original Stars Hockey League formed in 2004 to fill the gap with a four-on-four format and six teams. The idea lasted just two games. Meanwhile, prospects that might have made the NHL that fall played in the American Hockey League instead, and so did some NHL players. Scott Gomez joined his "home" team, the Alaska Aces of the ECHL; others went to Europe for the year, in many cases enjoying a lighter schedule than they would have in the NHL. Call it a return to "real" hockey, where money was not the primary motive for playing.

The really astute will recall, also, that a group led by Bobby Hull promised a revival of the WHA, a plan that did not pan out.

In all, it was a time when hockey was more alive than ever, but in different places than it had been before the lock-out. Local junior teams across Canada saw an increase in attendance, most notably the Calgary Hitmen and the London Knights. Fans, meanwhile, mused about whether they would even care when the NHL returned. Why put up with the antics of these overpaid guys and their irresponsible bosses, especially since it meant that ticket prices were through the roof in the cities where hockey mattered most—and those were, particularly, the six in Canada?

The second response fans had to gigantic salaries and the resulting work stoppage was to question the NHL's hold on the Stanley Cup. Why not do things like in the old days, people reasoned, and have the Cup once again become a challenge trophy, open to all comers? The NHL has awarded the Cup to its champion since 1926, but in its original conception, it was the Dominion Challenge Trophy, signifying the accomplishment of being the best team in the Dominion of Canada. Governor General Lord Stanley's idea was that anyone could vie for it.

The Governor General in 2005, Adrienne Clarkson, made what seemed to some like a good suggestion: why not award the Cup to the best women's hockey team in the country? Not too many people were fond of the idea, and the Clarkson Cup was created instead. But others thought that it wasn't fair for the Hall of Fame to continue to honour their contract with the NHL, since, in one sense, the league did not exist anymore. Of course, the plan to throw open the competition for the Cup to anyone did not come to fruition either, and the trophy was not awarded in the spring of 2005.

When play resumed that fall, it was to a wary fan base, and with chastened players. Many had seen the value of their long and rich contracts reduced. Just to take one example, Jeremy Roenick lost a good deal of money, and he spoke out about it. "We got our asses kicked," he said in response to the numbers that were worked out between the league and the players. He further suggested that fans who didn't like the way things were should just not come to games. Perhaps not the most Canadian of values, but then again, "JR" was born in Boston.

There was still a lot of mistrust and resentment after the lockout ended, but fans returned, prompted in part by their curiosity to see what the game would be like with a new set of rules and with the adoption of the shootout to break all ties. For purists, the shootout is still a gimmick, and it cannot be disputed that having three-point games ruins all previous records for wins, points and goaltending wins. But the real attraction of the new game was that it was so much like an old one, nearly forgotten, from 50 years earlier. Hockey had regained its purity.

Watch a game on tape from the 1950s or early '60s, and in black and white you'll see players whose primary engagement on the ice is with stick on puck. They don't hold and hook each other; their primary mission is not to get in the other player's way. Rather, they play the puck, with the goal of advancing it and eventually shooting on net. That sounds axiomatic—what else would a hockey player do? But look at footage of games in the decade or so before the lockout, and you'll see something much different. Wingers take five seconds after a faceoff to disentangle from one another. Centremen, too, once the puck has been kicked back to a defenseman, are entwined with their opposite number.

Going in on goal, a player is lucky if he doesn't have one guy wrapped around him from the back and another with a grasp on the shaft of his stick. The game moves like everyone is skating on butter, their hands slushing through molasses. It's also evident as far back as the 1970s, but during the height of the Gretzky era, say the '80s and into the early '90s, speed managed to overcome grabbing. Somehow, with the later stages of Wayne's career underway, clutching took over once more.

Post-lockout hockey was having none of that, and the speed and excitement of the game made people increasingly willing to spend their money to watch their teams play. However, that didn't heal the animosity fans felt for having lost a season, nor did it make the average Canadian less resentful of what were, still, enormous contracts.

Perhaps the biggest shift that the lockout produced was to the Canadian psyche. Never again would we view our game as a constant that would be there no matter what, and never again would it be possible to see the players as nice people just like us—only a bit better at hockey. Now, they would forever be highly paid experts doing something that would give them a lifestyle most of us could only dream about.

Gone are the gap-toothed warriors of the good old days whom fans could view as like them, only tougher and more determined and talented in the way they played the game. They have been replaced by men who are respected for their skills but who don't reflect the middle-class values of fans, at least as far as money is concerned. In ironic ways, this realization binds Canadian hockey fans to their American counterparts now more than before. Canadian and American autoworkers, for example, have accepted concessions over the past decade in order to keep their jobs, and through following these events in the news, people on both sides of the border have realized how tenuous employment is and how thankful they are to have work. Hockey players, by contrast, despite the concessions they made to return to work in 2005, are once again making millions of dollars, so that in the end, they represent values that separate them from the hard-working hockey fans all over the country, and in the U.S. too, who buy the tickets.

Hated Rivals

At the core, the values displayed through the game are rooted in conflict—us versus them being the primary one. Nobody who is serious about hockey plays to *lose*, after all. This has been manifested over the years in the animosity that is Habs versus Leafs, a dualism that mirrors the primary fissure at the heart of Canadian culture: the English-French divide. Almost from the time the organized game began, the aggressive spirit of hockey has provided an opportunity for French and English to play out their rivalries while maintaining respect for each other as strong adversaries, a contest that forces Canadians to ask themselves how deep the ethos of niceness really goes in their country.

The seeds of this enmity go back to the 1913–14 season, before either the Maple Leafs or the NHL existed. That year, the Canadiens and Toronto Blueshirts battled fiercely for the entire 20-game season. Along the way, the bond between the team from Québec and its Francophone followers was cemented. "These fans turned to their collective past to express their deepening attachment to the Canadiens," says D'Arcy Jenish. At the end of the season, Montréal had matched Toronto's record, and they met in a two-game, total-goals series. Toronto won going away, denying the Canadiens the chance to gain their first Stanley Cup. Perhaps the resentment for this loss lingers somewhere in Montréal fans' collective unconscious. Note that other Montréal teams had won before, including the Wanderers, the Shamrocks, the Victorias and a team simply identified as the Montréal Hockey Club, but the Habs were and are the soul of French Canada.

You might think that a rivalry that stretches back into hockey's history would make the most compelling drama ever seen in the game, and it has, at least at times. Since the early days of the organized professional game, the two teams have faced off in the playoffs 15 times (13 if you count only the period since the teams gained their modern identity as the Canadiens and Maple Leafs). However, things have cooled of late, with the most recent time the two teams met in the postseason being 1978–79. Even that last encounter was not a bloody and savage affair, as it might have been, but a 4–0 Montréal walkover in the quarterfinals (now the "Conference Semifinals"). This came at the end of Montréal's streak of four straight Cups.

The most intense period of head-to-head competition was in the early 1940s to 1967, when the teams played one another for the Stanley Cup five times—with Toronto winning three—and they met six other times, with each team taking three series victories. More recently, despite not making the playoffs from 2005 to 2011, the Leafs played Montréal to a dead-even regular season record in those years in terms of strict wins and losses.

The fact that Toronto and Montréal played each other only six times for the Cup from 1917 to 1967 (and haven't since) might suggest that their rivalry was not as emblematic of the divide in the country as memory suggests. But the difference between the two teams was played out not only in terms of Stanley Cups but also off the ice. The larger context of the rivalry between the two cities goes back to World War I and brings politics and national identity into the picture, illustrating again the niceness, or lack thereof, at the core of Canadian life.

During World War I, future Toronto owner Conn Smythe enlisted, serving as an artillery officer. He wore the Canadian uniform, the cap badge of which would later serve as the prototype of the Leafs' flag logo. When he returned home, he resumed his interest in hockey (he had played at the University of Toronto before he went to war), and he bought the St. Pats in 1927 and renamed them the Maple Leafs. Just to illustrate the level of the man's patriotism, note that after Canada adopted a new flag in 1965, the Leafs were quick to adopt a new logo, debuting a "five-pointed leaf [that] resembled the symbol in the heart of the Canadian flag," a change that prompted Smythe to weep. It was as if he were making the case when he approved the team name and logo that his team *was* Canada.

During World War II, Smythe was critical of Montréal (and Québec by extension) for not taking a greater share in the war. One account of history describes the tensions that war brought to Canada by saying, "Warmaking inflicted...deep wounds on the home front.... Both world wars rekindled the

French–English dispute when Parliament—after a national referendum in the second war—imposed conscription," then adds, "the social and regional rifts fomented in wartime between Québec and the rest of Canada persist as a perennial Canadian affliction." The Conscription Crisis of 1944 that pitted Anglophone government ministers against Francophones was emblematic of the problem, and the government's solution was to renew conscription, but only if it was deemed necessary.

The compromise didn't sit well with Smythe. Michael McKinley explains that many Canadian hockey players had signed up for home service, "a sop from the federal government to Québec, which was overwhelmingly opposed to 'conscription'…. [But] Conn Smythe hated home service. He had fought in the Great War, and though 45 years old, he wasn't going to let Hitler's jackbooted thugs run roughshod over Europe."

Smythe didn't confine his actions to the personal, though, but "made his 1939 Leafs take military training with the Toronto Scottish Regiment, and he urged all of his players to join a militia." McKinley doesn't say it, but the undertone suggests that the English-French cultural divide ran to the heart of Smythe's actions.

Smythe was injured by shrapnel while serving in France in 1944, this after having been a POW in Germany for over a year in World War I. His resentment must have been high when he surveyed what his archrival Montréal

Canadiens were doing to take (or evade, depending upon perspective) their part of the burden during World War II. As hockey historian Joe Pelletier explains:

> The war...shifted the power balance in the league, with Montréal placing building blocks that would make them the dominant team of the next few decades. The Habs... [found] jobs for players and prospects in essential industries like munitions and ship-building.... [T]he Montréal Canadiens kept their talent home, building the foundation for several Stanley Cup championships.

The Leafs continued to dominate in the immediate aftermath of the war, winning the Cup in 1945 and from 1947 to 1949, and again in 1951. But the Habs were catching up, and they won it in 1953 and from 1956 to 1960. Toronto reprised its three-in-a-row in 1962–64, gave it back to Montréal for a couple of years, then won its last championship to date in 1967. After that, as is well known, Montréal won the trophy eight times between 1968 and 1979. The Habs added two more, in 1986 and 1993, to make their total 24 Stanley Cups. Toronto sits at 13. But looking at the on-ice battles does not tell the whole story, not at all.

Aside from what happened during the war and after, the most famous flashpoint in the battle of language and culture was the Richard Riot of 1955, which occurred smack in the middle of the great Leafs–Habs glory years. As has been said, the event was less about hockey than it was about English oppression of the French. The incident was not related to Toronto directly, but Clarence Campbell became the focal point for the Québecois' resentment of how they had been treated by the English for decades when he suspended Maurice Richard for the balance of the season for punching a linesman during a fight with Hal Laycoe of the Bruins.

If the oppressed Francophone had a role model, it was Richard. For Francophones, Richard's struggle was their struggle. As noted author Roch Carrier says, the people saw Richard's defense of himself on the ice as their defense against oppression in their workplaces. Campbell, representative of the English-speaking majority, denied Richard his chance to finish the season and take the Canadiens to the playoffs when he suspended him. Jenish describes the reaction by saying that "the decision hit the city [Montréal] like a bomb."

Fans showed up to the next Canadiens home game to take their revenge on Campbell, who was in the crowd. You have to give him credit for bravery, because first one fan crushed two tomatoes against his chest, then another slapped him across the face, twice. Campbell stayed put. As a mob started to form and head his way, a smoke bomb exploded nearby, and the crowd moved outside, to where the cops were waiting. They had no hope of controlling the melee.

Carrier describes the scene vividly:

> *Madness reigns in the street. The Forum*
> *refuses to catch fire. The demonstrators can't*
> *get inside to wreak havoc there, so they go*
> *where there are store windows to smash,*
> *stores to loot. Is this the great anger of a small*
> *people? Is it a barbarian celebration?*

Before the chaos abated, the downtown section along Rue Sainte-Catherine had seen stores destroyed and cars burned. Still, the question of the oppression of the French speaker in Québec was not settled—the riot was about more than hockey, though it was fought out on a hockey battlefield. It is no great stretch to say that the Richard Riot heralded the Quiet Revolution of the following decade, in which the Québecois slowly took back their streets and their province. Of course, things came to a head again in the October Crisis of 1970, but that was altogether removed from the scope of the game.

The rivalry between Toronto and Montréal might have ended in 1967, at least as far as meaningful playoff encounters go, because that was the last time the two teams played for the Stanley Cup. That does not mean, however, that present-day players do not understand the spirit of competition that still exists between the two teams. Former Leafs forward Alexei Ponikarovsky, who is from the Ukraine, said in 2008 when he was with Toronto and about to play against the Habs, "It's the battle of Canada.... It's been like that for years." If a newcomer can perceive this division, what does it say about a country that views itself as being built on niceness? Maybe that once we look below the surface, Canadians are less united and more a product of opposing forces in tension with one another than we often think. That rivalry was never more true than when La Belle Province had two NHL teams.

Internecine Rivalry

With the Montréal–Toronto rivalry having cooled after 1967, some of the most violent encounters on the ice in the past few decades have occurred between what might have been thought of as brother organizations: Montréal and Québec City. Sibling rivals from the start, the Habs and the Nordiques were perhaps too close for comfort, playing just over 200 kilometres apart. The first coach of the Québec City club, who lasted only two games, was former Montréal great Rocket Richard, though the team was in the WHA back then. The ties went deeper when former Montréal superstar Guy Lafleur, who retired from the Habs in 1985 after his playing time became less frequent, came back to don the fleur-de-lis blue-and-white of the intraprovince rivals in 1989.

But it was during the playoffs of 1982, while "The Flower" was still with Montréal, that one of the most savage in-game brouhahas of all time occurred. The rivalry between the two teams, according to historian D'Arcy Jenish, was stoked by media speculation about which of the two clubs was more representative of French Québec.

"The first playoff encounter between the two teams," Jenish claims, "resembled warfare more than sport." Before the end of game four, every player on the ice except the goalies was fighting, and the referee only got things under control by dishing out 149 minutes in penalties and two game misconducts. The fight lasted 20 minutes. For Canadian fans, this was not out of the ordinary because the animosity between the teams was well established.

Internecine rivalry. It even sounds sinister, and although the NHL moved the Québec club to Colorado in 1995 citing the need to increase revenue in the form of corporate involvement as well as the need for a new rink, who's to say that New York wasn't thinking that maybe Montréal versus Québec City was too much like a civil war? From the perspective of the Americans who ran the league, having that rivalry play out in front of the hoped-for hordes of fans that the U.S. networks were supposed to deliver might have appeared unsavoury. It was the old "airing your dirty laundry" thing. Or maybe it was just unsaleable, as the issue sparking the rivalry is one that only vaguely resonates with Americans. (To this day, when I meet someone in the U.S. and say that I grew up in Montréal, the first question I'm asked is, "Is your family French?" Or "So you speak French, then?" The relationship between the English and French in Canada is a bit foggy for people south of the border, or at least for those in the southwest corner of the U.S., where I live.)

When the Nordiques moved to Colorado, the NHL did more than deprive Québec City of its team. It took away the forum where the question of Québec's continued place in Canada could be fought over. Suddenly, the space where this problem could be played out was not contested—it had to be Montréal. No sibling rivalry can exist where there are no siblings.

By the time of the move, the question was starting to lose some of its political resonance anyway. The referenda in 1980 and 1995 had come back to say "no," or "non," depending upon your linguistic preference. Québec did not get its citizens' sanction to seek a way to create itself as a separate nation through sovereignty-association or outright sovereignty. By the second go-round of separation voting, with the Nordiques playing in Denver, if there was to be a flag bearer in the game for the continued voice of the French, it had to be Montréal.

The problem by this point was that the Habs were a less Francophone team than they had been at any time in their history, and this, to some, suggested that the old oppression was still alive, long after Maurice Richard and Clarence Campbell had exited the hockey stage. The Canadiens' 1994–95 roster, for example, had 39 names on it. Of those, just 12 or 13 were French surnames. Nearly 20 years later, the battle continues, with complaints that the team is less French than ever. The French question will never die, of course. Saku Koivu, Montréal's captain for nine seasons, was much loved in the city but was also greatly criticized for not speaking French—despite the fact that he is from Finland and his second language is English.

Safely ensconced in Anaheim the second year after leaving the Habs, Koivu told me in a personal interview in January 2011, "I speak a little Swedish, and French as well. No, no French. Just three [languages]." It's a joke that, I have a feeling, he would have not made in Montréal. But he also remembered his time with the Canadiens fondly:

> Hockey in. Canada in general is even more of a passion and way of life and living than at home. Obviously, people are excited and interested in hockey back home [in Finland], but still, the difference after a win or a loss is different in Montréal. Everybody talked about it. You went downtown the next day, and it was just the way people spoke about the game the night before, you really felt it, and that's different. I don't think you can really experience that anywhere else than in Canada, in certain cities. That's what makes it unique. It makes it a real interesting place to live and play.

So Are We Nice, or What?

Canadians may be defined as being nice, but we are comfortable with the idea of duality. Two solitudes, if you like—hockey is all about that. Two teams. Two nets. One puck. At a faceoff, only one player can come up with the puck, and it can't be in your net if it's in mine. So I have to do whatever I can to make sure I protect my turf. Call this a negative value if you must, but if hockey represents who we are, it's at the core of the game, and the country, to thrive on a rival's failure.

If the history of hockey in Canada has been formed and sustained by the dualism that alternately pushes Montréal and Toronto apart and pulls them together, and which once meant that brother teams from Québec went all out to destroy each other, maybe the Canadian worldview has a harsher edge than we think. Each time there has been an attempt to change the pattern of opposition, it has failed. Remember Meech Lake? The idea was that Canada as a single entity would be strengthened. Failed. How about the Charlottetown Accord, with its "Canada Clause"? Failed.

Despite a history of increasing reconciliation between powerful owners and the players they employ, the divisions at the heart of Canadian culture will perhaps never be completely soldered over, nor should they be, but neither do Canadians live in a country with a simple, single set of values that are unconditionally accepted, nor are they always nice. Sometimes, events turn nasty, and we accept that contradiction to our normally placid existence, especially if it happens on a hockey rink.

chapter nine

Violence in the Canadian Imagination

The Connection Between Violence and Being Canadian

Violence. Canadianness. Does it start with hockey or end with hockey? The answer "may lie in the peculiarly Canadian hockey mindset that views hockey as war. For as long as men have made a living chasing a rubber disc over frozen water, that ice has been reddened by the blood of players," explains writer Lawrence Scanlan. He suggests there is an intricacy with which brutality is woven into the game.

Given Canada's reputation for being nice, the violence in our favourite sport should be unsettling, but it is tolerated and even encouraged and has been since the beginning of organized play. Fans see it in every match—the fights, the checks that leave players lying on the ice, the cuts and lost teeth. At the highest levels, our game is savage, yet we pride ourselves on being a peaceful country and often cite the much higher rate of violent crime in the U.S. as evidence of our superior character. Something doesn't add up.

One excuse we sometimes make for hockey's brutality is its containment within the confines of the rink. Plus, we tell ourselves, it's not average people out there in NHL games—these guys are the few and not a true representation of who the rest of us are. Take violence out of the hockey arena and put it into the context of Canadian history, though, and the "this is not who we are" argument falls flat.

It has become a cliché, or perhaps an oft-cited truth, that "Canada became a country that day"—the day in question being April 9, 1917, the Battle of Vimy Ridge. And maybe Vimy tells us that we're looking in the wrong place if we seek an apology for hockey's violence in excusing it as something that happens only on the rink. Maybe violence is more at the heart of the Canadian imagination than we'd like to admit. It's not something that we are proud of, but something that, as a culture, we must bear, an effect of the lingering trace of Vimy that lies underneath our placid exterior of niceness.

As part of our defining national myth, Vimy is retold to each new generation. Students learn about the battle in school, and it's dramatized many times in Canadian literature. For example, Joseph Boyden's recent novel *Three Day Road* shows readers, more than once, that through fighting at Vimy, Canadian identity at the level of country is confirmed. "We are an army to be reckoned with suddenly, no longer the colonials, as the Englishmen call us, looking down at us," the narrator, speaking from character Xavier Bird's point of view, explains after Vimy.

Frances Itani's bestselling novel *Deafening* reinforces the message, which we glean through a character's thoughts: "[T]he war showed no sign of being over. Every event reported was worse than the last—except Vimy Ridge, almost a year ago. That had been good news. A great Canadian victory." However, Itani also gives the counterpoint: "But rejoicing was bittersweet when thousands of boys went down. No one who lost a son, or brother or father, was jumping for joy after Vimy—despite what was written in the papers." This is refreshing—an honest appraisal of the sadness and cost of war, but seldom is this aspect emphasized in stories of Canada's glorious, self-affirming victory.

Keeping Vimy alive assures its place in defining Canada even after anyone who can remember it is gone—and that day is fast approaching, since a 10-year-old in that time would be over 100 now, and all of the soldiers have died. If Vimy were to disappear from memory, an important part of Canadian history and identity would go with it. Yet that will never happen because when you draw the line out from Vimy, it appears that hockey serves as a representation of it in our cultural memory. An interesting diagnosis of the situation comes from Don Cherry, whom Scanlan quotes as saying, "This [violence in the game] has been going on since 1918."

Scanlan adds, "For most of its history, Canadian hockey has been war." As with all wars, at the core of World War I, and Vimy in particular, is violence. The same is true with hockey at the elite levels, yet a curious double-coding of violence is present, because, just as with the Vimy victory, the terror of it is often ignored or excused, especially when its outcome results in a tournament won, or a Stanley Cup gained.

Violence as a Way of Life

Learning to tolerate an increasing amount of violence actually describes pretty well the young person's path of development in hockey. Right about the time a kid is old enough to understand how life works, he or she realizes that to survive on a hockey rink, it is often necessary to enact a set of violent behaviours. Checking, aggressively going after loose pucks with the threat of getting hit when you get to them, blocking shots. All of these ask a player to put pain in the background and, to invoke one of the oldest clichés in sports, "take one for the team." This is never a pleasant experience, nor one that comes naturally to a kid. In fact, many players can't live with the fear of hockey's physical side.

Those who can deal with the fear make it up through the ranks into the professional leagues. For them, there is a strange logic to how violence works. In a locker room conversation I had with him in November 2007, Shane O'Brien of Port Hope, Ontario, who has played for the Ducks, Tampa Bay, Vancouver and Nashville, said that he *had* to fight every

night in the AHL. The guys he fought were big men, but fighting them was his only hope of staying in the lineup and thus
eventually making the NHL. In the two years prior to his NHL
debut, he averaged 303 PIMs per season with the Cincinnati
Mighty Ducks and Portland Pirates. In O'Brien's first year with
the NHL's Ducks, had he played all 82 games, he would have
had about 185 PIMs. His high in the NHL through the end of
2011 was 196, in 2008–09 with the Canucks.

Fighting is the logic of the marginal player. If the
package you offer the team isn't seen by management as
quite complete without fighting, you fight. When young
players are interviewed at rookie camp, they often mention
that they don't mind dropping the gloves when it's called for.
When they make the league, they fight to prove that they're
okay with it. In the eyes of those who are evaluating their
performance, it shows that they're willing to stand up for
themselves, or to go to war for a teammate, and this reinforces the mindset of embattlement that must end, it would
seem, in violence.

To take another example, Jack Johnson, who joined
the LA Kings late in the 2006–07 season, got into a fight in
one of his first games. The TV commentary on the skirmish,
which was not quite a toe-to-toe and was won by ruffian
Daniel Carcillo, went something like this: "It's another thing
you want to get rid of…early in your career." As you watch the
video, it's obvious that Carcillo is doing the work of initiating

Johnson into the league, as he comes from nowhere and jumps him. Perhaps enamoured of his newfound skills, Johnson fought again in the game, this time against Shane Doan, although that was more of a pushing match. The cause was that Doan had run the Kings' goalie, Mathieu Garon.

Afterward, in a locker room interview, Johnson said the usual stuff: "it was going to happen sooner or later," "good to get it out of the way" and so on. But why is it necessary that the fight happened? He had played college hockey at the University of Michigan, where fighting is not a feature of the game, being strictly sanctioned. And in the time from the game mentioned until spring 2011, Johnson fought only three times. In the season following these "initiation" bouts against Carcillo and Doan, his first full one, he had no fights.

Johnson is not Canadian, having been born in Indianapolis, Indiana, but the point remains the same—hockey violence is somehow simply okay, and normal, to the millions of Canadians (let alone Americans) who play or follow the game at the NHL level, and even at other levels, from junior to senior amateur.

Filmmaker Brett Kashmere details the history of hockey violence and ponders its reasons in his documentary *Valery's Ankle*. The examples he portrays go from the slash by Bobby Clarke that broke Kharlamov's ankle in the Summit Series up through to more recent events in the game, including the Brashear-McSorley incident and the violence in minor league contests such as those in the North American Hockey League, said to be the most brutal league in the world. (With team nicknames like the "Rage," "Hitmen," "Monsters" and "Bandits," it's no wonder.)

Kashmere's voice is heard throughout the film, sometimes asking questions, sometimes revealing his own feelings about the game. He played in a contact league up until about the age many kids do, and then at 14, decided he'd had enough. He was, he says, "tired of the competition, the escalating violence, the culture of disrespect." His overriding question is framed in terms of the incident in the sixth game of the 1972 Summit Series: What might be discovered by thinking through the slash that Bobby Clarke delivered to Valery Kharlamov? Kashmere says that the game since 1972, and in particular more recently, has become tarnished by "continuous acts of gratuitous violence" that go well beyond fighting. "How can other forms of on-ice hostility be condemned," he wonders, "when bare-knuckle fighting, a criminal activity outside of the hockey arena, is still permitted?"

Perhaps the answer is that Canadians learn early that some players are marked for violence, while others turn from it. Fighting and horrid acts of on-ice misbehaviour aside, body checking is the great divider between "cans" and "can nots" in Canadian life. The ability to tolerate contact in the game is what first separates kids into groups. Up until the age of 10 or 12, there's not much distinction in the level of violence between one league and another, partly because the kids aren't coordinated enough to deliver body checks, even when these are allowed. But around Pee Wee, size differences among youngsters start to show, and those who don't measure up, literally, or can't deal with the violence, psychologically, relegate themselves to the non-contact "house" league, the shinny pond or they quit hockey altogether.

Everyone has seen little kids who hit each other and both go down to the ice like they were bouncing off a wall. They might have been going for the puck, but the contact is incidental, or accidental—most of the time, they don't even know the other kid is there. And they bounce right back up and go on. It's like watching children at a karate tournament. It seems cruel to put two six- or eight-year-olds wearing gloves and pads onto a mat and tell them to hit each other, until you see that they essentially can't. They're not coordinated enough. But shortly afterward, they get their skills working, and many quit at that point.

Similarly, in hockey, at the age when players can time their hits and deliver them with force and balance, things change. At first, kids learn to limit their aggression, to control their bodies so that they don't hurt each other. But some figure out that those who can hit without conscience inhabit a privileged world, because they get to play the game at a higher level. The advanced athletes, the ones who can master the fear of hitting and being hit, have a sliver of a chance to make it in hockey. The rest are washed out from that moment.

How does this translate into who a kid becomes? It depends upon whether he or she is a house-league or a travel-team player. The average kid learns that life is governed by rules that exist to ensure mutual respect and safety. As the house-league player goes to the rink week after week, the idea is reinforced. On the other hand, players on the select teams learn that their life has a special quality because they can behave in ways that not everyone can. And the free pass that comes along with that status is to be forgiven for acts of violence that would be punishable as crimes if committed out on the street.

When a kid decides to abandon the contact game and go house league, the hope of making a career in the professional game is left behind, but not the memory of violence. Those who remain fans into adulthood might go to major junior games to watch one of the 60 teams that contest for the right to go to the Memorial Cup tournament each spring. Their brains know that the players are kids, though the oldest of them might be 20, but the souls of the people in the stands tell them these kids are a breed apart—that they are somehow able to deal with the fear that every play must bring or are oblivious to it in a way that those in the stands could never be.

The days of being terrorized by opposing defensemen as you head into the corner hoping to wheel out with the puck before they squash you against the boards are put in the past when you quit contact hockey, but your sense that this violence goes on in arenas throughout your city is not lost. There is a residue that lingers, maybe of fear, maybe of relief, but also of the conviction that violence is one of the keys to success in a sport that a lot of Canadians would be proud to succeed at. Participation in the elite levels of hockey is reserved for a select few who can embrace the game's physical aspects. The rest of us enact our national identity by watching, without condemnation, what happens on the ice.

Violence Begets Peace

"Violence begets violence," someone might say, and certainly Kashmere's argument in his film supports that claim. But let's turn that equation on its head. For Canadians, violence on the rink begets peace in the world. Why? Because another way to view the great game is to say that hockey allows Canadians to suppress their impulse to act violently because they can get their fill of it in the arena. Of course, everyone understands that for a special group (soldiers in the real world, elite hockey players in the arena), and by their own consent, violence is sometimes necessary and part of their way of life. However, that too has a code that, at least in theory, governs behaviour.

Hockey players understand that strict rules govern their aggressions, something that translates off the rink and into adulthood into citizens who understand the need to control themselves. Perhaps that's why Canadian hockey fans have mixed opinions about the fighting aspect of the game. We want to see it, if there's a reason for it. But we don't want to see it just as a spectacle. We want to see the big hits that knock guys down and make them pay for the sin of not keeping their heads up, but we don't want to take that kind of hit ourselves, and most of us understand from a young age that such experiences are not for us because we don't play hockey at the select level.

Most of us who played in the house league learned to resist our urge to fight, no matter how strong it was. At that level, each player knows, further, that there won't be any "third man in." Going two-against-one is simply not fair, not how the game goes. You fight your own battles, if you fight at all, win or lose. That third guy is the one who ends up taking the brunt of the penalties. Even his own team frowns him off the ice.

This feeling has been internalized. For that reason, Canadians, to broaden the context to the international, are Pearson's UN peacekeepers. They are the men between, not the man in the fight, because they have developed the steely resolve to stand pat. Our soldiers have the guns, and they're trained to use them, but they have also learned that the outcome is better when a weapon is not used, and by standing ground and waiting, the message to the two potential combatants in a civil war situation is that you had better not mix it up, or there will be consequences.

Many Canadians didn't realize until recently how fiercely our military fights, because up until the last decade or so, we've thought of the UN-sanctioned soldier as analogous to a librarian shushing people who talked too loud. The news stories that came out of Kosovo changed that. We learned how chaotic keeping order can be, and we came to understand that the men and women who represented us there and who have done so subsequently in other places are often called upon to enact violence for a greater good.

Yet even our role in Afghanistan corresponds to the desire not to fight (though we are all familiar with the fight, and the losses, that Canadian soldiers have endured). The government's stated outcome for Canadian troops is to focus "on a targeted set of objectives in keeping with proven Canadian strengths," with priority on "maintain[ing] a more secure environment and establish[ing] law and order by building the capacity of the Afghan National Army and Police," as well as "providing jobs, education, and essential services, like water," giving humanitarian aid and maintaining the security of the border with Pakistan. Only the last of those goals borders on aggressive action, and it is notable that it appears as the final item on the list.

When Canada suggests fighting as the mission, it is as in this goal statement: "Canada is helping to...contribute to

Afghan-led political reconciliation efforts aimed at *weakening the insurgency* [my emphasis] and fostering a sustainable peace." The aggressive mission is downplayed, and peace is put forth as the goal. So again, Canadian culture sanctions that some will do the fighting, but it demands that it be done honourably and with limits.

Whatever our involvement in volatile areas of the world, our national self-image is still one of peace. Our military is not large, given the size of the country and its population (although with 2800 soldiers in Afghanistan at the end of 2009, Canada's role was "proportionally larger than the stake the United States [had] in Afghanistan" at the time, according to Professor Alan Henrikson of Tufts University as reported by CNN). Canadian news stories do not feature the newest and greatest innovation in warfare or video footage of the latest fighter plane. Rather, our way is to defer—to choose the path of non-confrontation, and certainly most recently, to say no to the Americans' request that we get involved in Iraq. When we fight, it is for a reason, at least in the most ideal circumstances.

With Afghanistan, it seemed at the outset that getting involved was the right thing to do. Rules were broken, and when someone is taking liberties with your skilled players, metaphorically speaking or literally, the enforcer has to step in. But the violence of the reaction is limited and governed by a set of codes that are clear (in the ideal situation).

Once the job is done, you retreat. You don't carry on looking for another fight. In the case of a hockey fight, when
the other guy goes down, the one on top stops punching.
In the case of Afghanistan, when peace reigns (or the Afghanis
themselves are capable of containing whatever violence
exists), we will leave.

When Violence Makes Sense

Despite Vimy's violence having formed our national
identity, Canadians are essentially pacifists. However, this
doesn't equate completely with nonviolence. Rather, our
aggression is controlled and channelled. We are accustomed
to standing on the bench and surveying the chaos going on in
front of us, and we know what should be done to maintain
fairness. But we also know when it's time to hop the boards,
choose a right-sized player on the other side and go at it.

To use the familiar example from hockey as stated earlier, the Summit Series began as a friendly exhibition. Soon,
it was posed as an epic battle between two ways of life: commu-
nism and democracy. The latter term was not, as it might easily
have been, "capitalism." Nor, really, was it "Canadianness."
The struggle was slightly more messy than that. It was our
way ("freedom") versus theirs ("conformity"). Being able to
label the division between "us" and "them" implied that we
knew what our way was, and that we were going to defend it.
This explains why the series turned into a war on the ice,
with everything from punching (by Team Canada players)

to kicking (by Red Army players) to the slash that broke Kharlamov's ankle (by Bobby Clarke) featuring in the action. But when it was over and we had won, the sense prevailed that maybe we didn't need to worry about these Russians after all. If we could beat them on the ice, then that was good enough for us. We shook hands and skated away.

Controlled violence for limited purposes, then, seems to be the Canadian way, providing a balance that keeps everyone in check, and we see this modelled every time we turn on a hockey game. Sheldon Souray provides a contemporary example that illustrates the connection between the skill of the game and its violent element. A defenseman with a big, hard shot, he doesn't go looking for trouble, but he's the kind of guy who doesn't flinch when he sees something happening that puts one of his teammates in a disadvantaged spot.

It was thought to be a natural move for him to leave the Canadiens to go to Edmonton in 2007. It was a chance to go home, since he grew up in Alberta, and provide the Oilers with the star they'd been missing. They were also building a big, skilled team, with guys like Dustin Penner and Kyle Brodziak filling out the ranks, players who would throw down the gloves if it became necessary. The hope was that by building this kind of team identity, the Oilers could regain their place at the top of the NHL.

Souray went West to fanfare and a big contract—five years and $27USD million. He wasn't going to be the captain of the team, but as a 31-year-old, and a veteran of the Montréal Canadiens, he knew what it was to play in a place where the expectations were high. No hiding out in Nashville or the U.S. south for him.

His first season, he got hurt and appeared in only 26 games. The point production he had enjoyed in his final year with the Habs (26–38–64) fell way off—to 10 points on three goals and seven helpers. The next year he put in almost a full campaign, missing just one game, and got back near his peak points total with 53. What he wasn't was as nasty as he had been previously. In the 2006–07 year, he had notched 135 PIMs. In 2008–09, 98. That's the equivalent of five fighting majors and one minor less.

The next year, he was back on track for large PIMs, getting 65 in just under half a season's worth of games (37), but his point total was again off (just 13), and fans were suggesting that he wouldn't be around after the trade deadline—too expensive for what the team was getting out of him. Meanwhile, Souray had given the Oilers a list of 10 squads he might go to, should they feel like trading him. They wouldn't get the chance, because an incident on the ice resulted in a radical change in plans.

The Oilers' storied rivalry with Calgary ran right through Souray on the night of January 30, 2010, when he found himself in a fight with Jerome Iginla. It was an attempt to settle a score, Iginla having put Souray into the boards earlier in the season, knocking him to the sidelines for 16 games. In the punch-up, Souray broke his right hand, and he didn't play another game all season. For Edmonton, this meant that the team couldn't deal the big defenseman, and they would eventually put him on waivers after the season ended, hoping someone would grab him, and his monster contract. When that didn't work, he was sent, on loan, to an AHL team in Hershey, Pennsylvania, a squad not even affiliated with the Oilers. The Oilers bought out Souray's contract after he once again cleared waivers unclaimed at the end of the 2010–11 season. Dallas signed him to a one-year deal that summer.

The good thing about this fight, if you look at the bigger picture, was that it showed that two premier players could settle their own score. The bad thing, for both teams, was the risk for their stars.

The message sent by Souray and Iginla's fight was that the us-versus-them (or better, me-versus-him) ethos that sparks violence lives, but that it's a set of values that most hockey fans would endorse because it also serves to contain further violence. However, sometimes, especially in hockey, the mechanism that is supposed to limit the violence doesn't work. In the aforementioned case, Iginla wasn't done for the season, and his subsequent actions indicate that violence crept past the level where it was "needed" to maintain order. In March, he took on San Jose's Ryan Clowe, a fight even his coach thought might have been a bit ill-advised. For Clowe, it was his 11th fight of the season, for Iginla, the sixth. Afterward, more than a few people with informed opinions said they thought the risk of him fighting Clowe was not worth whatever motivational reward the team might have gained from it. He wasn't settling a score, but trying to fire up his squad. Violence was being deployed for its own sake, and this is where the comfortable equation "violence begets peace" starts to get out of balance, looking more like violence begets peace...begets violence.

Living by the Code

Violence in the game is supposed to happen for a reason, to reinforce the message that there are limits to what one player may do to another. At its best, fighting works to even the score, putting bullies in their place, like it does in one of the greatest movies ever, *A Christmas Story*. Ralph Parker, the movie's nerdy hero, finally kicks the snot out of Scut Farcas, the bully who has terrorized every kid in Ralph's school, beaten them up and generally held sway with his violent ways. When Ralph finally gets even on behalf of all the kids, there's a genuine sense that this is right and to be enjoyed by spectators. (The film, by the way, is set in Indiana, despite being recognizably Canadian because of many of its shooting locations.)

Hockey violence ought to do what Ralphie's fight does, which is to even things up, with the guy who was wronged triumphing. But how often do you see a violent incident in a hockey game that truly settles a score on behalf of rightness? More often than not, new cycles of violence follow. Ask even a casual fan to name an incident of hockey violence, and you'll get a long string of examples, starting with the present and reaching back into the history of the game: Bertuzzi-Moore, McSorley-Brashear, Ciccarelli-Richardson, Clarke-Kharlamov, Shore-Bailey. Hockey, at its core, seems always to have been unrelentingly brutal.

Watch the Bertuzzi-Moore incident on replay, and your thoughts can't help but be, "He did that to him?" Even if you know why, and buy into the idea that it's okay to seek the kind of retribution Bertuzzi was wielding on behalf of his teammate Markus Naslund, isn't there a part of you that pulls back? Bertuzzi outweighed Moore by 30 pounds.

So-called "heavyweights" Brashear and McSorley weren't exactly innocent of violence. Shore was a known pest, Bailey a rugged left winger. None of the incidents that made their paths cross are analogous to the little guy getting revenge, as in the Ralph Parker model. So why and how do any of their actions reflect Canadian ideals? They don't, yet the logic of the rink justifies these actions even though they do not correspond to any lessons in moral reasoning you might learn in an ethics class. And because there is seemingly no check on what one player may do to another, when faced with the chance to act brutally, players inevitably do it.

In a few instances, violence in the rink has been, or has attempted to be, prosecuted as if it had occurred outside of the game, as in the early case of Loney-Laurin (hockey's first murder case, which happened in 1905 in the small town of Maxville, Ontario) and the recent cases of the aforementioned Ciccarelli-Richardson fight, where the former earned himself a day in jail, and Patrick Roy's son, Jonathan, who pled guilty to assault after he fought—actually pulverized—an opposing goalie during a major junior game in 2008.

What happens more often than not is that players who end up in court for their actions cite as a mitigating factor the eye-for-an-eye code that governs hockey. In the McSorley-Brashear incident of 2000, for example, the defense offered up by McSorley's lawyer in an attempt to avoid seeing his client jailed for his actions was plain: when you step onto the ice, contact is to be expected. The judge had a problem with the nature of the contact, a two-handed stick swing to the head by McSorley, and found him guilty of assault. McSorley said he never intended to hurt the other player.

When such an incident occurs, the reaction of a lot of hockey fans is shock. "What kind of horrible behaviour is that?" Actually, that's not the most common way of seeing it. Rather, most ask, "How could a hockey fight land you in court?" or "Why not let the players settle these things between themselves?" The reason these questions spring to mind is that the rink has always been seen as a special place, above the law, or outside of it. Fighting is part of that private world, and the people who participate are assumed to have given tacit permission to all of the others on the ice to act in ways that defy societal norms, so long as they are willing to take the consequences—on the ice.

Sometimes, there's an attempt at restitution. In the case of the Shore-Bailey incident, there was the aforementioned benefit game for Bailey, who never played hockey again. At that game, as Scanlan describes the scene, "He and Eddie Shore shook hands at centre ice in a charged and emotional moment." But that couldn't have erased Bailey's anger and resentment, nor does it do anything, really, to right any wrongs. It merely makes everything seem okay on the surface. The events that preceded the handshake still happened, and similar ones occur into the present, because Canadians are willing to give a moral bye to what their heroes do on the ice.

At its best, the hockey code says that when you hurt another player, you pay for it. It's primal, and sometimes, talking to hockey players, I feel uneasy as they describe why they have gotten into fights. After all, they're grownups, and we're a civilized society. But as former LA Kings winger Wayne Simmonds told me in January 2010, "You fight their best player in the second period [the Ducks' Ryan Getzlaf in this case], you know you're going to have to answer the bell in the third." The real player fights his own battles, one-to-one, when the code is working as it is supposed to. Scanlan, in his study of what he calls "our sweet and savage game," says that "the code" played out on a hockey rink "demands tribal retribution" for wrongs or perceived wrongs done to a teammate. The idea is that if you harass one of our guys, we have someone on our team who will return the favour.

It's logical that you can't have the so-called skilled players—often smaller guys whose abilities rest in finesse and not brawn—subject to the same kind of mistreatment that the bruisers suffer. Brian Gionta, Michael Cammalleri, Martin St. Louis or the Sedins, for example, make their living putting the puck in the net, not crashing and banging in the corners. So when they are harassed excessively, one of the tougher players on their teams takes charge. The problem is, the code is enforced in an oddly indirect way in the modern NHL.

Brent Severyn, a former enforcer in the league who later became a broadcaster, explained it this way to me in March 2007:

> *If I, as my team's tough guy, fight your team's tough guy and beat him up, it's like you're left with no protection. Think about the schoolyard. It's comforting to know that the big guy in your group of friends is going to be there to protect you if someone in the other group gets aggressive.*

Fair enough. But what doesn't make sense is why that deters *me* as a player from doing something to my opponent.

If I'm not going to pay, but the cost rather is my side's bully fighting their side's bully, why should I worry?

Think back to the fights of the 1970s, to Québec, Montréal, Philly and almost any other team you can name. Those were the days before the rules prevented players from jumping over the boards and getting into the melee. The images of the time are classic—everyone in the pool, with only the coaches left, often standing *on* the bench, yelling at the guys on the other bench, ties flying and clipboards waving from outstretched arms.

Back then, a big player wouldn't fight a small one. Guys approximately each other's size would be squared off, and they didn't just dance, hold and end up hugging, as happens today when you have the "pairing off" scenario among the 10 skaters on the ice. They slugged it out, but with the virtue that like player fought like, settling scores from earlier on-ice incidents. But eventually the league had had enough, putting in rules against the "third man in" in 1971 and against instigating a fight in 1976.

In so doing, the NHL created a bigger problem than it solved, because it institutionalized the ritualized fighting that exists today. The league subverted the honest rules of gentlemanly conduct that had come to govern the fisticuffs aspect of the game. Sure, it might have been ugly seeing Bob Gainey fighting with Jim Watson or Terry O'Reilly, but you knew that grievances were getting settled, one-on-one.

In our era, Scott Gomez watches while Georges Laraque or Travis Moen tussles with Colton Orr or Riley Cote, and that is somehow supposed to solve the situation of a slash delivered with two hands by yet someone else.

This kind of fighting, because it is often only indirectly related to the acts that precipitated it in the first place, doesn't solve anything. The next play, or the next game, someone else throws an elbow and knocks a player unconscious or checks a defenseless player from behind into the boards, because unchecked violence bearing no relationship to the code of right behaviour has become the norm in hockey of late. However, things are shifting, and fans seem, finally, to be willing to draw the line.

Have We Finally Had Enough?

The level of violence that fans will tolerate on the ice is a compelling and contradictory debate that has come to the forefront of public conversation recently, with many wondering whether the tipping point of too much violence has finally been reached. The question has been asked for decades but is being pondered more urgently now: at what point will fans rise up and demand a change in the way hockey is played?

In the summer of 2010, the death of a former NHL enforcer initiated a tide of change. Bob Probert, perhaps the toughest man ever to play hockey, lived by the code and fought literally hundreds of bare-knuckle bouts on the ice.

He also struggled with addiction, living as hard a life away from the rink as he did on it. He died relatively young, at 45, of heart failure. When scientists examined his brain, they found that he had a chronic degenerative condition called chronic traumatic encephalopathy (CTE). Brain damage, and it would have likely affected him more adversely as he got older.

It wasn't just his injury that made people sit up and take notice of the violence epidemic in hockey. Rather, it was that added to the demise of two skilful players hurt by concussions, they of course being Marc Savard and superstar Sidney Crosby. Savard made a heroic return to score a glorious goal for Boston in the playoffs of 2010. But a year later, he was still suffering memory loss, depression and other symptoms after having taken another whack to the head. His assailant is a cheap-shot artist whose name does not deserve the ink it would take to print it.

Crosby was knocked out of the game by two hits a week apart in early January 2011. Months later, he was skating, but with no timetable for returning to the Penguins' active roster. In the wake of this, news outlets began the crusade to ban checking to the head. The league, as it tends to do, responded by saying it would study the problem, that it didn't want to do too much, too fast.

Then in March, what might have been the final blow was levied when Zdeno Chara smashed Max Pacioretty's head into the stanchion next to Montréal's bench, breaking his neck and giving him a concussion. People flipped out. Fighting was one thing, but trying to decapitate a guy, which was what it looked like Chara was doing? Many thought it went too far. Surely, the league would have to act, to levy a suspension. Others weren't so certain, according to a poll taken at the time. In the end, no "supplemental discipline" was levied against Chara, the league offering its usual apologies—it was just a "hockey play," whatever that means, that happened so fast Chara probably didn't know who he hit and couldn't have known he would run the other guy into the pole. Most fans found that hard to imagine, with most agreeing that the NHL needed to ban checks to the head. In addition, many people said that they might be inclined to watch fewer games given the predisposition of the NHL version of hockey to violence. As *Maclean's* summarized things: "[This is] a potentially dangerous sign for a league that has always been able to count on its Canadian fans, come hell or high water." Still, NHL hockey went on as before.

And as if to add irony to the situation, it was Chara's teammate, Nathan Horton, who got the bad end of things in the Stanley Cup final when Vancouver defenseman Aaron Rome came across the blueline late and laid him out. The sight of Horton lying helpless on the ice, one hand grasping at a stick that was no longer there, his eyes open but glassy and his brain on another planet, should have been a big sign that read "Enough." Perhaps it was, as Rome was thrown out of the game and suspended for the balance of the series. The league's officials said at the time that they would also revisit "Rule 48," which concerns illegal checks to the head.

However, nothing will change until the culture of hockey changes. To some in the game, this kind of violence is simply the norm. Earlier in the playoffs of 2011, Boston's Patrice Bergeron was injured by an open-ice check from Philadelphia's Claude Giroux. Boston's GM, Peter Chiarelli, talked about the injury in a press conference, naming it as a concussion. The shocking thing, however, was the reaction on the TV show *NHL On the Fly*, where former player Bob Errey said of Chiarelli's truthful declaration about his player:

> *This is not good…. Do they have to report these concussions? I don't know why they would let anybody know, because you know the playoffs…anything goes. So if I know a guy is a little banged up and Patrice Bergeron comes back, I'm not that concerned with his health if I'm the Tampa Bay Lightning* [Boston's next opponent] *right now. This is about winning the Stanley Cup. This is about a childhood dream, and if Patrice Bergeron is out there he's going to be in a tight situation there when you're in a corner and can get an elbow up and, uh, you know, who knows?*

He added a sort of excuse by saying, "I hate to say that—that's the way the game is played on the ice."

Errey, without being conscious of it perhaps, encapsulates the discussion of violence in hockey perfectly: it happens. Certain people are chosen for it by virtue of their job as NHL players. The dream matters more than the consequences of your actions for another person.

Only time will tell whether the limit has been reached, but one thing is certain—nothing about the recent events is any different from the long history of violence that has characterized the game. Nothing, except perhaps that each of the five injured players from Savard to Horton is a skilled guy, not a scrub, and that each of them has the handsome good looks of someone you might imagine would marry your daughter— they can't be dismissed as inhuman thugs, in other words. Maybe, somehow, that is the tipping point between action and inaction to correct the seeming imbalance between the violence and niceness central to the game.

However, if nothing happens and the game remains as violent as it has been, the only conclusion is that, while most Canadians don't condone this type of behaviour, they reserve a spot for it in hockey, and that probably betrays the centrality of violence in the Canadian imagination that can be traced all the way back to Vimy Ridge.

A Country Called "Hockey"

More Than Canada

Canada may be synonymous with hockey, and the nation's history and values may be a product of the game, yet the sport has outstretched the physical boundaries of our country in recent days. Now, there's another, semi-mythical "country" whose boundaries overlay the U.S. and Canada. The entity in question is the country of hockey, and it's not a geographical construct, nor a political one. Perhaps it's better to call it the country of "Hockey," and Hockey has its own citizenship, bonding experiences, royalty, deities, a language and even a break-off nation within a nation.

Citizenship

With the salary cap in the NHL, it is most unlikely that the two greatest players in the game, whoever they are at a given moment, will ever play on the same NHL team at the peak of their careers. The fact that the best two right now—Crosby and

Ovechkin—are from different countries, Canada and Russia, also means that they will never play together in any meaningful international game (except for the NHL All-Star game, which as fans know, is nowhere close to the normal calibre of play in the league). Yet international hockey tournaments, like the Canada Cup of 1987, form bonds between players, and with fans, by uniting players who are normally divided by the boundaries established by their NHL affiliations. Former foes become heroes, and fans band together to urge them on to win. The aftermath of these tournaments points up the first feature of the country of Hockey—transnational citizenship.

In 1987, for the only time in their heyday, Wayne Gretzky and Mario Lemieux stepped onto the ice together on the same squad. They made magic in the Canada Cup series that will likely never be forgotten. The three games of the finals, Canada versus the Soviet Union, all went 6–5. The Russians won the first game. The second was captured by Canada in OT, Gretzky feeding Lemieux. The third was a similar feed, but at the end of regulation. Canada had won!

At the time, hockey seemed to be as pure and perfect as it could be, with Gretzky in the midst of his Oilers run and Lemieux just finding his stride in Pittsburgh. Little did anyone imagine that a year later, The Great One would be off to LA never to hoist another Cup, or that Super Mario would lead the Pens to two Stanley Cups to open the next decade. Fans knew only that their team had done what Team Canada had done 15 years earlier when they defeated the bitter Soviet rivals in 1972, gaining a victory that also reprised a Canada Cup loss to the Soviet team in 1981.

What mattered in the aftermath of 1987 was not that one of these guys was making his life in the U.S., nor that the Stanley Cup that each player was so desperate to win (or win again, in Gretzky's case) had recently spent four years living on Long Island rather than on Canadian soil. What mattered was that this victory bound these two great players to us, by creating a super-country called "Hockey." Who, after that, would dare to boo Lemieux when he showed up to play a game in an "away" NHL city? Only those people who were not part of the country of Hockey.

After the 1987 series, a fan could never forget watching these men and rooting for them. Even though the regular rivalries of the NHL took over once again as the NHL season rolled around, there was always the feeling of sympathy for players like Ray Bourque or Brian Propp or Kelly Hrudey, even when they later played on enemy turf, such as in Montréal or Toronto. And the superstars—Gretzky, Lemieux, Messier, Glenn Anderson and others—would be celebrated for the memories they had created for fans, no matter where they went. Loyalty to the NHL teams gave way to love for events like the Canada Cup. It was a moment in the past when something greater was at stake than the Stanley Cup, if that was possible.

Similarly, after the 2010 Vancouver Games, people who might have booed Crosby just out of spite, or given Luongo the works because he sometimes seems too big for the game, knew that these players and whichever man on their favourite team shared a spot on the Olympic roster with them were united at a deep level. Their gold medals would always, at least in an imaginary sense, be hanging around their necks and marking their affiliation as teammates.

Taking It to the Street

The social rituals that bond people as a community form the second feature of life in the country we call Hockey. The customs associated with the game rescue fans from their usual suburban malaise and create a vibrancy of public life not often experienced in contemporary North America. Think of a picture of any European capital on a summer's day. The image is of men with rolled-up sleeves playing bocce in the centre of tiny parks, or of people strolling about after a late dinner, or of kids playing soccer in alleyways. Each knows the other; everyone feels a part of something shared.

Canadians also have a vibrant urban life in the great cities, but largely speaking, even in places like Calgary, Vancouver and Montréal, the car reigns. It has become fashionable for the younger generation to live and work near downtown, perhaps living close to the office and enjoying nightlife in the evenings, especially on weekends. But when it comes time to have kids and raise a family, most Canadians do a similar thing: they retreat to the 'burbs and drive to work.

A large part of Canadians' memories of their childhood was formed by playing hockey on neighbourhood streets, but downtown was an alien zone. It was a place your class went to for a field trip but wasn't somewhere you would embrace. Is it any wonder, then, that to most Canadians, the street is not a place where shops and restaurants crowd the ground floor and the upstairs is the place where people live? However, in the country of Hockey, the street has been reclaimed as a zone of shared celebration—for the adults those street hockey players became.

When the days of March give way to the playoff nights of April, citizens know that it's time to party. It's exactly as philosopher Mikhail Bakhtin described when talking about the medieval version of carnival: "Carnival is not a spectacle seen by the people; they live in it, and everyone participates because its very idea embraces all the people. While carnival lasts, there is no other life outside it."

This need for a yearly Bacchanalia may in part stem from the fact that in Canada and the U.S., there is no nationally celebrated annual carnival (not forgetting the Québec Winter Carnival or New Orleans' Mardi Gras). It's different in Rio de Janeiro, where every February, everyone has a chance for a last blowout party—on the streets—to signal the beginning of the time of renunciation that is Lent. Citizens in the country of Hockey, by contrast, have internalized the idea that their carnival doesn't come on a religious calendar, but on the secular one devised each year by the NHL, and so when the playoffs start, so does the party. And the celebration only intensifies when a hometown team ends up making the Stanley Cup final, though this is probably more true in Canada than in the U.S.

In Calgary in 2004, the "Red Mile" became the site of revelry. In Edmonton in 2006, it was Whyte Avenue, dubbed the "Blue Mile," and in Ottawa in 2007, the "Sens Mile." In Vancouver in 2011, Granville Street absorbed the faithful. These spots were popular and were crowded with thousands of fans, even when the games were not being played at home.

The problem with these spontaneous street celebrations was that they got out of hand, at times turning dangerous. Some have questioned the situation in Calgary as exploitative in its practice of encouraging women to, politely stated, "show themselves." Public drunkenness also became an issue, so much so that by the 2006 playoffs, the police were involved, keeping things in order.

In one famous incident captured on film and shown on YouTube, two young women are showing the crowd their bodies, when somewhere an explosion is heard. You can hear the crowd cursing, but what's intriguing is that they seem more angry at the stupidity of the bomb-thrower than at the criminality of his actions. It's all in good fun, the tape seems to suggest. One person who commented on the video said it best: "It's not even hockey fans anymore, just idiots that are there just to make asses of themselves."

In Edmonton in 2006, fans gathered after the Oilers won a playoff game against the Sharks, and according to newspaper reports, a small group turned violent and ended up taking on the police, who were in riot gear. The celebrants were a little bit drunk, of course, but one of the cops makes an interesting comment: "I shudder to think what would happen if (the Oilers) in fact won the series here in Edmonton." Actually, Bakhtin addresses this behaviour, too, explaining that carnival is an event filled with violence and debasement. Was the crowd having fun? That all depends upon how you define "fun." Were they taking part in a bonding ritual? Certainly.

The tragedy in Edmonton was that two men were stabbed on the street, ruining the celebration and causing city officials to declare that the situation had gotten out of hand. One statement is particularly revealing for its understated, quite Canadian, way of describing the action. "There was also a significant amount of generally rowdy behaviour," reported the CTV. Ya think?

Is any of this rowdy behaviour a reflection on hockey itself? Well, aside from having been spawned in the shadow of the playoffs, there's a curious parallel, in the Edmonton case at least, to what happened on the rink during the Oilers'

1998–99 season. On that night, Joe Murphy and Mike Rathje ended up in a brawl that also involved some of their team-mates in the hallway between the players' benches. Was there a model here for future violence? Depends if you buy the Michael Moore argument in *Bowling for Columbine* that living near where they produce weapons of war infuses local kids with a violent sensibility. If you agree with Moore's theory, it's not a stretch to say that the Edmonton fans were merely re-enacting what they had seen their heroes do, albeit on a somewhat time-delayed basis.

The city of Ottawa revived the tradition of street celebration in 2007 when their team went on a run that ended in the finals, but it did things differently. First, the carnival was pre-planned, rather than spontaneous, as in Calgary. Second, the cops were involved from the start, saying that they would keep things in check. By 2010, when the Sens were again hopeful for playoff success, the institutionalization of the celebrations had gone all the way. "City council is expected to approve…[a] designation of the stretch of Elgin Street…as 'Sens Mile' on Wednesday [April 14]," according to news reports. A couple of local business owners came up with the idea in the hopes of creating some excitement (and, obviously, to bring in more customers). What you have here is the country of Canada starting to rein in the more wild and spontaneous country of Hockey.

As media reported on the event, they focused on how local businesses were encouraged to decorate for the occasion, and how fans were being asked to come out to support the hockey team. But they also warned of the limit that officials foresaw to the celebration: "If crowds get too large on game days, the city plans to control traffic in the area."

Ottawa's solution reveals a very Canadian reaction to the street partying. It starts with a grassroots movement, becomes institutionalized among citizens, gets out of hand and boom! The government steps in to "help." In so doing, whatever fun might have been had gets leeched out, and the party becomes a shadow version of its real self, accompanied by warnings of what will happen if things get, shall we say, "too real."

Of course, in light of the mess in Vancouver after the last game of the 2011 final series, it's perhaps good that such measures are taken if things get out of hand. The Stanley Cup final, as everyone knows, went to seven games that spring. People in Vancouver crowded the streets each time the Canucks played, whether at home or on the road. To many, the TV images of crowds estimated at upwards of 100,000 spoke of urban harmony and love of the game. And had the Canucks won the Cup, that's probably the story we'd all have come to know. But when the team lost, things changed from peaceful to riotous in a hurry. Explanations for the mayhem ranged from Mayor Robertson's declaration that the events were "disgraceful and shameful and by no means represent[ed] the city of Vancouver" to NDP MP Pat Martin's claim that "We have to remember that those weren't hockey fans trashing the most beautiful city in the world...; they were thugs and thieves and lunatics." Some of them, it might be argued, had been hockey fans a couple of hours before the looting started, but that doesn't fit all that well with this version of events. Martin went on, "Hockey is founded on a code of honour that prescribes dignified behaviour in victory and defeat."

True enough, but there's a long history of street violence related to the game (though saying so is not to condone it). To cite a final example, Montréalers turn their streets into a playground as often as they can. In 1955, it turned destructive, and in 2010, it was the same, with fires on streets marking the Canadiens' unlikely playoff series wins over favourites Washington and Pittsburgh.

Taking either a cynical or a realistic view, one official was reported by the CBC to have said that "more violence and looting in Montréal are inevitable as the Canadiens continue their quest for the Stanley Cup" after having won their first two series. City counsellor Claude Trudel said that further violence would come, "Simply because it happens time and time again. Time and time [sic] and game after game." A store manager said, "As a business, every time there is a [playoff] game...in Montréal, you are worried."

News outlets in other parts of the country and beyond were quick to pick up the story, and the U.S. version cited Montréal's history of hockey violence. ESPN talked about the looting that took place after the victory over Boston in 2008, and riots after the 1993 and 1986 Stanley Cup victories, and said, of course, "[t]he most famous was in 1955 when Canadiens great Maurice Richard was suspended and fans took to the street to cause such havoc that Richard had to make a public appeal for calm." In something of an echo of the Ottawa approach, Montréal set up a "Festive Zone" outside the Bell Centre, where people could have fun without fear of violence. The police believe that it was just a few hundred who ended up becoming violent as the night went on.

So there you have it. Calgarians and Edmontonians might have a newfound sense of the possibilities for public celebration, and Ottawa might have tried its own version on for size. But to really understand the place where hockey inspires at least some people to carry on a tradition of carnival violence (a practice going back 1000 years or more), you must head to Montréal, where some of the original rules of citizenship in the country of Hockey were formulated and continue to exist.

Sadly, the crowds in Vancouver after the Canucks lost their final series appeared all too aware of the lessons Montréal offers to those who see celebration as equivalent to a rampage of car burning and police baiting. And aside from the aforementioned explanations, one other surfaced days after the riot. Journalist Tiara Latourneau made the case that the disempowered in society can feel a part of the larger whole through hockey, but that their sense of belonging to something bigger than themselves is dashed when their team loses. The result is that their "contribution [to society] is summarily dismissed. Suddenly, shockingly, the disempowered national is...without an avenue for participation and contemptuous of a society in which she is not significant, honourable, or noticeable." Empowered people feel a similar loss, but they go back to their real lives as citizens who work, vote, and contribute to society. They know that "hockey is just a game." But is it? Latourneau, without being aware of it of course, makes a case for the power of the country of Hockey and its place in people's lives. Where she's mistaken is in claiming that for the empowered, it's easy to go back to normal life (she calls it "the real thing"). Neither for them nor for the disempowered does life go on the same way after a hockey-style carnival, especially the kind that results from their team losing.

To end on a positive note, one more example of fans attempting to take back the street is worth a look. This one grew out of the pure, organic spirit of sports as the excitement from the Olympic creed infused the city of Vancouver in the happier days of February 2010—it was related to the whole idea of the "essential thing is not to have conquered but to have fought well," which Olympians recite as their motto. Or maybe things got cracking because it was natural for the people spilling out of the main ice arena or returning to town from the other arena used for the tournament's matches to find themselves in a crush of other fans who shared their passions and joys, not just for the Games but for the game.

For fans of the home team, the Olympic hockey tournament in Vancouver went from low to high, with the street being, on one Sunday, the place for mourning, and on the next, for joy. On February 21, Team Canada lost 5–3 to the U.S. Buffalo-born player Patrick Kane described the events, putting them into perspective in how they played out on the streets. He was quoted as saying, "even downtown Vancouver was sullen. It's almost like we shut down the city."

A week later, as everyone knows, the Canadian men's hockey team won the gold medal with an OT goal. The red sweaters of Team Canada were everywhere, on Robson Street, through the back streets of Gastown and on every corner of Vancouver, as well as other places in Canada. Every news station in Canada and elsewhere documented the celebrations, but one account by journalist Frank Fitzpatrick seems particularly clever in capturing the spirit of the moment: "The red sea didn't part Sunday afternoon. It rose in a great wave of national elation." Is there any irony that this description appeared in an American newspaper?

Fitzpatrick adds, "Long after Canadian players had gold medals draped around their perspiring necks, the streets of Vancouver shook with excitement. Flags, voices and spirits were raised in a riotous celebration that extended deep into the night."

And just to give this writer, presumably American, his credit, note that he puts the victory into perspective: "These Olympics, but maybe especially today's riveting victory, had to erase some of Canada's inferiority complex about the United States. Now this hockey-mad nation has another memory to add to the 1972 win over the Soviets and the 2002 gold medal at Salt Lake City," he says.

Were all of the people celebrating this victory Canadian? Hard to tell, though probably most were. So how is it that an American commentator can so accurately capture the spirit of the situation? Because these revellers are not just citizens of the nation of Canada. They belong to the country of Hockey, and their passport doesn't require a maple leaf symbol inside it to allow them to be a resident of that nation.

It has become natural, it appears, for citizens of the country of Hockey to play out both their hockey sorrows and their hockey joys on the streets. While the history of such celebrations is sometimes tame—think of the familiar pictures of the Montréal Canadiens players riding in convertibles in 1971, politely smiling and waving as they wear their dated day-glow yellow and pink shirts—modern versions have tapped into a more primal side of life and perhaps even surprised a few people in their ugliness, which is why street parties have been reined in. But when such celebrations occur spontaneously and without violence, as in Vancouver in 2010, there's a beauty in them that isn't replicated anyplace else.

Hockey Royalty

Question: "How do you make a small fortune?"
Answer: "Start with a big one, and go racing."

It's an old joke, and you might substitute a few other things for "racing," but it seems generally true, as I was once told, that people who make a lot of money eventually end up buying one of two items—sports cars or art.

In Canada, some of the super-rich (like the Asper family of Winnipeg, whose fortune was made in the media business) endow museums or give to charities, but in the country of Hockey, the moneyed prefer to own a hockey team. In the 1980s, owners like Peter Pocklington became household names. In more recent days, it has been Oren Koules and would-be owner Jim Balsillie as well as Buffalo's new owner, Terry Pegula. As owners, they become a sort of royalty in the country of Hockey, watching from their luxury box, which becomes a de facto throne room.

Sitting up there, these owners occasionally get their mugs on TV (and don't think they don't know that that happens). As the playoffs go on, they are seen more frequently on the broadcast—the commentary always the same: "So-and-so is really a great owner. He and his family have done a lot for this town. They'll be deserving winners." The impulse on the part of the owner is not simply to hoist that trophy, though, or appear on TV, though goodness knows those are strong pulls. Rather, the idea must lurk at the corners of their minds that owning a hockey team will impart respectability and cement their position as rising stars in the establishment (or if they are Canadian, perhaps the "Establishment"). Of course, there's also the wish-fulfilment aspect, with the owner making up for his own failings as a player who didn't make it out of the house league.

In the old days, guys bought a team with the intention of running it—think of Conn Smythe in Toronto. He parlayed a bet on a football match into double what he started with, then did it again on a hockey game. With the money he won, he had the seed to gather a group of investors, and together, they bought the Toronto St. Pats. Then he proceeded to run the team his way.

Nowadays, owners generally take a more hands-off approach. Most of them, obviously, are successful business people who hire the best staff to manage their business and then leave them alone to do that. They are content to sit in the luxury box and watch the game, hoping someday to appear on the ice surface to take hold of the Stanley Cup.

While the owner stays nicely in the background, the team's GM runs the show. Actually, the examples that come to mind of this kind of owner run more to Americans—Mike Ilitch in Detroit, Henry Samueli in Anaheim. Each is a presence for fans, and recognizable at trophy time, but neither messes around with what the hockey guys are doing at other times. And both of these men have been successful with their approach.

U.S. businessman George Gillett, the former owner of the Montréal Canadiens, provides a similar example. He bought the Habs in early 2001 as an investment and because he had come to love the sport. Early on, he recognized that he ought to make the public aware of who he was and diffuse any lack of trust they might have had in him as an outsider. Then he left the operation to run itself. As Habs historian Jenish says, Gillett got all three keys right on the day he was introduced as the new owner: "He paid homage to the team's great tradition. He assured his audience that he would never move the Canadians out of Montréal. He promised to leave the management of the franchise to the professionals."

Occasionally, Gillett would check in, enjoying about half of the home games in a given year, and his son relocated to Montréal (from Colorado) to keep an eye on things. However, he never tried to usurp any of the glory and tradition of the storied team for himself, but allowed it to continue, making the team's best asset work for him. You kind of wonder how many Canadians, given the chance to own the Habs, would have played it that well.

Some owners—1980s bigshot Pocklington comes to mind—become stars in their own right. It's not very Canadian, this impulse to upstage the rest of the crew, and not very team-oriented. Maybe that's why such an approach usually ends in ruin. Pocklington ended up in California, the U.S. government after him for tax evasion after a bankruptcy. In the spring of 2010, he was convicted of perjury, with his sentencing scheduled on the beautifully ironic August 9, the anniversary of the day that he had traded Wayne Gretzky to Los Angeles 22 years earlier. The meting out of punishment was delayed, however, and he was sentenced near Halloween. Pocklington got six months home confinement, plus two years probation, some fines and community service.

Oren Koules parlayed entertainment business dollars into his ownership stake in the Lightning, but the dance didn't last long. Jim Balsillie, for his part, can't seem to get his chance at joining hockey royalty. Maybe the NHL thinks he would be too big for the job. In a funny, way, he seems more American in his approach than Canadian, perhaps proving that acting as royalty in the country of Hockey is not a matter of one's geographical country of origin, but of taking on a role that fits the way that owners are expected to act.

It ought to be noted, however, that Balsillie's effort to bring a team back home, relocating a U.S. franchise to Hamilton, is distinctly Canadian in its intention. Opinions are all over the map about whether this is a good idea, but logic seems to say that it makes more sense to try to sell a product where there's a ready market than where none exists. Many in the country of Hockey say "Long Live King Balsillie," and hopefully soon.

The Language Non-barrier

The country of Hockey has its own language. "We have to get our elbows up." "He's good at digging in the corners." "Who's going to wear the *C*?" "He's a little puck-shy." "It's like trading Gretzky!" Hockey gets its language from the rink, and all except the last example of hockeyspeak mentioned above appeal to the same value—courage. The trading Gretzky thing—well, maybe Mr. Pocklington is the one to ask for a definition of that. Where would hockey fans be without these kind of expressions to help explain what needs to happen when the going gets a little tough? Each time people use these phrases, they mark themselves as insiders whose frame of reference extends into a certain field of symbols. Fans, or citizens of this realm, don't worry about running up against a language barrier.

Other sports also have their own language. The most obvious comes from baseball. "Three strikes and you're out," which can apply to everything from guys trying to pick up women in bars to offenders sentenced to mandatory life terms after being convicted of three serious crimes. "In the red zone" means that a football team is inside the prime scoring area (from the 20-yard line to the goal line), but it can also mean a salesperson is about to close a deal. In cricket, "He tried to bowl me a googly" might sound somewhere between goofy and vaguely sexual in its reference, but it actually means something like, "He tried to pitch me a curve," which, of course, demands a special knowledge to understand.

For those new to the country of Hockey, the language occasionally demands translation or interpretation, and luckily for them, there are at least three hockey dictionaries on the market at the moment, including one that I helped write called *How to Speak Hockey*. It makes sense when you think about it, because when you enter a new country, speaking the language certainly makes life easier.

The flip side is players who come to the NHL from abroad. At first, they are hesitant in their interviews, not being comfortable speaking English. Pretty soon, they're chatting away when the microphone winds up in front of them. It's tempting to think, "Gee, that guy has picked up a working knowledge of English (or French, if he plays for the Habs) pretty quickly." In fact, he likely hasn't. He may know 10 to 15 stock phrases that will get him by regardless if his team wins or loses, or whether he scores or is responsible for a goal. But ordering a meal in a restaurant or trying to explain something to a plumber over the phone might be different. What matters, though, is that he can understand the lingua franca of the country he lives in, and that's the isolated world of his hockey team.

Deities

A few years ago, it was proposed that all potential new Canadian citizens be given a test to determine their fitness to live in Canada. This was in addition to the standard set of questions that every applicant for citizenship between the ages 18 and 54 must answer. If the country of Hockey ever decided to institute such a requirement, one of the best questions might be this one: "Do the hockey gods exist?" If the applicant stuttered out a startled "Of course" with sufficient conviction, that person's application would immediately be accepted. And what of the applicants who replied "No"? Well, the "government" would require a little more time to check up on their cases.

The hockey gods are a lot like Santa Claus, a famous Canadian (at least if you go by his H0H 0H0 postal code). Most people vaguely believe Santa exists, but at certain times in their lives, he is easier to believe in than at other times. The hockey gods, likewise, are more real in certain moments and situations, and less so in others. They can affect the outcome of a game, from the mundane to the spectacular.

Consider goalies who are hot in the playoffs, taking their teams far past where they should have gone. Or goals that bounce off four bodies—so-called "seeing-eye shots"—that can change the course of games. How else can these events be explained except as the power of a deity?

But the hockey gods' work often is more impressive than that. Consider the case of Bill Barilko, who scored the last goal in Toronto's Stanley Cup win in 1951, putting a puck past Montréal's Gerry McNeil in overtime of game five. That summer, he disappeared while on a fishing expedition. The Leafs at that time were enjoying their fifth Stanley Cup in seven years. Though Detroit was about to assert itself, winning three of the next four, and Montréal was going to take over for the latter half of the 1950s, the Leafs were the preeminent team as the decade began.

Barilko's goal was the last one that would end a season for Toronto with a Cup victory for 11 years. But it's not just that they won again in 1962 that is remarkable. The hockey gods come into things in that it was in this year that Barilko's remains were discovered with the small plane he was in when he died. Odd coincidence? Maybe to some, but to members of the country of Hockey, it was proof that there is a Supreme Being in the picture, or rather, a pantheon of them.

A Breakaway Nation

The curious case of Toronto, the breakaway nation within a nation, is the last element of the country of Hockey. This place, often called "Leafs Nation," is part mythical and part real and is where dreams ought to go to die. Instead, they live on in ghost form, giving citizens of this place a way of defining themselves that makes them a part of the larger group of hockey fans. Yet at the same time, they are separated from the rest by their obstinate refusal to look at life as it really is and accept the mediocrity of their team. For the other citizens in the country of Hockey, the existence of the Leafs, and their supporters' stubborn persistence, provides a contrast to the everyday devotion of the average fan, showing that we should care more about our team and what it gives us, win or lose.

Like a rogue republic in the former USSR, Leafs Nation is a place unto itself. If Toronto is Canada's New York City, then it must be significant that the Maple Leafs are a complete inversion of the Yankees. In fact, one Winnipeg reporter said just that a few years ago. "The Leafs are like the Yankees, except for all the winning, of course. But the reality is the Leafs are the biggest cash cow in a herd of Canadian hockey jerseys."

The New York team spends money like mad—their payroll dwarfs those of the other teams in MLB—and they win. For a while, they had a fallow period, not taking the World Series between 1978 and the mid-1990s, but then they started to win again, becoming World Series champions in 1996 and again from 1998 to 2000. Even casual fans probably remember the postseason in fall 2001. In the shadow of 9/11, Mayor Rudy Giuliani sat in the stands, often accompanied by his son, and watched while the Yankees contested for their fourth World Series in a row, albeit in a seven-game losing effort to the Arizona Diamondbacks.

They didn't become champions again for several years, and then they changed residence, across the street. "The New Yankee Stadium," they called it, and people might have wondered if the ghosts had accompanied the move—the situation resembling the Habs' trying to take the spirit of the old Forum with them when they moved to what is now the Bell Centre. They did that by lighting and extinguishing a torch in the Forum, then lighting another in the new arena. The Yankees did it with a closing ceremony after the baseball season ended in 2008. It didn't take long to prove that they'd done it right. That first fall in their new home, 2009, the team won its 27th World Series.

The Leafs, in stunning contrast to the Yankees' record of success, have been perennial underachievers since NHL expansion, despite generally being among the league's big spenders, salary-wise. This wouldn't be remarkable, except that their fans are so rabid, so intense and so confident that things will turn around that they make it difficult not to feel a sense of helpless frustration as the years of losses mount.

The period of Toronto's dynasty is long in the past. Since the team won its last Stanley Cup in 1967, all the other teams in the Original Six have won at least one. Eleven expansion teams had also hoisted the Cup as of the end of the 2011 season. Rather than being an example of strength and virtue, the Maple Leafs are a flop, digging themselves ever newer holes to fall into.

Are the Leafs Canada's team? Ask people in rural Ontario who they follow, and for many, it will be the Leafs. But others hold onto Boston, perhaps going back to their interest in Orr's career. Still others favour Montréal, because it was the team whose games they could listen to on the radio or watch on TV as youngsters. But ask most anyone in Toronto, and the answer will be the same: "Leafs Nation. I'm part of it." Is it peer pressure? Or is it an attempt to create self-definition or the sort of pride that motivates outsiders and underdogs the world over?

It makes sense that Canada would choose Toronto over Montréal. If the language divide played a part, then a large portion of the fans in our country could take comfort in being with the blue and white. The Leafs do, after all, wear the symbol of the country on their sweater. But being a member of Leafs Nation also subjects fans to continued battering, disappointment and defeat. It's almost as if there's a badge of pride to be earned for sticking with the team even though they have been so bad for so long.

Why don't the Leafs get any better? One of the reasons is that they have a history of trying to fix things too quickly. It's easy for a new GM to blow up the old roster and sign a bunch of new guys for too much money. Look at the move to acquire Jason Blake. A bust. Granted, he was ill during his first year in TO, and it's a miracle that he played at all, but if he was going to play, he should be judged by what he did on the ice, and that was not much. Funny enough, when he went to Anaheim, he reverted to form with .58 points a game to finish out the 2009–10 season. What happened once he escaped the vortex of Leafs Nation? Perhaps Toronto's expectations were simply too high. But that's got a long history in the city.

The Leafs' failure as a club might suggest a hollowness at the metropolitan core of our sparsely settled nation. Toronto seems like another world when someone from the nearby cities of Oshawa or Peterborough steps into it, with its tall buildings and cosmopolitan sense. Watch the Toronto news, and you'll see stories of what we like to call U.S.-style violence played out in neighbourhoods that seem alien in their makeup to most Canadians. Toronto has a gritty side, like New York City. In some ways, TO is a hard place to live in, and it's becoming harder. In such a place, people need something to hang onto.

The trouble is, the hockey team that represents the city, far from holding up a flag for organization, drive and success, seems to espouse an ever-changing and never-clear set of values. Maybe in some ways that makes sense. While Canada, demographically, is relatively uniform along the French-English divide, Toronto has a mix of dozens of different language groups and people from all over the globe. That's all good—except that strategies need to be developed to help newcomers accommodate to their new surroundings.

Until that happens, chaos, at least in limited terms, will be a part of life in the big city.

Leafs Nation might be a response to the sprawling disorganization that is modern Toronto. Over against an increasingly fragmented and violent environment, people can hold onto one common core value in following the team. It binds them and erases their differences by incorporating them into a larger whole. Maple Leafs hockey gives the country's newest residents, a good number of whom land in Toronto, a quick ticket to acculturation and a relationship to the country of Hockey.

Being a member of Leafs Nation might also be a way of showing strength, but as a form of denial. Standing together is a signal to others that says, "Hey—we're not going to discuss our failings with you. We can talk about them among ourselves, but you butt out." There is strength in numbers.

If there was some kind of curse to fall back on, like the Red Sox used to have, or if there was a kind of "loveable loser" mantle to wear like the one the Cubs and their fans don, it might be a little bit less embarrassing for the Leafs. As it is, nobody has come up with such an enabling myth for their failure, and so the team, and the fans, soldier on year by year, ever hopeful that the newest renovation plan will work. It might be a good if one of these years, one of the strategies did succeed. Leafs' fans would not be less loud, but their winning would allow the rest of the hockey world to point to the team's record of achievement and offer an invitation back into the country of Hockey based on their no longer needing to take pride in their outsider status.

The problem with the great hopes and dashed expectations in Toronto isn't just that the Leafs don't win the Cup. Twenty-eight other teams every year don't, either. The issue is that members of this tribe see themselves as being in the centre of the hockey universe. Although the league isn't run from TO, the Hockey Hall of Fame is there, after all, and the expectations are that the team will represent more than the town—it will represent the game. Citizens of the country of Hockey would likely offer another opinion, suggesting that no *one* place can definitively label itself the centre of the hockey world. That's because Hockey is a country without borders, defined more by the spirit of its inhabitants than by its geographical location.

That's a Wrap

All the elements necessary to define a country have been covered, from a ruling aristocracy to gods to common culture to the oddball cousin who is, somewhat regretfully, still a part of the family. This country of Hockey is not quite coincident with the country of Canada as a whole, overlapping in some places but diverging in others, but that's okay because it suggests that the hockey-mad citizens of the nation to the south can also belong, with geography being less important than passion.

Afterword

Hockey Is My Country

My country is hockey. But it's not entirely so. These days, there are a lot of Canadians who don't value the game, don't play it, don't watch it or haven't grown up with it. That might be because they were raised elsewhere, or it might be that their culture is not hockey-centric. Scarborough, Ontario, it was recently reported in the *Globe and Mail*, has lost about three-quarters of its hockey-playing youngsters. The population of the city is largely made up of immigrants and their children, and soccer is now the game of choice. It is played year-round indoors. The city recently even changed one of its hockey rinks, the Clairlea, into the Scarborough Soccer Centre. To many, that's a sad reflection of a demographic shift away from a core set of shared experiences and, hence, values, of being Canadian.

In the end, the formulation I have been using in this book (and as its title) might need to be reversed. Instead of "my country is hockey," for a significant number of people in Canada, "hockey is my country." That is, the game is a refuge for them, a place of comfort in the face of a changing Canada. Hockey offers people a place to go, literally and figuratively, when the world outside their front doors isn't giving them what they want. As such, hockey might just be the last vestige of the Canada that many of us yearn for.

In the 1970s, Pierre Trudeau predicted a future multi-cultural Canada. At the time of the 1972 Summit Series, the country's population was about 21.8 million, the majority descended from Western European immigrants. Nearly four decades later, the non-Canadian-born population, more than half of whom are from places other than Europe, is over 5.4 million, according to Stats Canada. If hockey is the glue that holds the culture together, then it's obviously incumbent upon those who love the game, maybe even the country, to bring these new folks into the fold.

Yet perhaps our proselytizing for hockey betrays a fear that the Canada we've known won't be the Canada of the future if we fail to recruit people without hockey backgrounds into the country of Hockey. And what if it doesn't work? What if indoor hockey rinks are continually converted into indoor soccer venues or facilities for other sports? That can't happen for two reasons. For one, those who love the game won't let it happen. The second reason that hockey can't vacate the centre of our common culture is that the game is much bigger than it appears to be. It's not just something people watch a couple of nights a week in front of their TVs or play in beer leagues or discuss around the office water cooler. The game is everywhere in Canada, and it is as strong as its history and its heroes.

Those who love the game and want to share it with non-hockey-philes are making significant efforts to capture a new generation whose background doesn't include hockey. Turn on the radio during a Leafs game, and you'll hear a broadcast in Punjabi. Even the recently revived 1970s icon of the game, Peter Puck, has become bilingual. (Now you know what he was doing on his long hiatus.)

How successful has this attempt to bring new Canadians into the game been? Shortly after the Punjabi experiment in Toronto began, the broadcast boasted 100,000 listeners. And what does the fact that it is being attempted say? That Canadians want to be inclusive. We embrace the chance to share this game we love with our newcomers. And perhaps for the cynical, there's also the commercial revenue potential in including this new group of fans.

The Healing Power of Hockey

Perhaps the greatest attribute of hockey—and one reason it will survive the onslaughts of Canada's changing people-scape—is its healing power. How can this be if the game is so fierce, and if it has been the staging ground for as bitter a rivalry as the one which divided Montréal and Québec City, for instance, and led to those all-in fights of a few decades ago? Consider that the game becomes a refuge for people who lose a limb via its iteration as "sledge hockey," and you have your answer.

This sport, invented in the 1960s and part of the Paralympics since Lillehammer in 1994, sits players on tiny sledges, or sleds, and has them propel themselves with picks on the ends of their sticks. It's a full-contact game as played at the Olympic level, and it's rough. The 2010 gold-medal-winning Canadian player Raymond Grassi, for example, says that when he hits someone and they fly into the boards, "It's like hitting a brick wall." But if that sounds like more of the same good old hockey violence, consider that many of the players who come to the game do so after horrible events in their lives, which at first, seem like they would take away all hopes of an athletic career.

Jean Labonte served as captain of the 2010 squad that won the gold medal for Canada in Vancouver, and in August 2008 when I interviewed him over the phone, he described the game as a refuge, an antidote to the loss of his leg to cancer. After his surgery, he tried other sports, able-bodied ones, but when he sat on the sled and realized the power and speed of the game, he knew it was his passion.

Another way to look at sledge hockey is to marvel at the way that Canadians see hockey as an antidote when times are bad. People turn to the game as an escape from negative preoccupations. As the 2010 Canadian Paralympic goalie Paul Rosen says, "Through sport, you can have another life.... You know what, it's only a leg..." he continues. "Once you get over that, you realize life can be as good or better then [*sic*] before."

Terry Fox did not get famous for playing hockey, obviously. He grew up playing basketball in BC, but when he was a teenager, he lost his right leg to cancer. If he were alive today, he might have taken up sledge hockey, but back in the 1970s, the athletic outlet that inspired him was running.

His Marathon of Hope was as solitary as any personal journey could be, and the video of him out on vacant highways taking his shuffling hop-steps is almost heartbreaking, except that while you watch him, you might imagine Fox as a kind of mythical embodiment of all you know to be good about hockey players. He was courageous. He was oblivious to pain. He understood that he was the solitary leader, the captain, so to speak, of a team that was invisible yet ran alongside him every step of the way. Interesting to note is that when he made his stop in Toronto, Darryl Sittler, then captain of the Maple Leafs, gave Fox his 1980 NHL All-Star sweater, saying that Fox was the real superstar.

As is well known, Fox did not complete his cross-country journey. Cancer claimed him first. But Rick Hansen, inspired by Fox's efforts, undertook to circle the world in his wheelchair in the mid-1980s. He accomplished his Man in Motion World Tour in 26 months, and since that time, he has raised over $250 million for spinal cord research. A powerful symbol of what a person with a vision can achieve, he was honoured by being one of the people to participate in the Olympic Torch Relay for the Vancouver games. Like Fox, Hansen's venue was not hockey, but his spirit shares the qualities of the players who display the most grit and the deepest values of commitment to the game.

Had Fox and Hansen taken to the ice, they likely would have been the Bob Gainey or Doug Gilmour type. Not flashy or glamorous, but committed to the cause, able to make everyone on the ice look better because they did what they did. The modern-day equivalent can be seen in Ian Laperrière. He literally put his face in front of shots, and punches (though he also dished out a few of those), for the sake of the guys whose uniform colour he shared, whether that was blue, purple, burgundy or orange.

The bodies of these men aren't beautiful by the time the game is done with them. Fox had a stump where his leg should have been. Hansen cannot use his legs. Laperrière has a nose that hooks wildly. A bunch of his teeth are not his own. He is scarred. Gilmour, too, was missing some chompers before he had a fake set screwed in near the end of his career. But both of these hockey players, like Fox and Hansen, somehow made the best of the body that they had. With these guys, beauty is not what you see. It's what motivates them from deep in their gut, and those who play with them get it. Maybe there is another sport, perhaps boxing, where the sacrifices are similar and the devotion as severe. But no other sport has heroes with such vital human qualities.

There are twin themes here: that hockey is a tonic, and that the game is not played at a lesser level because it is the preoccupation of players who differ physically from the rest of the population. In fact, it is in the halting steps of the new skater—the bumpy path across natural ice trying to follow a puck that hops and skips away—or in the age-slowed progress of the fun league player that hockey lives its most vibrant life for most who love it and play it.

Playing for the Love of the Game

Perhaps the best way to measure the continued strength of the game and its ongoing presence in Canadian life is to look at women's hockey. The women's game, it is worth noting, is less like the NHL in certain respects and more like the game most of us play, although obviously the skating and puck handling are far superior at the elite level. Yet maybe the game women play is the repository of values that are purely Canadian—healthy competition in an atmosphere of restraint.

This could explain why we have so heartily embraced the achievements of the women who represent the country. Think about the Games in Salt Lake City in 2002. The men's team won, as hoped, and Canada went mad. But the women's team won gold too, and for them, it was revenge for having lost the first Olympic tournament their gender had been invited to, in 1998. Canadians enjoyed the men's win, but they knew that the next evening, or the one after that, these guys would all be back on their NHL rosters, earning somewhere around $25,000 per night for their work, some much more than that.

The women, however, would not be going anywhere else to play for money (with the notable exception of Hayley Wickenheiser, who played 23 pro games in Finland the following season). They would continue to toil for the symbol on the front of the sweater, as the old cliché goes. Now, this is not to discount that some of them could make bucks doing appearances or nabbing commercial contracts, and that's all great. But to get richer by the minute playing the game, that was not an option for them.

Eight years later, at the 2010 Olympics, the women's game was stronger, but the money still wasn't available. Fans in Vancouver seemed to get that the team was doing it purely for love of country. The crowd at the gold medal game, and outside the arena afterward, was jubilant—this win was pure, because for these women, hockey meant everything.

Women's hockey may be the last vestige of a time when the game was played for something other than pure profit. A former coach in the NHL, who will remain unnamed, once told me:

> It's amazing what takes over these guys.
> In my day [he played in the 1980s], guys hoped
> to retire with some money. But you knew
> you had to work the rest of your life. These
> days, the guys bring in those Condé Nast
> magazines, and they compare the prices of

beach-front vacation homes while they suit
up for practice. We would have never
dreamed of something like that.

What a contrast to a generation earlier. Musician and
writer Dave Bidini reports that his friend compares professional hockey players of the '60s and '70s to professional
musicians: "[B]oth took long bus rides, earned sparse incomes,
spent endless time in bars, stayed in countless bland hotels,
ingested a mountain of bad food, and played to half-full
houses." Both groups played for love.

For women in the game, it's about sacrifice more than
profit, and what is gained is pride. To take an American example, Cammi Granato, perhaps the greatest women's player ever,
if not one of the top two or three, says that she sacrificed, will-
ingly, a lot for hockey, including putting off starting a family
until she was in her late 30s. She also explained to me in
a phone interview in 2009 that every time she and her teammates went to the U.S. Olympic Center to train, it was like
being in college all over again, living in a dorm-type situation.
The only other adults who choose to live in similar conditions
are those who make a commitment to the armed forces!
Granato's reward, aside from a slew of medals including the
1998 gold, is a spot in the Hockey Hall of Fame.

No woman has yet made the NHL, though most people
recall that Manon Rhéaume came as close as any woman has,
playing two exhibition games for Tampa Bay a year apart in the

early 1990s. Richard Harrison captures her spirit most effectively in his poem "Rhéaume" when he describes her desire:

To be a woman and have it be her play that counts.
To stop the puck where the best are men....

This is what keeps a hockey dream alive and allows any person, regardless of gender, to state, "Hockey is my country."

The lesson we can take from the women's game has to do with the spirit of fair play, hard work and doing something just because it's the right thing to do. This is what inspires women to seek out hockey careers at the highest levels. U.S. player Angela Ruggiero delayed her off-ice career to go for the gold medal at the 2010 Games, according to a *USA Today* story, and after the game, she explained that "you really give your life to it, make a lot of sacrifices...so you're hoping to win that gold medal."

If someday one of these heroines manages to come forward and present the ability to compete with men, good for her. She'll deserve every Mercedes that her NHL salary will buy her. But the rest, players who give up their social life and time with family (or time spent viewing games on TV or watching others play) to pursue a hockey dream are like most Canadians. They know that no pot of gold awaits them at the end of this rainbow, but they also sense that they would not be happy if they abandoned the pursuit.

And so they go on, juggling jobs and practice times, living with the injuries and letting career aspirations outside the game wait, simply because the lure of hockey is so great. They will never win the Stanley Cup, most likely, but that doesn't matter. Neither will most of the rest of us. But that doesn't stop us from donning equipment late at night in the rec league to face the same foes we played against last week under the exact same circumstances. Bidini describes his own moment of realization of what hockey means as he ponders his amateur career: "Suddenly, I saw hockey for the subculture that it was—tribal, fetishistic, Canadian—a ritual that had been cloaked against much of the outside world, sort of like mumming or falconry." The game's value in life is much more than can be measured in dollars—it is what makes us who we are.

In all parts of hockey country, the dreams of young kids continue to be invaded by visions of Stanley Cup glory. Every player interviewed after winning the Cup says the same thing—that he had already won it 100 times, or 100,000, in his imagination. That sentiment is true for many Canadians, and if the irony of these dreams is that, sometimes, they keep you from living your real life, then what is a "real life" without hockey, anyway?

"The Hockey Sweater," Roch Carrier's great short story, captures the flavour of the game in a boy's life: "The winters of my childhood were long, long, seasons. We lived in three places—the school, the Church and the skating-rink—but our real life was on the skating-rink." No matter what the contradictions in modern Canada, our country will remain hockey because our deepest and truest values are shaped by the game.

Notes on Sources

A book like this builds on the work of writers who have explored similar events and themes. These days, many sources are available to the researcher, from books to print articles to web-based information. What follows is a list of my sources by chapter; print sources are listed first followed by web-based sources. I gratefully acknowledge the efforts of all those represented here.

Note that because of the variety of citation formats offered in electronic sources, and because I sometimes quote people who are themselves quoted within both print and electronic sources, the name of the person as mentioned in *My Country Is Hockey* is indicated in parentheses at the end of some entries for clarification.

Introduction
Brunt, Stephen. *Gretzky's Tears: Hockey, Canada, and the Day Everything Changed*. Toronto: Knopf Canada, 2009.

Holman, Andrew C. "Introduction: Canada's Game? Hockey and the Problem of Identity," in *Canada's Game: Hockey and Identity*. Andrew C. Holman, ed. Montreal and Kingston: McGill-Queen's University Press, 2009.

http://content.usatoday.com/communities/gameon/post/2010/02/usa-canada-hockey-most-watched-sports-program-in-history-in-canada/1
http://individual.utoronto.ca/mfkolarcik/blueandwhite.html
www.hockeycanada.ca

Chapter One
Boswell, Randy. "Canada's Game Not So Canadian: Earlier Version of Hockey Played in Scotland in 1700s." *The Vancouver Sun*, May 15, 2010.

McKinley, Michael. *Putting a Roof on Winter: Hockey's Rise from Sport to Spectacle*. Vancouver: Greystone–Douglas & McIntyre, 2002.

Owen, Gerald. "The Origins of 'Hockey,'" in *Total Hockey*, 2nd ed. Dan Diamond, ed. New York: Total, 2000. (Cowper)

Scanlan, Lawrence. *Grace Under Fire: The State of Our Sweet and Savage Game.* Toronto: Penguin, 2002.

Robidoux, Michael A. "Imagining a Canadian Identity through Sport: A Historical Interpretation of Lacrosse and Hockey." *Journal of American Folklore,* 115, 2002.

Willis, Ed. *The Rebel League: The Short and Unruly Life of the World Hockey Association.* Toronto: McClelland & Stewart, 2004.

"Birth of the Canadian Flag" www.pch.gc.ca/pgm/ceem-cced/symbl/df3-eng.cfm

http://bruins.nhl.com/club/news.htm?id=447439

http://vancouver.ca/commsvcs/planning/stats/poptrends/index.htm

www.birthplaceofhockey.com/evolution/hfx-rules.html

www.birthplaceofhockey.com/evolution/mtl-rules.html

www.canadianencyclopedia.ca/index.cfm?PgNm=TCE&Params=A1ARTA0003794

www.cbc.ca/hockeyhistory/episodesummary/01/post/featurestories.html

"The Kraut Line Goes to War" www.facebook.com/note.php?note_id=299476280851

www.hockeycentral.co.uk/nhl/origins/Origins-Kingston-Ontario.php

www.hockeyshome.ns.ca/birth.htm

www.queensjournal.ca/story/2005-10-04/features/hockey-night-kingston/ (Fitsell)

www.queensjournal.ca/story/2010-02-05/sports/halifax-or-kingston-who-owns-hockey/ (Tichinoff)

Chapter Two

Carrier, Roch. *Our Life with the Rocket: The Maurice Richard Story.* Translated by Sheila Fischman. Toronto: Penguin–Viking, 2001.

Hughes, Morgan, et al. *Hockey Chronicle: Year-by-Year History of the National Hockey League.* Linwood, IL: Publications International, 2003.

MacIntosh, Donald, and Donna Greenhorn. "Hockey Diplomacy and Canadian Foreign Policy." *Journal of Canadian Studies,* 28.2, 1993.

"Fedotenko Scores Both Tampa Goals" http://sports.espn.go.com/nhl/recap?gameId=240607020

"Frank W. Mahovlich–Liberal Party of Canada" www.parl.gc.ca/common/senmemb/senate/isenator_det.asp?senator_id=137&sortord=N&M=M

"Hockey on Carpet over Doan: Parliamentary Committee Summons Hockey Canada over Shane Doan's Captaincy" www.thestar.com/News/article/209309

http://montreal.ctv.ca/servlet/an/local/CTVNews/20050216/dryden_ambrosedebate_20050215?hub=OttawaHome

http://sportsillustrated.cnn.com/2009/hockey/nhl/08/27/demers.senate/index.html

http://sportsillustrated.cnn.com/olympics/2002/ice_hockey/news/2002/02/25/loonie_luck_slam/

http://tomhawthorn.blogspot.com/2010/04/bob-attersley-hockey-player-and.html

www.cbc.ca/news/background/liberals/leadershiprace.html#kd

www.cbc.ca/news/background/liberals/leadershiprace.html#sd

www.cbc.ca/sports/story/2007/04/30/doan-captain.html

Chapter Three

Falla, Jack. *Home Ice: Reflections on Backyard Rinks and Frozen Ponds.* Toronto: McClelland & Stewart, 2001.

———. *Open Ice: Reflections and Confessions of a Hockey Lifer.* Mississauga: Wiley, 2008.

———. *Saved.* New York: Thomas Dunne-St. Martin's, 2007.

Kennedy, Brian. *Living the Hockey Dream: Interviews and Personal Stories from NHL Superstars and Other Lovers of the Game.* Edmonton: Folklore Publishing, 2009.

Lee, John B. "When I Was a Boy and the Farm Pond Froze" in *Going Top Shelf: An Anthology of Canadian Hockey Poetry.* Michael P.J. Kennedy, ed. Victoria: Heritage House, 2005.

Meyer, Bruce. "Road Hockey" in *Going Top Shelf: An Anthology of Canadian Hockey Poetry.* Michael P.J. Kennedy, ed. Victoria: Heritage House, 2005.

www.asc-csa.gc.ca/eng/canadarm/default.asp

Chapter Four

Brunt, Stephen. *Searching for Bobby Orr.* Toronto: Knopf Canada, 2006.

———. *Gretzky's Tears: Hockey, Canada, and the Day Everything Changed.* Toronto: Knopf Canada, 2009.

Connors, Tom. "The Hockey Song." *Stompin' Tom and the Hockey Song.* Boot Records, 1972.

DeCock, Luke. "Piracy Lives in California." *The Hockey News Greatest Masks of All Time, Collector's Edition*. Toronto: The Hockey News, 2009.

Jenish, D'Arcy. *The Montreal Canadiens: 100 Years of Glory*. Toronto: Doubleday Canada, 2008.

Maggs, Randall. "The Last Faceoff" in *Night Work: The Sawchuk Poems*. London, ON: Brick Books, 2008.

——. "What I Liked About Bars" in *Night Work: The Sawchuk Poems*. London, ON: Brick Books, 2008.

McFarlane, Brian. *Team Canada 1972: Where Are They Now?* Etobicoke: Winding Star, 2001.

McKinley, Michael. *Hockey: A People's History*. Toronto: McClelland & Stewart, 2006.

Petty, Tom. "Two Gunslingers." *Into the Great Wide Open*. MCA Records, 1991.

"Stapleton Admits He Has Summit Series Puck" www.thepeterboroughexaminer.com/ArticleDisplay.aspx?archive=true&e=1295972

http://generationx.yaia.com/definition.html

http://voices.washingtonpost.com/dcsportsbog/2010/04/brooks_laich_changes_a_tire_af.html

www.cbc.ca/canada/british-columbia/story/2010/03/10/bc-sedin-hospital-donation.html

www.cbc.ca/greatest/top_ten/

www.habseyesontheprize.com/2009/11/26/1174682/25-years-ago-today-the-surprise

www.hockeydraftcentral.com/1983/83078.html

www.rachelmarsden.com/columns/reagan.html

www.sportsnet.ca/hockey/2008/08/05/gretzky_trade_reports/ (Taylor)

Chapter Five

Henderson, Paul, with Mike Leonetti. *Shooting for Glory*. Toronto: Stoddart, 1992.

Hewson, Kelly. "'You Said You Didn't Give a Fuck About Hockey': Popular Culture, the Fastest Game on Earth and the Imagined Canadian Nation" in *Now Is the Winter: Thinking About Hockey*. Jamie Dopp and Richard Harrison, eds. Hamilton: Wolsak and Wynn, 2009.

Ludwig, Jack. *Hockey Night in Moscow*. Richmond Hill: Pocket–Simon & Schuster Canada, 1974.

MacSkimming, Roy. *Cold War: The Amazing Canada-Soviet Hockey Series of 1972*. Vancouver: Greystone–Douglas & McIntyre, 1996.

Mercer, Rick. "One Thing I'll Say for Bruce Carson." *Maclean's*, May 2, 2011.

Richards, David Adams. *Nights Below Station Street*. Toronto: Emblem–McClelland & Stewart, 1997.

Sinden, Harry. *Hockey Showdown: The Canada-Russia Hockey Series*. Toronto: Doubleday Canada, 1972.

Team Canada 1972: Part 1. VHS. Markham, TV Eye Entertainment, 1997.

Team Canada 1972: Part 2. VHS. Markham, TV Eye Entertainment, 1997.

Tragically Hip. "Fireworks." *Phantom Power*. Fontana Universal, 1998.

Tzu, Sun. *The Art of War*. Translated by Thomas Cleary. Boston and London: Shambala, 1991.

"God is Canadian" http://archives.cbc.ca/sports/hockey/clips/1005/

"Ping Pong Diplomacy" www.chinadaily.com.cn/60th/2009-01/07/content_8636697.htm

www.ocregister.com/articles/hockey-233508-canada-canadian.html

Chapter Six

Blake, Jason. *Canadian Hockey Literature: A Thematic Study*. Toronto: University of Toronto Press, 2010.

McKinley, Michael. *Putting a Roof on Winter: Hockey's Rise from Sport to Spectacle*. Vancouver: Greystone–Douglas & McIntyre, 2002.

Shakespeare, William. *King Richard the Second. The Complete Works of Shakespeare*. Lexington, MA: Xerox College Publishing, 1971.

"CBC to Go in New Direction with 'Hockey Night' theme music" http://sports.espn.go.com/nhl/news/story?id=3428440

www.thehockeynews.com/articles/40476-Largest-known-portrait-of-Queen-may-return-to-Winnipeg-along-with-NHL-team.html

Chapter Seven

Coupland, Douglas. *Souvenir of Canada*. Vancouver: Douglas & McIntyre, 2002.

Hay, Elizabeth. *Late Nights On Air*. Toronto: Emblem–McClelland & Stewart, 2008.

Hodgins, Jack, *Broken Ground*. Toronto: Douglas Gibson–McClelland & Stewart, 1999.

Kashmere, Brett. *Valery's Ankle: An Essay-Film*. Canada, 2006.

Lorinc, John. "Game Changers: This Week's Boldest." *Globe and Mail*, March 27, 2010.

MacGregor, Roy. "One for the Road." *Today's Parent*, September 2003.

Pond Hockey: A Documentary Film. Directed by Tommy Haines. Minnesota: Northland Films, 2008.

"Banning Street Hockey Endangers our Children's Healthy Development" in "Nurturing Resilience: Raising Children to be Competent and Caring" by Michael Ungar. *Psychology Today* blogs, April 22, 2010, http://www.psychologytoday.com/blog/nurturing-resilience/201004/banning-street-hockey-endangers-our-childrens-healthy-development

www.cbc.ca/sports/story/2006/01/30/crosby_streethocke060131.html

www.hockeycentral.co.uk/nhl/origins/Origins-Kingston-Ontario.php

www.iihf.com/nc/home-of-hockey/news/news-singleview/article/road-hockey-illegal-crazy.html (Podnieks)

www.thepassinglane.ca/2010/06/toronto-considers-rescinding-street-hockey-ban.html

www.thestar.com/sports/gthl/article/829749--parents-sue-gthl-after-sons-cut-by-team?bn=1

Chapter Eight

Carrier, Roch. *Our Life with the Rocket: The Maurice Richard Story.* Translated by Sheila Fischman. Toronto: Penguin–Viking, 2001.

Cole, Stephen. *The Last Hurrah: A Celebration of Hockey's Greatest Season '66–'67.* Toronto: Penguin, 1996.

Denault, Todd. *Jacques Plante: The Man Who Changed the Face of Hockey.* Toronto: McClelland & Stewart, 2009.

Ferguson, Will. *Why I Hate Canadians.* Vancouver: Douglas & McIntyre, 1997.

Gohier, Philippe. "No French Connection." *Maclean's*, October 4, 2010.

Jenish, D'Arcy. *The Montreal Canadiens: 100 Years of Glory.* Toronto: Doubleday Canada, 2008.

Kreiser, John. "On Thin Ice: The Recent Bankruptcies of the Senators and Sabres Demonstrate that the NHL Needs More Than a Zamboni to Smooth Over its Rough Spots." *Hockey Digest*, April 2003.

McKinley, Michael. *Hockey: A People's History.* Toronto: McClelland & Stewart, 2009.

——. *Putting a Roof on Winter: Hockey's Rise from Sport to Spectacle.* Vancouver: Greystone–Douglas & McIntyre, 2002.

Mollins, Carl, ed. *Canada's Century: An Illustrated History of the People and Events that Shaped Our History*. Toronto: Key Porter, 2001.

"Rule 11.7, Masks." *NHL Official Rules 2008–09*.

Turner, Randy. "Our NHL in Heaven Compared with '97." *Winnipeg Free Press*, November 8, 2007.

"Leafs-Habs Rivalry on Display During Hall of Fame Weekend" www.thestar.com/article/533107 (Ponikarovsky)

"Legend Found: Pete Mahovlich" http://insidehockey.com/?p=559

"One on One with Ted Lindsay" www.legendsofhockey.net/html/spot_oneononep196607.htm

http://economistsview.typepad.com/economistsview/2011/02/public-sector-unions-in-the-us-vs-canada.html

http://en.wikipedia.org/wiki/Original_Stars_Hockey_League#North_America

http://mapleleafs.nhl.com/club/page.htm?bcid=his_1920s

http://sportsbiznews.blogspot.com/2007/05/first-bankruptcy-bowl-then-stanley-cup.html

www.cbc.ca/sports/story/2005/06/26/roenick050626.html?email

www.greatesthockeylegends.com/2008/11/war-and-hockey-history.html (Pelletier)

www.thecanadianencyclopedia.com/index.cfm?PgNm=TCE&Params=A1ARTA0001859

www.usatoday.com/sports/hockey/nhl/2005-07-13-roenick-labor_x.htm

Chapter Nine

Boyden, Joseph. *Three Day Road*. Toronto: Penguin, 2005.

Gatehouse, Jonathan. "Hockey Violence: It's Time to Draw the Line." *Maclean's* March 28, 2011.

Itani, Frances. *Deafening*. Toronto: HarperPerennial, 2004.

Kashmere, Brett. *Valery's Ankle: An Essay-Film*. Canada, 2006.

NHL On the Fly, NHL Network. USA. May 7, 2011.

Scanlan, Lawrence. *Grace Under Fire: The State of Our Sweet and Savage Game*. Toronto: Penguin, 2002.

"North Star On Ice" http://sportsillustrated.cnn.com/vault/article/magazine/MAG1067721/index.htm

"Roy's Son Pleads Guilty" http://sports.espn.go.com/nhl/news/story?id=4538948

http://afghanistan.blogs.cnn.com/2009/12/07/canadas-role-in-afghanistan/

http://archive.chicagobreakingsports.com/2011/03/ex-hawk-bob-probert-suffered-from-brain-disease-cte.html

http://sportsillustrated.cnn.com/hockey/nhl/news/2000/10/06/mcsorley_assault_ap/

www.afghanistan.gc.ca/canada-afghanistan/priorities-priorites/index.aspx

www.hockeyfights.com

Chapter Ten

Bakhtin, M.M. *Rabelais and His World*. Translated by Helene Iswolsky. Bloomington: Indiana University Press, 1984.

Barmak, Sarah. "Fans 'Ashamed' of Hockey Riots: Violence Erupts, Vehicles Set on Fire in Vancouver as Canucks Lose Stanley Cup Final." *Toronto Star*, June 18, 2011. (Robertson; Martin)

Fitzpatrick, Frank. "Canada Ends Up with Hockey Gold Mine, But U.S. Still Has a Silver Lining." *McClatchy-Tribune New Service*, Washington. February 28, 2010.

Jenish, D'Arcy. *The Montreal Canadiens: 100 Years of Glory*. Toronto: Doubleday Canada, 2008.

Letourneau, Tiara. "The Lost Citizens of Hockey Need to be Engaged." *Vancouver Sun*, June 17, 2011.

SI Presents: Team Canada: 2010 Olympic Champions. New York: Time Inc., 2010. (Kane)

"41 Arrested in Mayhem in Montreal" http://sports.espn.go.com/nhl/playoffs/2010/news/story?id=5185068

"Oilers Revelry Turns Ugly on Edmonton's Blue Mile" www.canada.com/calgaryherald/news/story.html?id=76fcefe9-2866-409c-920d-811a384ea601

"Peter Pocklington Sentenced" http://sports.espn.go.com/nhl/news/story?id=5733374

"Sens Mile" www.canada.com/ottawacitizen/news/story.html?id=5f37beb9-e64b-4762-a467-cef15d0eb37c&k=89106

"Violence on 'Blue Mile' Mars Oilers Celebration" http://ctestp.ctv.ca/servlet/an/local/CTVNews/20060513/oilers_arrests_060513?hub=CP24Sports

http://en.wikipedia.org/wiki/Red_Mile

http://ottawa.ctv.ca/servlet/an/local/CTVNews/20100414/OTT_Sens_Mile_100414/20100414?hub=OttawaHome

www.cbc.ca/canada/montreal/story/2010/05/13/montreal-habs-post-game-riot.html

www.cbc.ca/canada/ottawa/story/2010/04/13/ott-sens-mile.html

www.legendsofhockey.net/htmltimecap/GamesSummaryCCUP1987.shtml

www.mapsofworld.com/olympic-trivia/olympic-motto.html

www.thehockeynews.com/articles/33823-Puck-stops-here-Peter-Pocklington-to-plead-guilty-to-perjury-in-California.html

www.thehockeynews.com/articles/40634-Largest-playoff-crowds-yet-clog-Vancouver-as-Canucks-two-wins-from-cup.html

www.youtube.com/watch?v=dlCGz0V4qEA

Afterword

Archbold, Rick. *Canada, Our History: An Album Through Time.* Toronto: Doubleday Canada, 2000.

Bidini, Dave. *The Best Game You Can Name.* Toronto: McClelland & Stewart, 2005.

Carrier, Roch. "The Hockey Sweater" in *The Hockey Sweater and Other Stories.* Translated by Sheila Fischman. Toronto: Anansi, 1979.

Harrison, Richard. "Rhéaume" in *Going Top Shelf: An Anthology of Canadian Hockey Poetry.* Michael P.J. Kennedy, ed. Victoria: Heritage House, 2005.

McQueen, Ken. "Golden Moments: Vancouver's Party Resumes, On a Scale Unprecedented for the Paralympics." *Maclean's,* March 29, 2010. (Grassi; Rosen)

"NHL Play-by-Play in Punjabi Scores Big Time" www.thestar.com/article/588194

http://urbantoronto.ca/showthread.php?8131-Swapping-blades-for-cleats-in-Scarborough&p=224858

www.rickhansen.com

www.usatoday.com/sports/olympics/vancouver/hockey/2010-02-25-canada-usa-woman_N.ht

Brian Kennedy

Brian was born and raised on the outdoor rinks in Montréal, and although he now lives in California, he remains a true Canadian, especially when it comes to Hockey (with a capital *H*). Brian holds a PhD in English and teaches at Pasadena City College, but his freelance sports writing is his real calling. He feels particularly lucky to cover the Anaheim Ducks and the LA Kings, which allows him to meet many of the famous players of the past and present and to ask them all the burning questions he has always wanted to.

He is the author of two other hockey-themed books, but in *My Country Is Hockey*, Brian was able to dig deeply into the Canadian psyche and discover how the game of hockey is an integral piece of our Canadian identity.